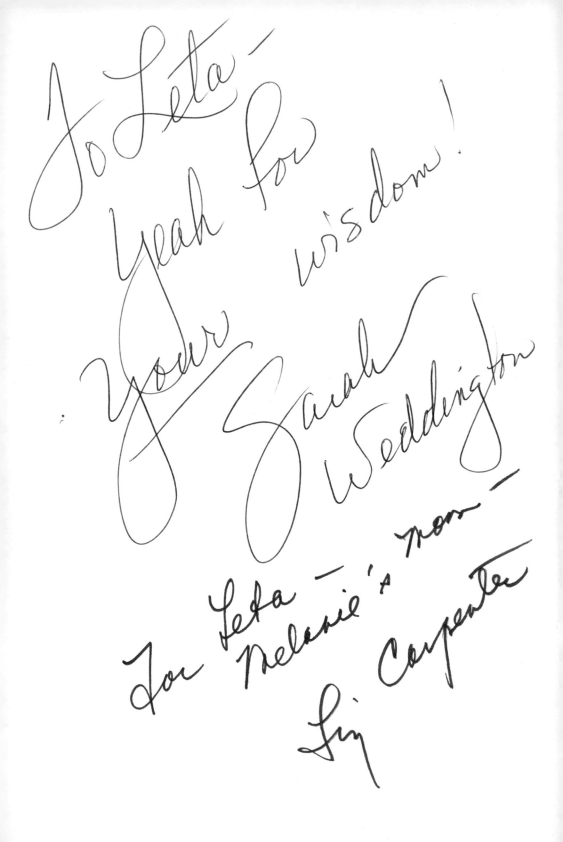

To Leta —
Yeah for
Your        wisdom!

Your

Sarah
Weddington

For Leta — from
Melanie's mom —

Liz Carpenter

*"Let me tell you what I've learned"*

For Leta —
a native
Texas wisewoman
from Childress —
my neck - of - the -
woods —

PJ Pierce
2002

CARMEN LOMAS GARZA

BOOK FOUR

**LOUANN ATKINS TEMPLE WOMEN & CULTURE SERIES**

*Books about women and families, and their changing role in society*

TEXAS WISEWOMEN SPEAK

# "Let me tell you what I've learned"

## PJ PIERCE

FOREWORD BY LIZ CARPENTER

*University of Texas Press, Austin*

The Louann Atkins Temple Women & Culture Series is supported by
Allison, Doug, Taylor, and Andy Bacon; Margaret, Lawrence, Will, John,
and Annie Temple; Larry Temple; the Temple-Inland Foundation;
and the National Endowment for the Humanities.

LIBRARY OF CONGRESS CATALOGING-IN-PUBLICATION DATA

Pierce, Paula Jo.
    Let me tell you what I've learned : Texas wisewomen speak / PJ Pierce ;
foreword by Liz Carpenter.
          p.      cm. (Louann Atkins Temple women & culture series ; bk. 4)
    Includes bibliographical references and index.
    ISBN 0-292-76593-2 (cloth : alk. paper) — ISBN 0-292-76594-0 (pbk. : alk. paper)
    1. Women—Texas—Interview. 2. Women—Texas—Biography. 3. Oral
history. 4. Texas—Biography. I. Title. II. Series.
CT3260 .P54 2002
920.72´09764—dc21                                   2001055651

*For my mother,*
**PAULINE DURRETT ROBERTSON,**
*the wisest woman in my life,*
*and for my daughters,*
**HEATHER ELLEN** *and* **SUMMER ROBYN,**
*who become wiser every day*

# CONTENTS

Foreword by Liz Carpenter   *ix*
Acknowledgments   *xi*
Introduction   *1*

Barbara Jordan   *13*
Liz Carpenter   *21*
Marj Carpenter   *33*
Jody Conradt   *43*
Wilhelmina Delco   *55*
Linda Ellerbee   *67*
Juliet Villarreal García   *79*
Carmen Lomas Garza   *91*
Glenna Goodacre   *103*
Kay Bailey Hutchison   *115*
Barbara Jacket   *125*
Edith Irby Jones   *135*

Ninfa Laurenzo   *145*
Amy Freeman Lee   *155*
Sarah McClendon   *167*
Diana Natalicio   *177*
Violette Newton   *189*
Guadalupe C. Quintanilla   *201*
Louise B. Raggio   *213*
Irma Rangel   *225*
Ann Richards   *237*
Mary Lou Robinson   *249*
Sarah Weddington   *261*
Judith Zaffirini   *273*

Epilogue: Pauline Durrett Robertson   *285*
Appendix A   *293*
Appendix B   *295*
Bibliography   *297*
Index   *299*

# FOREWORD

The creative author PJ Pierce has done us a great favor. She has gleaned from twenty-five strong women with a variety of experiences the essence of living a full and useful life. I predict it will prompt not only thoughtful self-analysis but also a round of parlor games and dinner table conversations to answer: what have I learned from life?

For the novelist Edith Wharton, a long life of living vitally is possible: "In spite of illness, in spite of even the archenemy sorrow, one can remain alive long past the usual date of disintegration if one is unafraid of change, insatiable in intellectual curiosity, interested in big things and happy in small ways."

This formula is borne out in PJ's circle of wisewomen. All of them are not only unafraid of change but have prodded it along.

Speaking personally, when she popped the question "What have you learned from life?" to me, I quickly replied: "Not enough." That's still my answer, but my formula gets some additions.

When I was twenty, I knew that a sense of humor would serve me well. By the time I was into a writing career at thirty, I added a sense of purpose to my requirements for happiness. Now—at eighty—I know that a sense of history opens your eyes to all the connections between the people you know and the things you have done. Because national politics is my favorite sport, I have known personally or professionally twelve presidents of the United States. I am stimulated by looking down that long telescope of history and seeing the ebb and flow of change, the hits and misses, through a wider lens.

One of the wisest people I know—John Gardner, who founded Common Cause—once said, "It's what you learn after you know it all that counts."

At age eighty, I have witnessed a lot of Texas history, known a lot of its heroes and some of its scoundrels, and like many daughters and great-great-granddaughters of pioneer Texans, thrilled to the great variety that is Texas. My people came here in 1829, long before the words "feminism," "networking," "choice," were part of the female dictionary. There were certainly bossy and pushy women then, but Texas wouldn't have made it without them.

In the contemporary women's movement, which started in 1971 when the Texas Women's Political Caucus followed the national caucus, we stopped trying to please men as our priority and began to popularize women helping women, i.e., networking. We also learned not to let the insults go unanswered. We learned to talk back and laugh—two deadly weapons.

We learned to run for office and sometimes get elected. For years, Texas had been electing women as county clerks and county treasurers without really noticing. This time, we teamed up, ran State Treasurer Ann Richards for governor, and got her elected. Ann was mother of four and a savvy political operator. And she started appointing women to everything, including the Board of Regents of Texas A&M and the Texas State Highway Department, which had been the private preserve of men.

We helped open up the law schools, and then on to the U.S. Supreme Court. Sarah Weddington, a twenty-six-year-old Texas lawyer, took the *Roe v. Wade* case there. She did it without pretense. She found the case, took her old car, drove to Washington, stayed with friends to save money, and won the case for legalizing abortion if you choose to have one.

So today, because of Ann, Sarah, and many others, we women assume we can do whatever it is that needs to be done. I say: Take risks, open doors for other women, and make your own performance so worthy that the doors never swing shut again.

I urge readers to absorb the words of the wisewomen in this book. Don't rush through the words. Test them on your own life. You'll be a wiser person when you do.

**LIZ CARPENTER**

# Acknowledgments

I am profoundly grateful to all the women who gave so willingly of themselves and their wisdom to make this book happen. Each invested her time during the interview and afterward, reading her chapter and correcting facts. While reading their chapters, many added additional bits of wisdom they hadn't thought of during the interview. Getting to know these remarkable women was the most satisfying part of writing this book.

Without my lifelong friend Candace O'Keefe, this book would not have happened. Together Candace and I conceived the idea one summer afternoon during a casual discussion about strong women whose wisdom goes unrecorded. As executive director of the Foundation for Women's Resources, Candace became my main consultant and cheerleader as the book took shape. It was her friend (and now mine) Liz Carpenter who granted me the interview that became the sample chapter in my book proposal to the University of Texas Press. Candace has gone on to become executive director of the Women's Museum: An Institute for the Future, which opened in September 2000 in Dallas.

I thank Liz Carpenter for agreeing to be the guinea pig for the fledgling project, and my daughter Summer Robyn, a professional photographer, for traveling with me to various corners of the state, photographing and tape-recording most of the women. Summer's typical good nature and patience made this project even more a pleasure. I thank my daughter Heather Ellen, an advertising executive, for her technical help with other interviews closer to home.

Thanks to Stephanie Sobotik and Ashlie Griswold at the Foundation for Women's Resources for their help in locating many of the women who were interviewed. My mother and six sisters are an unending source of support. I especially want to thank two of my sisters, Robyn Montana Turner and Ellen Robertson Neal, both journalists, for their ideas and encouragement concerning this project. I am grateful to my many friends who read chapters and wrote in the margins: Rebecca Bingham, Dinah Chenven, Maxine Dorris, Beth Freeby, Barbara Gamble, Sallie Herring, and Sara and Bill Hilgers. Thanks to authors Ruthe Winegarten and Susan Wittig Albert for reading the entire manuscript, offering their suggestions, and pronouncing the book "valuable literature."

I thank Austin author Mary Beth Rogers for writing her well-researched and insightful book about Barbara Jordan. Since I was not able to interview Barbara before she died, I relied heavily on Mary Beth's book, *Barbara Jordan: American Hero*, for information.

Theresa May, editor-in-chief at the University of Texas Press, believed in this project from the start. I am grateful for that trust. Her dry humor, encouragement, and good advice kept me on track and entertained as I waded through the long process of writing and publishing. Art Director Ellen McKie read my mind and then came up with pages that were even more inventive than the images in my head. I thank both of them for their genius, their humor, and their friendship.

Thanks to the hundreds of people whose eyes have lighted up when I talked about this project. Such enthusiasm has kept me assured that the wisdom of our female tribal elders is something people want to hear.

Most of all, I thank my husband of thirty-one years, Jack, for his quiet patience and constant support and enthusiasm during the writing of this book.

*"Let me tell you what I've learned"*

" *I don't know here this afternoon what will be next for me. I won't know what the next step is until I get there. I know that when I went to Boston, and Austin, and Washington, I took with me everything I had learned before. And that's what I will do this time. That's the point of it, isn't it? To bring all you have with you wherever you go.* "

BARBARA JORDAN,
COMMENCEMENT ADDRESS, HARVARD UNIVERSITY, 1977
(CONTEMPLATING WHAT THE NEXT STAGE OF HER CAREER
WOULD BE AS SHE PREPARED TO LEAVE THE U.S. CONGRESS)

This book of wisdom, *"Let me tell you what I've learned": Texas Wisewomen Speak,* came to life on January 17, 1996, the day Barbara Jordan died. Like others, I wasn't ready to lose her. Just shy of sixty years old, Barbara contained too much wisdom yet unspoken. As a baby boomer, I had come to respect the advice of this wisewoman, especially on ethical matters that face us in good times and bad. At the time of her death, she was a teacher of political ethics to many lucky students at the LBJ School of Public Affairs at the University of Texas at Austin.

During that same period, Barbara was serving as the unpaid advisor on ethics to former governor Ann Richards and as a member of President Clinton's U.S. Commission on Immigration Reform.

How do people like Barbara Jordan become wise? Barbara spent a lot of time being quiet and listening. After careful thought, she would begin to speak in her deep, authoritative voice, enunciating every word, as if God herself were talking. Perhaps Barbara's wisdom came from all her accumulated experiences. As she said, "I [take] with me everything I [have] learned before. . . . That's the point . . . isn't it? To bring all you have with you wherever you go."

If so, then we should all be quiet and listen—searching for wisdom. We gather knowledge more easily than we gather wisdom. Knowledge is merely an accumulation of facts. My nineteen-year-old son, Ian, is full of facts. When I asked him, at age fourteen, how he knew a particular obscure fact, he said, "I just picked it up along the way, Mom."

Wisdom, on the other hand, is an understanding that comes from experience and seasoning. Wisdom is something we learn from our grand-mothers. It takes a lifetime to ripen. In older cultures, elders were revered for their wisdom. Traditionally, young people in Native American tribes went to the tribal elders for advice.

In today's youth-worshipping society, that reverence for age and its wisdom is almost lost in our fast-paced era of computers and advertising. And we are suffering from that void.

*"Let me tell you what I've learned"* is this native Texan's attempt to pre-serve some of the wisdom and advice I gleaned from going to our "tribal elders."

Although thousands of Barbara Jordan's words have been recorded for future generations, I haven't seen her answers to the questions I wanted to ask: "What have you found to be most important about life?" "If you were a young woman starting out to build your life today, what would you do differently? What would you do the same way?" "What is most important to tell the generations coming behind you?" "How has your upbringing in Texas influenced the way you have lived your life?" "What new insights have you had since you have gotten older?" "What excites you about the future?" And more.

It was too late to record such particular wisdom from Barbara Jordan, so I vowed not to let the chance slip away again with other wisewomen from Texas. I began gathering names of women whose hearts and minds I wanted to pick. More than just hearing their life stories, I wanted to hear what they had learned from their experiences. I set up a list of core questions, which I posed to each woman (see Appendix B). It was typical for one woman to relate to some questions and another to relate to differ-ent ones. If one was clearly uncomfortable with a particular question, I would take the subject as far as she was willing to go and then move on to another question. Later in the interview, when she felt more at ease, I might broach the uncomfortable area again. That tactic provided a chance for her to reconsider, sometimes opening up a course of discussion that she became willing to pursue. If not, I left it alone. During the course of the individual interviews, impromptu questions would naturally come up as each conversation took its own path.

The typical interview lasted two hours or less. Each chapter contains the woman's own words, taken from her interview and edited for clarity and space demands.

Before settling on the twenty-five individuals I would eventually interview, I set down criteria. Every woman must have passed the half-century mark of her life and thus be old enough to say with conviction, "Let me tell you what I've learned to be important after all." Each must have become well known in her field, whether regionally or nationally.

The group as a whole must represent a cross section of career paths and ethnic groups, and all geographic areas of Texas must be represented. Each person must have lived a significant part of her life in Texas. Some who were not born in Texas have lived here most of their adult lives, and thus they wear the brand.

Why include only Texas women? America is full of wisewomen. But a perception exists that Texas women are different—feistier perhaps, more likely to think that anything is possible. It is a theory that some call "the mystique of the Texas woman." Whether the mystique holds water is up for debate. But it does seem to be there. Distinctive Texas traits were there when we were battling the elements on the frontier, and the same traits remain to this day, when Texas women have come onto the national scene as strong politicians.

We Texas women haven't perpetuated the myth all by ourselves; we have had help from others. I hear the myth from my friends in other states and from my European friends. My Austin friend Dinah Chenven, who grew up in New Jersey, says it this way: "I had always thought that professional women needed to present themselves as humorless and sexless to be taken seriously. When I got to Texas, though, I saw respected professional women presenting themselves as they really were (or wanted to be)—earthy and fun, unafraid of being compromised by makeup and high heels. I was amazed by that."

Naomi Wolf, of Washington, D.C., author of *Fire with Fire: The New Female Power and How It Will Change the Twenty-first Century,* said during a visit to Austin in October 1995 that Texas women seem to welcome power much more than do some other middle-income women. They aren't afraid that power will defeminize them. "Maybe it has something to do with the state's history," she said. "Women here seem very solution-oriented."

It was the quest for solutions to injustices that spurred many of the women in this book to make meaningful changes in the system. Society is now more fair to women, in particular, since these wisewomen pushed their ideas to the forefront on the state and national levels.

Attorney Louise Raggio devised solutions that changed the lives of all married women in Texas when, in 1967, she headed up the otherwise all-male Marital Properties Task Force in the Texas State Bar and helped push new laws through the Texas legislature. For the first time, married women in Texas could buy or sell property, secure a bank loan, start a business, and have credit in their own names.

Sarah Weddington, attorney, won a solution for all American women in 1971 when, at age twenty-six, she successfully argued the landmark *Roe v. Wade* case before the U.S. Supreme Court. By a seven-to-two vote on January 22, 1973, the court finally announced its decision: a constitutional right to privacy gives women the right to choose whether to continue or terminate a pregnancy.

Shortly after *Roe v. Wade* became law, journalist Liz Carpenter joined forces with other powerful American women to form the National Women's Political Caucus. Liz handled the press during those years of organizing female political caucuses nationwide and campaigning to get the Equal Rights Amendment passed. Although the ERA did not pass, the groundswell caused by that fifteen-year effort helped prepare the nation for today's successful female politicians.

Along with a handful of other women journalists, Linda Ellerbee broke ground in the national broadcasting arena and paved the way for younger women to become household names as broadcasters on national networks. Juliet García and Diana Natalicio became two of only a handful of female university presidents in the United States, Juliet being the first Mexican American woman ever to hold that position in this country. Both immediately began fostering innovative, nontraditional solutions to allow women and other minority students to overcome hurdles in higher education. Today their programs are models for other institutions all over the country.

Senator Kay Bailey Hutchison, after having been stalked herself, passed federal legislation to prosecute stalkers, most of whose victims are women. When former Texas legislator Wilhelmina Delco saw problems in education for her children and other black students, she devised solutions by becoming local PTA president, then school board member, and then a state legislator. The results of her efforts have affected the lives of thousands of Texans in positive ways.

Solutions were also on the mind of Ann Richards when she became governor of Texas in 1990, at age fifty-seven. Ann appointed women and minorities to positions of power in state government, making the power structure look more like the actual population of Texas. When disenfranchised female Vietnam War veterans commissioned artist Glenna Goodacre to sculpt a statue to represent their contributions to the effort in Southeast Asia, she spent more than a year creating a solution. About the Vietnam Women's Memorial dedicated in 1993 and installed on the mall in Washington D.C., Glenna said, "I am proud to have created something that means so much to so many."

Black female athletes had few outlets for their talents at Prairie View A&M until coach Barbara Jacket created the first women's track and field team at that historically black college in the 1960s. That solution provided many young black women with another reason to make it through college. Through the years, she turned out fifty-seven all-American female athletes, many of whom went on to become Olympic contenders and coaches.

Most of the powerful women you'll meet point to the atmosphere in Texas as being a strong influence on their success. Barbara Jordan was proud to be Texan. In 1989 she told a *National Geographic* reporter: "I get from the soil and spirit of Texas the feeling that I, as an individual, can accomplish whatever I want to, and that there are no limits, that you can just keep going, just keep soaring. I like that spirit."

Others echo Barbara's sentiments. Ann Richards comments, "When you grow up on the frontier, or close to it like I did, you believe there is nothing you can't do."

Artist Carmen Lomas Garza says, "Tejanas are different from the Mexican American women in California where I live now. Tejanas are much friendlier . . . and more celebrative. I think we inherited these qualities from our Tejana ancestors, who through their camaraderie had learned to survive the harsh physical environment of South Texas."

Linda Ellerbee says, "Even at a time when women were supposed to be meek and quiet, I think most Texas women weren't good at that. My family certainly had women who spoke their minds."

Kay Bailey Hutchison quotes her great-great-grandmother, who in 1849 wrote home to Tennessee: "Out in this new country, I see no one but strangers, but they are the kindest people I have ever met with." Says Kay, "That's the kind of stock from which we [Texas women] come."

Many women have wisdom to impart; all women have a story to tell. I chose the women you will meet in these pages because they broke barriers and rose to a level of distinction that has brought them recognition. They overcame obstacles to succeed. They changed stereotypes of what it meant to be women in their thirties and forties. And they are continuing to change stereotypes of women in their fifties and beyond.

These are women who have lived extraordinary lives. Journalist Sarah McClendon is still covering the White House at age ninety. These women are not ones to say, "I am too old for that now," as their mothers and grandmothers might have said.

From more than one hundred women whose names I had gathered, I finally chose twenty-five who, I feel, represent hundreds of other Texas wisewomen. They range in age from fifty-three to ninety-three years.

- Sixty-five percent are mothers.
- Thirty-one percent are widowed, 17 percent are married to their original spouse, 30 percent are divorced, 8 percent are remarried, and 13 percent have never married.
- Two are only children.

In this book, their common theme is "What I have learned to be most important in life." All have the same intention: to share insights learned through decades of living so that generations coming behind them can profit from their experiences.

These female pioneers took paths not open to women in their time. And today they still look at life differently than most people do. They see what needs to be done and figure out a way to make it happen.

For instance, coach Jody Conradt took the obscure sport of collegiate women's basketball to the forefront and began filling arenas to capacity with her national championship teams. Jody had no predecessors—no female mentors to show her the way. Now, female coaches all over the country look to Jody as a mentor.

In 1947 Edith Irby Jones applied to medical school in the South, although no black person had ever been accepted to a white medical school below the Mason-Dixon Line. Today in her seventies, she still runs her solo medical practice so she can do it her way.

Guadalupe Quintanilla overcame the label of mentally retarded thrust on her by an Anglo school system that decided she couldn't learn—simply because she spoke no English. Today she is a university professor and wealthy business owner who teaches cultural sensitivity to those who work in the public sector. Her three children, who also were once labeled slow learners, now have doctoral degrees.

Every woman I interviewed was eager to share. My only frustration is that each shared more wisdom than could be included in these pages. Each understands that once you have success, it is important to pull others up behind you. Yes, there is a feeling of "sisterhood" among successful women that corresponds to the "good old boy system" among men. The difference seems to be that among most women nurturing overshadows competition.

Even in competitive Washington, on the floor of the U.S. Senate, Kay Bailey Hutchison, a Texas Republican, has crossed party lines on many occasions to join forces with other female senators on issues that are important to all of them as women. She and the eight other female U.S. senators in 2000 collaborated on the book *Nine and Counting,* which draws a road map for women as they try to break barriers in politics, business, and other fields.

Sounding a similar theme, Juliet García, president of the University of Texas at Brownsville, talks about the *confianza*—a familiarity, a rapport—among women that is lacking in our relationships with men. We can drop a comment about our children or grandchildren into the proceedings at a business meeting of women and no one will think less of us. In fact, she maintains that such comments can build instant rapport, breaking down cumbersome layers that often keep people from learning from each other.

Each woman you will meet in these pages has taken the "journey" approach to life, believing that the experiences along her path are at least as important as the destination. She has taken opportunities where she has found them and has not hesitated to walk into uncharted territory.

For each of these women, life is still an adventure involving risks and rewards.

Taking chances as they have come, Louise Raggio describes her journey in a pithy metaphor. She says it's sort of like catching on to the ring of a carousel as it comes by. Now in her eighties, Louise stands ready to catch the next ring.

Spontaneity also comes naturally to journalist Liz Carpenter. She says, "In my generation we didn't have five-year plans like my daughter has. You just walked through the open door or backed away from it. And I generally walked through it."

I was delighted with the honest responses I got from these women and with their willingness to talk for as long as it took to convey their convictions. They took their assignment seriously—to share their wisdom with coming generations.

I took one or both of my daughters, who are in their twenties, with me to assist in most interviews. Heather, an advertising account executive, took notes and operated the tape recorder. Summer, a professional photographer, shot portraits. Of course, their assistance was not the only thing I valued about their coming along. My ulterior motive was for my daughters to garner wisdom for their own lives.

Heather, Summer, and I began seeing similarities among the subjects—similarities that paint a picture of the qualities necessary to allow one to stand apart from the crowd. All of these women are enthusiastic. All have persevered through hard times and never enjoyed self-pity during their life struggles. They think in the long term instead of the short term; they aren't concerned with meeting the demands of the popular culture.

They are optimistic about the next generation's abilities and about what the future holds for the world. They genuinely like teenagers and young adults and like to associate with them.

These women share a sense of social responsibility and are willing to lead. Most had strong parent figures (either one or both parents) who gave them self-confidence and advocated for them. The politicians, in particular, had fathers who encouraged them.

But it was when they talked about close relationships with their mothers that many began to shed tears. It was not uncommon for these strong women to become emotional when talking about the love they received during their formative years and what that early support has meant to their lives.

All grew up as risk-takers and are not afraid to fail. They are organized, fast thinkers (even at age ninety) and are accustomed to thinking "outside the box." They know how to use their time efficiently, and all have boundless energy. They are opinionated and at ease, although both Sarah McClendon and Linda Ellerbee, journalists, maintain that they are really shy people hiding behind a notepad. It seems to me, however, that they must have outgrown their shyness. Both were outgoing and funny during our interviews—and were anything but timid.

All are flexible and have several projects going at the same time. Most were so busy that it took a while to find time in their schedules for an interview. Most are fiercely protective of their weekends, although Louise Raggio, Barbara Jacket, and Violette Newton each gave up part of a Saturday for me.

All are enthusiastic about their work and proud of their achievements. Although they are well known for their accomplishments in their professional fields, without exception, the fifteen mothers in the group said that their children are their greatest achievements. They have raised strong families, and their children are successful, happy people.

Accomplishments often edge out friendship. Many lamented that they had given up their women friends along the way to concentrate on careers, where they usually were surrounded by males. Their families took up the rest of their time. It is typical of the fifty- to sixty-year-olds to be without close female friends because their careers are still in high gear.

This age group mentioned that they need to begin spending more time enjoying life, more time laughing with friends. Most of the women over sixty have cultivated female friends now that their children are raised and settled and their careers are allowing them a bit more time for friendships. Many have joined groups of like-minded females for professional and social interaction.

Social interaction, however, does not mean partying. Few like to go to big parties. They have lost interest in that diversion. Most like to be with family and small groups of friends around the kitchen table.

Not one of these women has ever quit being productive. At age ninety-three, Sarah McClendon says that she doesn't have time to stop working every day as a journalist. There are too many things to accomplish. She is still too curious. At age seventy-six, Marj Carpenter is getting ready to travel to China, her 116th country, to keep Presbyterians in the United States updated about their missions abroad.

Perhaps the most compelling reason to take all this wisdom to heart is that most of us are on track to live many more years. Our long lives will be increasingly affected by the choices we have made earlier. Surveys show that 80 percent of baby boomers in the United States say they plan to work well past age sixty-five. Perhaps the secret to staying vibrant in old age is continuing to be productive in some capacity and finding balance in your life so that work doesn't consume you. Although the women in these pages love what they do professionally, most of them nurture themselves, allowing time and energy for exercise, the arts, friendships, and fun.

One in three American women has passed her fiftieth birthday. A woman who reaches fifty today and remains free of cancer and heart disease can count on celebrating her ninety-second birthday, according to Dr. Kenneth Manton, demographer at Duke University. A quarter century from now, the number of older women in the world will have doubled.

Given our probable longevity, it is important to examine the quality of our lives. It is my hope that you, the reader, will find within these pages wisdom that is timeless, quotable, timely, poignant, funny, encouraging, upbeat, and optimistic about the future. I hope that you'll want to highlight passages and write in the margins.

I feel wiser for having been privy to so many lifetimes of learning. All of the taped interviews and transcripts of the interviews are archived in my personal files. Every woman has read her own chapter and has attested to its accuracy. Interviewing these women was exhilarating.

Whether you are from Texas or elsewhere doesn't matter. Nor does it matter whether you are female or male. My hope is that, as you read, you will feel some of that same exhilaration and that you will savor the distilled wisdom of these twenty-five outstanding women of Texas. May what you find help you along your own life's journey.

# BARBARA JORDAN

*Barbara Jordan, former U.S. Representative (D–Texas) and educator, May 7, 1986.*
*Photo by Frank Wolfe. Courtesy of the LBJ Library Photo Archives.*

"*I believe*

*that*

*I have*

*a spirit*

*that*

*is not*

*going to*

*disappear.*"

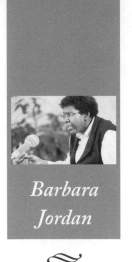

## Barbara Jordan

B. 1936,
**HOUSTON, TEXAS**
D. 1996,
**AUSTIN, TEXAS**
*She was buried in the Texas State Cemetery,*
*twenty-seven years after she had written a bill*
*to outlaw segregated cemeteries in Texas.*

Barbara Charline Jordan grew up in the Fifth Ward of Houston, Texas, the third of three daughters. Her father was a warehouse clerk and later a Baptist minister, and her mother was a maid and a housewife, dominated by her husband. Barbara's father often commented disapprovingly about her skin tone, which was much darker than his, her mother's, or either of her two sisters'. Early in life she decided for herself: "You've got to be able to love yourself—love yourself strongly, and not let anybody disabuse you of your self-respect."

Barbara was most influenced by her grandfather Patten, her mother's father, in whose junkyard Barbara learned some of the most important lessons of her early life. "Just remember the world is not a playground, but a school room. Life is not a holiday, but an education," he would tell her. Grandfather Patten taught her self-confidence and a respect for education.

Barbara became an outstanding speaker in high school and went on to all-black Texas Southern University, where she learned much of her now-famous speaking flair from the debate coach, Tom Freeman. The high point of her college debate career occurred when Harvard's debate team traveled to Texas Southern to debate her championship team. The debate ended in a tie, which Barbara privately saw as a "win."

When she entered the Texas legislature in 1967 at age thirty, it was a first for a black woman. On top of that, she was the first black senator since 1883 and the only woman in the Senate. Behind her back, there was lots of grumbling from some of her fellow senators, most of whom represented the white, racist, conservative tradition of old Texas politics. After her swearing-in ceremony on opening day, one especially powerful old senator from San Angelo commented to a friend, "I'm not going to let no nigger woman tell me what to do." But within a few months' time, Barbara had won the respect of even that senator with her thoroughness, hard work, and pertinent questions. Perhaps the defining moment occurred when the old senator, along with another powerful older senator, pulled Barbara into his office to ask her help in devising a way to break a filibuster—over glasses of scotch. As a freshman senator, Barbara had been accepted into the inner sanctum—an unheard-of feat. By session's end, she was unanimously voted outstanding senator.

That was just the beginning of her remarkable thirty-year career in public service. When she left the Texas Senate six years later to take her place in the U.S. Congress, her portrait was hung in the Senate Chamber. In 1974, as a member of the U.S. House Judiciary Committee, she captured the imagination of the nation with her televised "my faith in the constitution is whole" speech during the Watergate hearings on President Richard Nixon's impeachment.

In 1979, as she was becoming more and more incapacitated with multiple sclerosis, Barbara began the phase of her career that gave her the most pleasure—teaching at the LBJ School of Public Affairs at the University of Texas in Austin. Her classes were so popular that students had to compete in a lottery to win admission into her classes. One student said, "I've never met a person who believed so strongly that we can actually change the world, and that gives me confidence that we really can."

Her career was cut short when, at age fifty-nine, she died of complications of multiple sclerosis and leukemia. Her body lay in state at the LBJ Library in Austin for twenty-four hours. At her funeral, Houston's Good Hope Missionary Baptist Church was packed with fifteen hundred people, among them dignitaries such as Presidents Bill Clinton and Jimmy Carter. Hundreds more stood outside the church in drizzling rain, listening to the proceedings on loudspeakers. Among the eight people to offer reflections on Barbara's life was former governor Ann Richards, who said, "There was simply something about her that made you proud to be a part of the country that produced her."

*Barbara
Jordan*

## SPEAKS

**CHALLENGING YOURSELF:** Life is full of challenges. And we often measure ourselves and our success in life by how we meet those challenges. . . . Challenge validates our aliveness and often disturbs the order of our lives. *(1990) Mary Beth Rogers,* Barbara Jordan, American Hero *(New York: Bantam Books, 1998), p. 299.*

**POWER OF THE FEMALE:** One overdue change already underway is the number of women challenging the councils of political power dominated by white-male policy makers. That horizon is limitless. What we see today is simply a dress rehearsal for the day and time we meet in convention to nominate . . . Madame President. *Keynote address, Democratic National Convention, July 13, 1992.*

This country can ill afford to continue to function using less than half of its human resources, brain power, and kinetic energy. *Keynote address, Democratic National Convention, July 13, 1992.*

**THE AMERICAN DREAM:** What people want is simple. They want an America as good as its promise. *Commencement address, Harvard University, June 16, 1977.*

**GETTING INVOLVED:** It is not enough to say, "right on, brother" or "we shall overcome." . . . You must become part of the decision-making process. *Paul Slater, "Freedoms Attached, Senator Tells Meet,"* Corpus Christi Caller-Times, *May 14, 1970.*

**THE CONSTITUTION:** My faith in the Constitution is whole, it is complete, it is total and I am not going to sit here and be an idle spectator to the diminution, the subversion, the destruction of the Constitution. *House Judiciary Committee, "Debate on Articles of Impeachment," p. 60, July 25, 1974.*

**POLITICS:** I am here simply because all those people in the Eighteenth District of Texas cannot get on planes and buses and come to Washington to speak for themselves. They have elected me as their spokesperson, nothing else, and my only job is to speak for them. *Charles L. Sanders, "Barbara Jordan, Texan, Is a New Power on Capitol Hill,"* Ebony, *February 1975.*

Those who hold the public trust must adhere to the highest ethical standards there are. The job requires it, and the public must demand it. *Remarks at the University of Texas at Austin, February 22, 1991.*

**RESPECTING OTHERS:** If you respect differences, you will also respect the ability of other thoughtful people to struggle internally with a problem and come to an answer that is somewhat different than your own. *Keynote address to the Southern Africa Grant-makers Affinity Group, Council on Foundations, Chicago, April 21, 1991.*

I am a born optimist. I find that if you can just cut off the layers, the rhetoric, the superficiality, and get to the inner core—the heart [of a person]—that you will find a responsible human being. *Liz Carpenter, "Barbara Jordan Talks about Ethics, Optimism, and Hard Choices in Government,"* Ms., *April 1985.*

**EQUALITY:** It was immigration that taught us, it does not matter where you came from, or who your parents were. What counts is who you are. (Speaking as chair of the U.S. Commission on Immigration Reform.) *Quoted by Rep. Sheila Jackson-Lee (D-Texas) speaking before the U.S. House of Representatives "Tribute to the Late Hon. Barbara Jordan,"* Congressional Record, *January 24, 1996.*

**ETHICAL BEHAVIOR:** You need a core inside you—a core that directs everything you do. You confer with it for guidance. It is not negotiable. *Scott Williams, "Jordan Praises Stockman,"* Daily Texan, *November 23, 1981.*

**DIVERSITY:** One thing is clear to me: We, as human beings, must be willing to accept people who are different from ourselves. *"All Together Now,"* Sesame Street Parents, *July–August, 1994.*

Speaking for myself, I wish that we would get past all the hyphenations that seem to be dividing our society. We must let all Americans be Americans, regardless of where their ancestors were born. Social cohesion requires it. Public policy should support it. *"Focus: Legal Immigration/Naturalization,"* CIR News *(newsletter of the U.S. Commission on Immigration Reform) 2, no. 1 (February 1995).*

**HARMONY:** A spirit of harmony can only survive if each of us remembers, when bitterness and self-interest seem to prevail, that we share a common destiny. *Keynote address, Democratic National Convention, New York, July 12, 1976.*

**YOUNG PEOPLE:** I have faith in young people because I know the strongest emotions which prevail are those of love and caring and belief and tolerance. *In* On Campus, *Friday, February 14, 1994.*

**TEACHING:** I find teaching extraordinarily satisfying. I realize that probably through my entire political career I was in training for this. . . . I'm teaching young people who will move into local, state, and federal positions of power. . . . Some will run for political office. It's a remarkable opportunity to have an impact on the generation that will succeed me. *Malcolm Boyd, "Where Is Barbara Jordan Today?"* Parade, *February 16, 1986.*

**MARRIAGE:** Where a man was concerned, the public perception was that he was supposed to get out there and lead and do and make decisions and the rest of it; and no one said to him that he needed to care for babies, or iron the curtains or clean the johns. That was not expected of him. What was expected was that he'd marry a woman to do it for him. *Barbara Jordan and Shelby Hearon,* Barbara Jordan: A Self Portrait *(New York: Doubleday, 1979).*

**SELF-CONFIDENCE:** You must understand that I have a tremendous faith in my own capacity. *Molly Ivins, "A Profile of Barbara Jordan,"* Texas Observer, *November 3, 1972.*

**SILENCE:** There is a part of me who enjoys to speak when I have something to say. And if I don't have anything that I feel needs to be said, then I don't say it. *Bruce Nichols, "Rep. Jordan, at 41, Considers Political Future,"* Dallas Times Herald, *November 27, 1977.*

**PATIENCE:** I'm not long on patience. Sometimes I'm more abrupt with people than I ought to be. I always regret it afterward. *John Pierson, "Barbara Jordan's Star Reaches Dizzy Heights for House Sophomore,"* Wall Street Journal, *February 6, 1975.*

**LIVING ONE DAY AT A TIME:** I live a day at a time. Each day I look for a kernel of excitement. In the morning, I say, "What is my exciting thing for today?" Then I *do* the day. Don't ask me about tomorrow. *Malcolm Boyd, "Where Is Barbara Jordan Today?"* Parade, *February 16, 1996.*

**FAITH:** I believe that I have a spirit that is not going to disappear. That my body will die and disintegrate, but there is that basic law of physics, that matter is neither created nor destroyed. Now the skin and bones will go back to dust, but the spirit of that individual, the presence of "isness" of me, I feel will live. *Liz Carpenter, "Barbara Jordan Talks about Ethics, Optimism, and Hard Choices in Government,"* Ms., *April 1985.*

# LIZ CARPENTER

*"Lots of solutions happen around a casserole. If you can put a meal on the table, you will find that it comes in handy, even if you are plotting a revolution."*

*Liz Carpenter, journalist. Photo by Summer Pierce © 2001.*

*Liz
Carpenter*

B. 1920,
**SALADO, TEXAS**
CURRENT HOME:
**AUSTIN, TEXAS**

∾

Liz Carpenter is a descendant of six generations of Texans. She was born the middle child in a family of five children in Salado, Texas, a small town close to Austin. Shortly after graduating from the University of Texas with a bachelor's degree in journalism, Liz began her journalism career in Washington, D.C., at age twenty-one.

She and husband, Les, operated their own news bureau in Washington from the time they married in 1944 until 1961, when Liz became then Vice President Lyndon B. Johnson's executive assistant. During LBJ's years as president, 1963–1968, Liz served as press secretary and staff director for Lady Bird Johnson. Of her White House years, Liz has commented: "I survived two White House weddings, five White House dogs, and raft rides down the Snake River with cabinet members. I danced in the East Room with two presidents, a king or two, and innumerable prime ministers and ambassadors. Heady stuff for a girl from Salado."

Liz was one of 271 founders of the National Women's Political Caucus in 1971 and emerged as spokeswoman for the organization. The group's purpose was to organize caucuses in Texas and other states to urge women to run for office and to help get them elected. She was co-chairperson of the Equal Rights Amendment Initiative in 1976–1981 and served as assistant secretary of the U.S. Department of Education in 1980–1981 during the Carter administration.

She has authored four books: *Ruffles and Flourishes* (1970), *Getting Better All The Time* (1987), *Unplanned Parenthood: The Confessions of a Seventy-something Surrogate Mother* (1994), and *Start with a Laugh* (2000), a how-to book about giving memorable speeches. Her quick wit and storytelling ability have made her a sought-after lecturer.

Liz moved back to Austin in 1976, two years after Les died. The couple had raised two children, Scott and Christy. In 1991 Liz took on the job of rearing her two nieces and one nephew, all teenagers, whom she "inherited" after her oldest brother, Tom, died.

At age eighty, in 2001, she became one of the fourteen new members of the elite Texas Institute of Letters, an honorary organization for writers. Liz is a member of the Texas Philosophical Society, she is a Distinguished Alumnus of the University of Texas, and she was inducted into the Texas Women's Hall of Fame by Governor Mark White.

Liz often begins her morning before dawn, writing at the computer in her glassed-in office at home overlooking the skyline of downtown Austin and the green Texas Hill Country.

**AUTHOR'S NOTE** *Spending time with Liz Carpenter almost always involves a lot of laughter, good food, and liberal politics. Liz always manages to make everyone feel at home in her cozy house made of Texas limestone rock and shaded by seven Texas live oak trees. The day she moved in, she named the house and the acre of land Grassroots because she was back home in Texas. It sits on a cliff hidden away in the hills of West Austin.*

*I get a taste of Liz's hospitality during the handful of visits I make throughout the course of writing this book. Each meeting starts in her sunny, comfortably cluttered office overlooking the Austin skyline. But we usually end up at the dining table—either over a cup of her delicious, strong coffee and pastries or over sandwiches with whoever else happens to drop in that day. But Liz never stops working, even at the dining table. She puts down her sandwich from time to time to answer phone calls from friends across the country who invariably have some interesting question or request.*

*Liz Carpenter*

## SPEAKS

**TEXAS WOMEN:** My mother always admonished me: "Remember who you are. Make something of yourself." She was really proud of her family that was here in Texas in 1829. She was a very calm woman of faith. I knew something was expected of me.

We Texas women are close to our history—to those women who came across the river carrying a rifle. The ranch woman is in all of us to a degree. Women on the frontier were in charge because we had to be. The open spaces made us a lot spunkier. I think Texans are shaped by blue skies, optimism, and more space. And I think Texas men like spunky women.

I think Texas women have strong genes. But then, I have known some other very strong women who didn't have the benefit of growing up in Texas. (Laughs.)

**MENTORS:** I seem to have chosen as mentors outspoken women who worked to change things for everybody, rather than women who quietly followed the rules and worked to change things just for themselves.

Minnie Fisher Cunningham of Waller, Texas, who was active in the suffrage movement, told me all about it—so vividly that I thought I had been there. (Texas made women's suffrage legal before it became legal nationally.) One of her important lessons was: "Address the envelope and stamp it before you write the letter. Then you'll be sure to write the letter." She also said, "To have a stepping-stone, you have to be one." It is glorious when you make the phone call that gets somebody the interview.

My first boss—a woman—taught me lots of things. One that has stuck with me through the years: Never make a decision solely on the basis of money. If you really want strawberries and they are $5.00 a pound, get the strawberries!

**POLITICS:** During my Washington years, I began to realize that it will take *women* to make important changes in society because we are the nurturers. We make a difference in politics when we speak up, because we try to find the commonsense basis for doing things.

I watched and learned from Frances Perkins, secretary of labor under Franklin Roosevelt. Frances—with that tricornered hat—used common sense and created most of the New Deal legislation. She walked into FDR's office with a little handwritten list: unemployment compensation, minimum wage. . . . (I can't tell this without crying.) All those things made up the New Deal. And it wasn't all those swashbuckling Harvardites that pushed it through the Hill. Instead, it was a woman who insisted on it. Most people don't know that.

And then during the 1970s and 1980s, we campaigned for the Equal Rights Amendment. We came to understand that we couldn't realize our feminist potential unless we did it through politics. We had to have more clout.

So Shana Alexander summoned me to that meeting at the Statler Hilton in July 1971 where 271 women founded the National Women's Political Caucus. Our mission was to urge women to run for office and sometimes get elected, to get the Equal Rights Amendment passed, and to organize caucuses in all the states. I was put in charge of handling the press and getting what was said by these women leaders into the newspapers—Betty Friedan, Shirley Chisholm, Gloria Steinem, Bella Abzug, Virginia Allen. . . .

I remember saying to Shana, "These women shouldn't be using such strong words." And she said, looking philosophical and beautiful, "But these are strong times!"

And that convinced me that the ERA movement would soon find its way into the population. And it did—to such an extent that I doubt that young women today have any idea of how much sweat and sacrifice was given. It was taking your whole damn weekend! You might be playing to twenty-five or a thousand. And you were mostly paying your own way.

Campaigning for the ERA went on for about fifteen years. It was the most exciting thing that I had ever done because it was such a gamble. I was terribly disappointed when the ERA didn't pass. But still I have faith that it will pass because it is right. I think it will probably pass in a whisper sometime.

If the generations are going to be there for each other, it will be because women did it. We're not going to get anywhere on world peace if we keep looking at Brooks Brothers suits walking out of a summit meeting. That scene offends me so I can hardly keep from throwing something at the television set!

**ANGER:** Anger is a good motivator. You need to use the adrenaline that anger engenders in a constructive way. Women used to be taught to take whatever is said to them and remain silent. But you need to talk back. You shouldn't take somebody's orders or arguments, simply to be polite, when you know what has been said is unfair and untrue. If you can do it with humor, you do better.

For example, when Pat Schroeder of Colorado was a young woman in the U.S. Congress in the 1970s, a male representative said to her, "How can you be a congressman and the mother of two small children?"

Schroeder said: "Because I have a brain and a uterus, and I use both!"

**PRINCIPLES I LIVE BY:**

- "See humor in the situation," my mother would tell me. She had a good sense of humor and valued it. So humor has always been a part of my life, maybe because you needed it in such a big family. And you certainly need it in politics and in all of the other fields I have been associated with.
- Hate will devour you if you let it. I don't allow myself to hate people.
- Be there for others. It's a pleasure to share other people's needs. It's the sins of omission that haunt people.
- Be loyal to your friends. I'm heavy on loyalty and on not letting people down. Lyndon Johnson reinforced that lesson in me. He never asked you to do something he wasn't willing to do. He gave friendship and he got it.

**CAREERS:** I went into Washington when World War II was under way, in June 1942, and men were leaving. So, for the first time, a newswoman could get a job doing something other than being a society reporter (a behind-the-palms intelligence service). We knew that Eleanor Roosevelt had made it possible for us to have a job because she made news, and she held press conferences that were limited to women. By discriminating in this way, she forced newspapers to hire women reporters to cover her.

In my generation we didn't have five-year plans like my daughter has. You just walked through the open door or backed away from it. And I generally walked through it.

Most young women just entering the workforce today don't feel that there will be problems for them because they are female. I think they are going to have to get burned before they realize that women are still fighting an uphill battle for equality. They'll have to be discriminated against—and they *will* be. I think that within the first ten years of being out in the workplace, they are going to get really angry because they will see that they are not treated equally. And they're going to think that they are the first ones to discover it.

**CORPORATE WORLD:** Young women—especially those in their thirties and forties—are finding that the corporate world does not feed their soul enough. They are working fifty- to sixty-hour weeks but are not finding satisfaction. Few corporations really encourage the human side of their employees. Young women in the rat race need to live a little slower, talk a little slower, and go places where they are likely to meet somebody who is their mental equal and inspires courage.

**CHANGING CAREERS:** Young women are interested in shaping themselves for one job. And yet, if statistics are true, they will each hold six or seven jobs in their lifetime and move five or six times.

I think that today's young woman has ahead of her a lot of time in which to do things. Because people are living much longer, a woman has time to follow her bliss, change jobs several times, be with her family, and then carve out what she wants to do the rest of her life.

**WRITING YOUR OWN JOB DESCRIPTION:** You should be willing to take risks. Don't be too scared. It has been said that men are made anxious by failure, but women are made anxious by success. Lots of women want the job description spelled out for them because they are fearful they can't live up to it. But you should go into a job and fill up the job description the way you want it to read.

**GETTING A JOB:** On your résumé, don't put "references available upon request." You aren't going to hold anybody's attention for more than ten seconds. So you had better list the most influential people you know on your résumé.

During a job interview, talk in a voice the interviewer can hear. The whole TV generation seems to be talking in falsetto voices, and these girls want older people to extract information from them. You should remember: Anybody who can give you a job worth a damn probably has a hearing impairment. So speak up and don't put a strain on them!

**COOKING:** So many young women have lots of talent and education, but they can't cook a damn thing! It helps to use whatever nurturing instincts you have. Lots of solutions happen around a casserole. If you can put a meal on the table, you will find that it comes in handy, even if you are plotting a revolution.

**SATISFACTION:** Life holds lots of satisfaction for me. Those times that stand out as most satisfying are when:

- I look at my two children, Scott and Christy, and my grandson, Les, and I see them being vital and involved in good works. It makes me realize that growing up in an intense media-political world did not turn them off. Instead, it helped them to grow.
- I am being used to my utmost (and I survive it). For example: when, during the horrible events just after the Kennedy assassination, I was there to write those fifty-eight words for Lyndon Johnson to say to the American people when he landed in Washington, D.C.

  I was the only writer aboard Air Force One on the way from Dallas to D.C., and some higher force propelled me to realize that LBJ would have to speak when he landed in Washington as president. So, instead of waiting for an assignment, I rose to the occasion. LBJ delivered those fifty-eight words on the tarmac at

Andrews Air Force Base, Maryland, on November 22, 1963: *"This is a sad time for all people. We have suffered a loss that cannot be weighed. For me, it is a deep personal tragedy. I know that the world shares the sorrow that Mrs. Kennedy and her family bear. I will do my best. That is all I can do. I ask for your help—and God's."* (LBJ Library: Statements of Lyndon Johnson, Box 89, "Remarks of the President upon Arrival at Andrews Air Force Base, Nov. 22, 1963.")

- Words come to me in my writing. For me that is early in the morning when my mind is clearer. I can't imagine not meeting the computer every morning. It's like a husband beckoning: "Come play with me."

- When I wrote my first book, *Ruffles and Flourishes,* and I had those eighteen chapters spread out on the floor. It was like tiptoeing through the tulips. The thrill of it! Feeling that there was my life thus far! I felt like swimming in that life and drinking champagne.

- When I make a speech that people identify with. When I make one that's a dud, it's not satisfying.

**FAITH:** When my plans start falling into place, I begin to think that it must be an affirmation from God or from some spirit greater than myself, telling me that I am on the right track. When nothing is going right, I begin to question whether I have made the right decision. When everything starts getting in your way, that may be a way of telling you, "Kid, you are on the wrong path."

So many things I need fall right into my hand—unexplained. A book that tells me something I didn't even know I was looking for—or a phrase in a paper. I listen for words because that is my business. And they come my way, so I know that it's not just an accident. It happens too often. I do have to open my ears—my mind—to the fact that maybe there is somebody helping me.

I am surprised that some of my contemporaries are agnostics and atheists. I think that they just haven't realized that there is some order to the universe. I've always had faith that there is a God, and the closer I get to what hopefully will be heaven, the more I listen for it. You are better off if you walk hand in hand with the universe.

I plan to haunt this planet—swing from the chandeliers of the White

House. Hopefully I'll be able to impart some golden knowledge back between heaven and earth.

**FRIENDSHIP:** Without all of my good friends, life wouldn't be nearly as grand. Families are often not around to be supportive when you need them, and friends have been a salvation to me.

You have to create a network of friends or you can't operate in the world. Wherever I have lived, I have always had good neighbors. Networking was important before it was a word. I could call my neighbor and say, "Go pick up Christy. She's sick." We did that for each other. It was about being a friend.

I count among my good friends both men and women. My group of singers (Getting Better All the Time Singers—GBATS)—our bodies are beginning to fall apart, and we are trying to be there for each other. We check on each other.

I have four really good male friends. But women friends are usually my first choice because I can talk about anything with them. We women have gotten to where we really bare our souls with each other, and men have a harder time doing that. Women have discovered that women friends are the best friends.

However, females seem to be associating more with males on a platonic level today. That's good. Since I have been raising my two teenage nieces and my nephew, I have seen young men—like my nephew, Tommy—becoming gender blind and color blind. He has friends of both sexes and all colors. I know because they are around my house all the time.

**MOTHERHOOD:** My kids have turned out fine. But now I realize I wasn't with them enough when they were little. I wish I had been around them more. But my career was important, too. I was so much more excited by what was going on on Capitol Hill than with their little mannerisms.

I wish God had made us so we had kids later—because when you are under forty, you are young and ambitious and ready to put your energy into a career. I hate to say this since I am so close to the cemetery, but I think God should have done it differently. He made a mistake by having our reproductive life last till only about age forty. After forty, you are ready to spend time with the children, and you don't resent the time away from work.

**BRIDGING THE GENERATION GAP:** There is a lot to learn about the generations being there for each other. Conferences are being held on the subject.

We are the storytellers. We are the ones who need to remind our grandchildren, nieces, and nephews about their roots. About my teenage uncle who at seventeen died at the Alamo. Whether we are kin to younger people or not, we need to make them appreciate the past. They need to realize that life did begin before Ronald Reagan.

But we also need to listen to the younger generation. We don't seem to listen to each other enough.

**MARRIAGE:** I was lucky to have been married to my best friend. We worked together and we played together in Washington, but we also gave each other some space to do our own thing.

I learned some things a long time ago from psychologists who were gathered at Betty Friedan's house. (She always had a lot of psychologists around her; they liked to study her.)

I said, "What's the main cause for divorce?" They said, "Two people who don't grow at the same rate." I saw that problem happen especially with marriages in the political arena.

**WIDOWHOOD:** When Les died, I spent two unsettling years trying to deal with life without him. Then someone gave me the best advice I ever got about being widowed: "God has given you a chance at a second life." (Since then, I have passed that message of freedom on to a lot of other widows.) Death had robbed me of my husband. But it also allowed me to change my life. Most couples neutralize their friends. During my marriage, I got cut off from some real characters I enjoyed whom Les didn't like. So we had people over that we both liked.

After Les died, I began inviting some of those characters into my house and life. By having them at my house, I felt almost like I was getting back at death. That sounds heartless to say, but it's true. It's a way to cope.

**GETTING OLDER:** I have just been to the White House Conference on Aging. The fastest-growing age group in America is the eighty-and-up group. And they are staying vital longer. There are thirty-four million people over sixty-five and only 5 percent are in rest homes. So we are living vitally and changing, and are able to follow our bliss longer.

I think it is a market that hasn't been recognized. I try to sell magazine stories about people who are as old as I am. The editors say, "Oh, that person is yesterday. We are playing to the thirty-five-year-old." They are targeting the Jerry Seinfelds of the world—the yuppies. The magazine industry just hasn't figured out yet that people my age buy magazines, too.

**RETIRING:** I wouldn't urge anybody to retire and do nothing, because when you stop being productive, you don't feel needed. And the need to feel needed is primary in us. When I go to nursing homes with the GBATS, my group that sings (somewhat), I see so many empty faces. People may think they want to retire and sit on the porch and rock, but those people could die tomorrow and it wouldn't make any difference. I feel that I always need to find something else to lose sleep over!

# MARJ CARPENTER

"*Excess is wrong:*

*excess of drink,*

*excess of food,*

*excess of gossip,*

*and excess of piety.*"

**Marj Carpenter**

B. 1926,
MERCEDES, TEXAS
CURRENT HOME:
BIG SPRING, TEXAS

Marj Carpenter was a rugged West Texas newspaper reporter and news editor for twenty-eight years (1950–1978) in Pecos, Andrews, and Big Spring. Her life as a journalist was filled with chasing car wrecks and fires, politicians and football coaches—all while she was raising three children. Marj was one of three journalists at the *Pecos Independent* nominated for a Pulitzer Prize in the early 1960s when they uncovered the fraudulent activities of Texas wheeler-dealer Billie Sol Estes. She became a widow in 1965. Her children were fifteen, thirteen, and nine years old.

After the children were grown, Marj spent ten years (1978–1988) as news director for the Presbyterian Church U.S., headquartered in Atlanta, followed by six years as manager of news services for the newly reunited Presbyterian Church (USA). Since 1980, Marj has visited and reported on almost 600 Presbyterian mission stations in 115 countries. Her travel has taken her deep into African jungles, into famine-stricken Ethiopia, and into leprosy camps.

In 1995, the year after she retired from the Presbyterian headquarters, Marj was elected to the highest office of the 2.8-million-member Presbyterian Church (USA). As moderator, she traveled throughout the Presbyterian world, preaching the message that got her elected: Presbyterians should stop bickering over sexual issues, stop worrying that they are losing members too fast, and go back to what they do best: mission. She is an elder in her home church, First Presbyterian Church in Big Spring. Her books, *To the Ends of the Earth* and *And a Little Bit Farther,* are conversational accounts of her travels to Presbyterian mission stations abroad. At seventy-two, Marj still makes a few trips abroad each year to visit mission sites and to report on them. Her schedule is booked a year in advance to speak each Sunday to Presbyterian churches around the nation.

Marj was president of the National Federation of Press Women in 1992–1993 and has interviewed eight presidents, as well as many other political leaders. She believes strongly in freedom of the press and served on the First Amendment Congress under President George Bush.

**AUTHOR'S NOTE**    *Marj is anything but pious. In fact, many who think of church leaders as being staid and proper might find her downright irreverent. I find her excessively refreshing. My favorite of her platitudes: "Excess is wrong: excess of drink, excess of food, excess of gossip, and excess of piety."*

*She is still the rugged West Texan she always was, even though she lived in Louisville and Atlanta for sixteen years during her career at the Presbyterian national headquarters. When she retired in 1995, Marj was homesick for West Texas, and so she moved back home to Big Spring.*

*Straight-spoken, friendly, humble, and down-to-earth, Marj has a West Texas practical, no-nonsense approach to life. Her dry sense of humor, hearty laugh, and broad West Texas drawl accompany her everywhere. She is so busy in her "retirement" career in her seventies that she had to look three months ahead in her calendar to find a free hour at home so that we could have an uninterrupted interview. Marj has jotted down notes beforehand to make sure she gets important points covered. Once a journalist . . .*

*Marj Carpenter*

**SPEAKS**

**PRINCIPLES I LIVE BY:** When I reflect on the most important things I have learned in my life thus far, the following are at the top of the list.

- Love the Lord.
- Praise your children and grandchildren as they are growing up, so that they end up as confident adults.
- Take the Gospel into all the world.
- Have fun.
- Care for those in real trouble.
- Stand up for what you think is right.

**MENTORS:** My high school English and journalism teacher in Mercedes, Texas, Amy Cornish, was the one who inspired me to go into journalism. There is no question. She made me learn to be a proofreader. She gave me all sorts of assignments that I didn't really want.

When I first learned to drive, she sent me up to McAllen to cover an opera singer I really didn't want to hear, and on the way back I came upon a train wreck. The train had hit a group of migrant workers and had killed over thirty people. I had two pictures left in my camera. It was like the massacre scene in *Gone With the Wind* when the dead soldiers were lying all over the depot. I got in the car and cried all the way back to the paper. It was the first time I sold a photograph to a newspaper. I was sixteen.

**SETTING GOALS:** I really didn't want to major in music, but I did it to please my mother. She had always wanted to major in music, and she had all her hopes pinned on my doing it. She thought that women could always teach school if they couldn't do anything else. So I got a teaching certificate.

But the first week I was in college, I ran upstairs into the attic to the Pub Office where the students worked on the annual and the newspaper. I volunteered to work on the newspaper because journalism is what I really liked. I was the only nonjournalism major who ever edited the paper at Texas A&I. I have always been glad I did that. I ended up being a journalist the rest of my life.

My dad kept telling my mother I wasn't meant to be a music teacher, that I was meant to be a reporter because things seemed to happen around me. And through the years that has been true. When I was twelve and on top of the Empire State Building, a woman jumped off in front of me. My kids always joke that because things always happen around me, it makes you scared to go anywhere with Mama. (Laughs.)

**CAREER CHALLENGES:** I went to work for the newspaper in Pecos when my kids were little. When my paper helped expose Billie Sol Estes, things turned into a real zoo. Reporters came from all over the world. I corresponded for papers in West Texas, Dallas, and even the *New York Times*. I even sold an article to *Fortune* magazine. And suddenly I was just real deep into a kind of journalism that I never dreamed I'd be in. I was meeting journalists from all over the world. It was interesting, but it was also scary. In those years a brick was thrown through a bedroom window in my house, and a snake was put in my car. Somebody set our newspaper office on fire twice. My children even received a threat or two during that time. Those were not years that I particularly like to remember.

**STANDING UP FOR WHAT YOU BELIEVE:** I've learned that you don't have to die in every ditch. When faced with something you really want to stand for and argue about, sometimes you need to wait a bit, listen a little, and see how things are going to turn out before you get in there and fight that battle. Otherwise you just seem to be fighting battles all the time.

I've learned to count my ditches and fight just for the things that I find really important. Part of that wisdom came out of the Billie Sol Estes episode in 1962 when we were fighting in every ditch. I think that can wear you down until you become ineffective.

I have learned that if you lose a fight, maybe there was a reason.

**CHANGING CAREERS:** After twenty-eight years as a newspaper reporter, I got a call from the headquarters of the Presbyterian Church in Atlanta. They asked if I would be interested in becoming the news director of the Presbyterian Church. And I said, "No, I'm too rough for that. I have been covering sporting events and crime news and murder scenes and plane crashes, and I don't think that I would be suitable for that task." But they asked me to come for an interview. I went, thinking that it was all just a funny joke, that they wouldn't hire me, that I had too many rough edges. But they hired me. (Laughs.)

I never regretted it, except during that first month when I thought, "I have gotten into something boring that I do not like and I have made a big mistake. I should have stayed in newspapers." Then I got to go to Brazil on a Presbyterian Church trip and it changed my whole outlook. Sometimes somebody up there knows better than you do about how your life should turn out.

**WRITING YOUR OWN JOB DESCRIPTION:** When I saw the worthwhile things our church was doing in Brazil, I thought, "There are all sorts of things the church is doing out here in the world that the Presbyterians don't know anything about. If I can get out there myself and report to people back home what is going on, I will enjoy this job." There wasn't any money for a reporter to cover the church around the world, so I have always raised it through Presbyterian friends who want to hear what their church is doing abroad.

**TRAVEL:** Having been on more long trips than most people, I can give some real practical advice I have picked up along the way.

Travel light. You don't have to take all of the clothes you own, because you are not going to be in the same place all that long. The person you see today won't know that you wore the same thing yesterday. Be able to clean your own clothes along the way if you need to—wash them and hang them out to dry. Don't carry a lot, but do carry whatever medicine you need. I take along something for indigestion, diarrhea, and constipation—just those basic things. Always take those along. It saves you lots of grief along the way.

It is harder for me to travel now than it used to be. I walk a little slower, but I get there. I like to walk in airports as much as I can for exercise, and I always check my bags now so I can do that.

**LOOKING TOWARD THE FUTURE:** I'm doing less overseas travel now. I am planning on going back to China. Before they had to leave, the Presbyterians were heavy into mission in China, and the results are now very apparent. I used to go to eight countries a year, but I have slowed way down, and now even one country a year is just fine with me. Eventually I would like to get into Iran and Iraq, where there are some Presbyterians. Our missionaries were driven out, but the church is still alive there. I would like to go to Siberia, where some of our Alaskan Presbyterian missionaries are starting churches.

**CHURCH:** Now I am serving on the session (board) of the local church. When you are back in your local church, it doesn't matter what you've done out in the larger world. You are just one of the members at your home church. My local church doesn't give a darn that I have gotten to do all these fun things all over the world. They are not the least bit interested in my advice. (Laughs.) It is humbling.

I have had some real fierce arguments about what I think our local church should be doing differently because I have seen what the church is doing out in the world. I have worked in many ecumenical groups. I think we need to cooperate among denominations.

**FAITH:** Life is short. I used to think that life went on forever, but I am beginning to realize that it doesn't. We do need to believe in some kind of God—in a higher being. We need to believe that there is something after life is over on this earth.

When times are tough, tie a knot and just hang on. Although families are important to us, we have to have something else to believe in when life gets tough.

**WIDOWHOOD:** My husband died in 1965, when the kids were still young. I have always been so busy that I haven't had time to worry about not being married again. I have had one or two opportunities that could have developed into remarriage, but I really wasn't interested because I was scrambling, trying to get enough together to give my kids a good college education. The three children and I were very, very close. We got through it the best way we could. I haven't regretted that. We are still close.

It wasn't easy, but I don't remember having any real terrible problems, except that it seemed that I had to work all the time. Sometimes I would hold two jobs. I would work at the paper and then do substitute teaching at the school because I had a teaching certificate. Just anything to earn money. We figured all kinds of ways to get scholarships and to borrow money so they could go to college. All three of my children have a college degree; one has two degrees. We got all the money paid back.

I managed to get them all some kind of used car to drive. A car was really important to teenagers back then, too.

**CHILDREN:** When children do something well, tell them so. Tell them you are proud of them, brag on them, tell them how glad you are they did good. When they do something wrong, tell them that, too, but easily. Tell them how they can do it better. The children who grow up with all kinds of problems are those who have always heard "shut up" or "get out of the way."

You need to give kids as much freedom as you can, but you also need to discipline kids and not just turn them loose to do anything they want. I don't mean harsh discipline. Make some rules and stick with them. Be consistent.

**FAMILY:** Always be supportive and caring about your family. Being with them every minute isn't what counts. People who are constantly together may get tired of each other and become less caring. Let your family know that you care about them and that you are glad when you can be together.

I feel most alive when I am with my three grandchildren. This may seem ridiculous given all the scary and interesting things I've done, but grandkids are what you pass on. Long after you're gone, hopefully they will be out there doing something good.

**PROUDEST ACCOMPLISHMENT:** My proudest accomplishments are my children and grandchildren—no question. They are people you like to be with.

Next to that, I am proudest of what I have been able to do for the Presbyterian Church. I was the only reporter ever elected moderator of the Presbyterian Church. Usually moderators are preachers or professors.

**NURTURING YOURSELF:** I do a lot of things for fun. I love to play with my grandchildren and to visit my friends. I have friends everywhere I go and a lot of friends here at home. I enjoy good old-fashioned conversation.

I play the piano. It is a great relief to me to sit down and plunk out honky-tonk tunes on the piano. When I'm frustrated, I really bang on those keys.

I read a lot, sometimes just for fun. I read lots of detective stories and all of Agatha Christie's stuff. I also read heavy books for the church, but not a steady diet of them.

I relax in the evening by taking a couple of scotch and waters. That is a good Presbyterian drink, so it's all right. (Laughs.) I'm Irish, Scottish, and German. What a wonderful combination!

**FRIENDSHIP:** I'm excited about the fact that I am living in a part of the world I love—out in West Texas—and that I have good friends here. I get together with a group of women here once a week at noon, if possible. We eat together and laugh and joke. I hang out with all kinds of people of all faiths, even a pair of atheists. (Laughs.) I like variety.

One of my professional friends from the old days is Sarah McClendon. I stayed in Sarah's home in Washington during two of the four presidential inaugurations I have attended. Sarah stayed in my home in West Texas one time to hide out. She was traveling as a reporter with the Goldwater campaign, and she got tired of it about Midland, Texas. I was over there covering it and she went home with me to Pecos and hid in my house for three days and nights and worked in my kitchen while they were hunting her.

Finally somebody remembered that I knew her, and they called from Washington and said, "Have you seen Sarah McClendon?" And I said, "Just a minute." And I went into the kitchen and said, "Sarah, they found you." And she said, "Oh, well. Three days. That was pretty good!" We are still friends. She calls me once or twice a year to ask my opinion on something she is working on, and I really appreciate that.

**TEXAS WOMEN:** I think that, maybe, Texans are too proud. Maybe we are too loudmouthed about it. But we're proud of our history, our heritage.

Texas women tend to be different from other women. They don't ask you about how big or important you are. Texans could care less about who your ancestors are. Instead they ask you where you are going, what you're doing.

Texas women have always been outspoken. Maybe they had to be outspoken in the early days in Texas to survive. I think they are strong. Sometimes they are what keeps the family going—the pillar of the family. It seemed like my mother and grandmother were.

Texas women have a good sense of humor. When I was staying with Sarah McClendon during Ronald Reagan's inauguration, my feet were hurting the night we were to go to the Texas Ball. Sarah objected to my going in my long dress with tennis shoes. But I was comfortable. (Laughs.)

**HUMOR:** I try to keep a sense of humor. I think if you don't, you're done. My kids all got my sense of humor. We wouldn't have made it through our lives without it.

**GETTING OLDER:** Would you believe my favorite ages have been my sixties and seventies? These last ten years have been the best of my life. I've gotten to go to interesting places. My first grandchild was born ten years ago. When I see people who give up at age sixty and go on the shelf, I just wish they'd get up and get at it. Because there is so much left out there to do.

# JODY CONRADT

"*If our society could practice all the things that we learn from being part of a team, then we wouldn't have many problems.*"

*Jody Conradt, coach. Photo by Summer Pierce © 1998.*

*Jody
Conradt*

B. 1941,
GOLDTHWAITE, TEXAS
CURRENT HOME:
AUSTIN, TEXAS

∿

With close to eight hundred wins at this writing, Jody Conradt has won more games than any coach in collegiate women's basketball. Only one other active collegiate basketball coach—a man—has more career victories.

Jody has been the head women's basketball coach at the University of Texas at Austin since 1976, when she took over the fledgling program. Within three years, the Lady Longhorns ranked among the top five in the nation. During Jody's tenure, the university has emerged as a national basketball power, winning the 1986 NCAA National Championship, dominating play by winning ten league titles, and sending numerous Texas student athletes into the professional basketball ranks. She added the duty of director of women's athletics in 1992 and oversaw eleven women's athletic programs until 2001, when she gave up that position at age fifty-nine to concentrate again solely on the women's basketball program.

In 1998 Jody became the second women's basketball coach in history to be inducted into the elite Naismith National Memorial Basketball Hall of Fame in Springfield, Massachusetts. She has been called a great teacher of the game of basketball, as well as the ultimate player's coach. On the court, she has directed a program generally acknowledged as one of the two or three pacesetters—one whose overall marketing, public relations, media efforts, and winning ways showed the world what women's basketball could be.

Jody has been National Coach of the Year four times and earned the title of Southwest Conference Coach of the Year five times. She was inducted into the International Women's Sports Hall of Fame in 1995, joining such sports greats as Wilma Rudolph, Chris Evert, and Martina Navratilova.

Ninety percent of Jody's players have earned their college degrees. She has produced four U.S. Olympic team members and nineteen all-Americans. More than a million fans, averaging more than eight thousand per year, have watched Jody's teams play at home.

Jody grew up in Goldthwaite playing sports. Her father, who was a semi-pro baseball player and a Little League coach, and her mother, who played softball, encouraged her. Her mother still makes the hundred-mile trip to Austin from Goldthwaite for every Lady Longhorn home game.

**AUTHOR'S NOTE** *My husband and I have sat at court level—directly across the court from the UT players' bench—at each Lady Longhorn home game for the past twelve years. From that vantage point, we can observe Jody Conradt's every facial expression as she paces back and forth in front of her players on the bench, concentrating on each play on the court. As a bench coach, Jody keeps a poker face and is known for her poised, intense demeanor during games.*

*We can sometimes hear her words over the roar of the crowd on the rare occasion when she scolds an umpire who has clearly misjudged a call.*

*Although I feel as if I have known her for years, today is the first time we have actually met. Instead of a well-tailored skirt, blazer, and heels (her usual game-night attire), she is wearing her office attire: khaki pants and a short-sleeved blue denim shirt with an orange longhorn embroidered above the pocket. And in place of her solemn game-day face is a relaxed, smiling one as she welcomes me into her cozy book-lined office.*

*Jody laughs easily and often, and I delight in her fluid conversation. I like this Jody even better than the serious one I have come to know on the basketball court.*

*Jody Conradt*

## SPEAKS

**TEXAS WOMEN:** If you grow up in Texas, you develop a sense of pride early on about this state. That pride builds confidence, a can-do attitude. We know we are a little bit different and that's okay. I feel that more is expected of Texans, and therefore we are motivated to reach those expectations. The perception exists that something is a little bit different, a little bit special, a little bit bigger about our state. And we are all by birth challenged to fulfill that prophecy. That goes for women as well as for men.

**POWER:** I think that both Austin and the University of Texas are more accommodating to women in power than other places. And I have always used that as a selling point when we try to recruit athletes to this environment. We are one of the few universities in the United States in which the women's athletic department is separate from the men's. Female student athletes at UT observe women being bosses, particularly in athletics, which is usually a male domain. The head of our athletic training staff is a woman. The athletic director is a woman. The compliance director is a woman. Everyone who is in a position of authority in the women's athletic department is a woman.

We have had many women leaders in our state government. We have had a woman governor. And many of those women have been strong supporters of our women's basketball team. You have always been able to see powerful women at Lady Longhorn games—Barbara Jordan, Ann

Richards. . . . And those women didn't start coming because they liked basketball. They probably didn't know a thing about basketball. They came because they identified with the perception that women athletes are strong women. They saw the UT women's basketball team excelling where women hadn't excelled before.

By the time Barbara Jordan had been a regular fixture at Lady Longhorn games for a few years, she felt she knew more than I did and she was helping me coach. (Laughs.) But initially she didn't know anything about sports. She had never been an athlete; she had never played.

**WOMEN'S SPORTS INFLUENCING SOCIETY:** Barbara Jordan excelled in a field where few other women up to that time had been successful—in the political arena. That was certainly a nontraditional role for a woman.

Today society is accepting lots of roles for women that were not at all traditional a generation ago. It didn't occur to many women in my generation to become doctors, lawyers, coaches, or construction workers because we didn't see women doing these things. The limitations that we placed on ourselves back then have been removed.

I think that women's presence in sports is one of the reasons that women are moving into "men's" professions. Men and boys are changing their perception of women—sometimes just because they have seen women playing sports. Little boys and little girls are playing together on the same court.

**LIFELONG SKILLS:** The best laboratory for learning lifelong skills is sports.

It really pleases me that a whole generation of little girls out there is going to have an opportunity to learn lifelong skills. It doesn't mean they have to be good enough to get a scholarship or even to pursue the sport into high school. But I can't think of a better avenue (than sports) for teaching skills that are going to be beneficial in life. Skills such as: setting goals, finding a way to make your niche, feeling good about yourself, communicating, learning to deal with losing, learning to deal with winning, learning to be tolerant. If our society could practice all the things that we learn from being part of a team, then we wouldn't have many problems.

**GROWING UP IN SPORTS:** I was lucky to have been encouraged in sports as a child. When I was growing up, social life in the small town of Goldthwaite revolved pretty much around the church and the school. And everyone played on teams. In fact, if everybody didn't play, you didn't have enough for a team. In my neighborhood there was always some kind of game going on, such as touch football or baseball, and I was always involved.

My dad was a Boy Scout leader and I was a Boy Scout before I was a Girl Scout. It seemed to me that the Girl Scout activities were not nearly as much fun as what the boys got to do. The boys got to camp and play sports.

Basketball was *the* sport at school. There weren't a lot of options. Girls played half-court basketball in Texas back then. I played forward. Even when I came to the University of Texas they were still playing half-court basketball.

**COMPETITION:** When a young woman enters the workforce today, she has it easier if she has been part of an athletic team because she has learned to compete in a team atmosphere.

My generation of women was socialized to be noncompetitive, nonaggressive. Being competitive was not feminine. Thankfully, women today are beginning to realize competitiveness and femininity are not exclusive qualities. But we still have a way to go in that area. Women of my generation who didn't get to be on a competitive team when they were younger often ask me, "What's it like to be part of a team?" They have no idea. It's almost like a part of their life is missing.

I am competitive. When I exercise, I have to keep score. I love to play golf. But I have finally learned not to look at my golf score to determine whether my day has been bad or good. (Laughs.)

As a coach, I have had to teach a few good but timid players to be competitive. It's not a pretty process and it's not particularly fun. I have to tell a player's teammates, "Just push on her. Beat on her. Be physical with her." It's reinforcement, over and over. The timid player finally reaches the point of retaliation. Her feelings sometimes get hurt in the process. But such a player is proud of herself when she finally is able to break through and become aggressive on the court. I think it translates to life later on as well.

**MENTORS:** As a teenager, I never envisioned being a coach because all my coaches were men. Until I got to college, I thought that women didn't have the ability to coach. Because I was one of the first successful women coaches, I didn't have many female coaches to learn from.

My coaching mentors have been ones whom I have watched from afar—people like John Wooden, who was basketball coach at UCLA in the 1960s and 1970s. His teams won ten consecutive national championships. I admired what he and other coaches like him did, and they influenced the decisions that I made.

**SETTING GOALS:** To be successful, you have to be able to establish goals. If you know what you want, it is not difficult to make a plan to get there. I believe that people can be whatever they dream, although I never actually dreamed my career. I wish I had been able to dream more when I was a young woman starting into my career. I wish I had had more options in my dreams. My career kind of happened. There wasn't a grand plan.

I have followed my passion and I have been fortunate to be able to make a living at it. I think you should enjoy what you do. I can't imagine having a job that I didn't look forward to.

**COACHING:** If I weren't challenged, if I didn't have fun going to practice every day and working with young people, I wouldn't be coaching. A lot of things about coaching aren't fun. But when you see your team achieve, that overshadows all the hard times. There are enough of those good times.

**WHAT MAKES ME FEEL ALIVE:** I feel most alive when I am able to

- bring a group of individuals together and help them become a team,
- work with young people and see them improve on a daily basis, and
- see them reach farther than they thought they could.

**TEACHING:** Coaching is teaching. I don't think there is any significant difference, except that as a coach, you get some of the most motivated and highly skilled students. Coaching involves breaking down what seems to be a complex problem into simple parts. That's what teaching is in my mind. Organization, breaking things down—all those things are pretty natural for me.

**TEAMWORK:** Teaching teamwork is a whole other subject. Players coming to the Lady Longhorns from high school have been the top players on their high school teams and usually are somewhat egotistical. But as they evolve into college players, their individual goals become secondary to what they want for their team. The really astute ones become effective as individuals within the framework of a team.

Teams that are really fun to coach are the ones that become stronger as a group than they were as individuals. A natural enthusiasm permeates throughout those teams.

Most of us are part of a team—not necessarily an athletic team. A team is a group of people brought together for a common purpose. Most team members have the same goals:

- to be exceptional in what we do,
- to bring our strengths to the group, and
- to have the group be stronger and able to accomplish things that, as individuals, we couldn't possibly do.

I guess there was a time in our society when you could start a task and finish it yourself, but now, everything we do depends on somebody else.

**CONFRONTATION:** Teaching girls to confront their problems head on is something I deal with almost daily as a college coach. If a person can't confront, she can't move forward. Most girls have been socialized to be nonconfrontational. Instead of discussing the problem with a person she is having trouble with, a girl typically talks behind that person's back. But I encourage players to confront. It is in my personality to be to-the-point. I want to tackle the problem and fix it.

**ADVERSITY:** When a team gets through adversity, it can be a big breakthrough. In fact, a team can't reach its potential unless it has gone through some adversity. I think the same applies to life. It is when you experience personal tragedy or are going through a difficult time that you learn to reach out.

**DIVERSITY:** A team needs to be diverse in terms of race, personalities, and height of players. Diverse teams are fun to work with and more successful than teams on which everybody is just alike. Members of a diverse team tend to develop tolerance and appreciation of individual strengths and skills.

**WOMEN'S BASKETBALL THEN AND NOW:** Through the years, we have been able to achieve more diversity on our teams, partly because of racial integration and because of the Title IX legislation.*

In the beginning there were no fans. Now there are fans. Now there are scholarships. Now there is travel. Now there are a lot of glamorous things that go with being a female student athlete. That wasn't the case initially. Back then, the only reason to be a female college athlete was that you loved it. You enjoyed the closeness of the team, the camaraderie. And you played for that reason. Now that female athletics has evolved, there are a lot of other things—scholarships, travel, prestige, all of those things—and sometimes the student athlete makes those things a higher priority than the sport itself.

It is sometimes a little harder to get to the good part of basketball now than it was back then. I think that we all look back with nostalgia—for some parts of our lives when everything seemed much simpler, less complex, less stressful. But I have worked for a long time to help win acceptance in our society for talented women athletes. Women athletes are finally enjoying financial support and scholarships and are being able to compete in the same kind of arena that their male counterparts compete in.

Now that women are looking at the possibility of going professional, I'm not sure that we will be any better than the men in dealing with the urge to throw away a college education in order to go pro. The temptation is going to be there for us. I hope that we can learn from their experience. Right now, in the women's pro leagues, the salaries are not six

~

*Title IX of the Educational Amendments of 1972 is the landmark legislation that bans sex discrimination in schools, whether it be in academics or athletics. Title IX states: "No person in the U.S. shall, on the basis of sex, be excluded from participation in, or denied the benefits of, or be subjected to discrimination under any educational program or activity receiving federal aid."

figures, and the women pro athletes still have to have another career that earns money. Making $5,000, as Danielle Viglione did last summer, was not enough to keep her from coming back here and finishing her degree.

**ACADEMICS:** It is my responsibility as a coach not to recruit student athletes if they don't have the skills to be successful at UT. Athletes are not bound by the same admission standards as the general student body, but they are going to be in the classroom with people who have very high test scores. So they have to be able to compete with those students. Putting a natural competitor in an environment in which she doesn't have the skills to compete can be disastrous. She is going to feel like a failure.

**FAILURE:** Most successful people have a real fear of failure. It's not the successes that motivate us. It's the failures.

I am physically sick every time we lose. And I don't feel any better until I get to practice the next day and we start to do something tangible toward improvement. I feel challenged and determined and I want to work real hard because I don't want to feel that bad again.

I am a bottom-line person. Things are black or white. You win or you lose. Even if you lose by one basket, it's still a loss. The only thing that could make you feel good after a loss is knowing that you played the absolute best that you can. But you never feel that way. (Laughs.) There is always that missed free shot, always a turnover. It is the pursuit of an impossible dream, I guess. People say I am a perfectionist. And I think that is probably true. (Laughs.)

**HANDLING CRITICISM:** I am also very sensitive. I don't think most people know that. But I take to heart every criticism and I struggle with it. Over the years, I have become able to deal with criticism a bit better and to put it aside a little bit quicker and move on. I guess I have learned to rationalize.

When you are unfairly judged, you can react in one of two ways. You can just say, "This isn't worth it and I'm not going to subject myself to this anymore." Or you can say, "I'm not letting the suckers get me down!" I have been tempted many times to throw in the towel, but the next morning when I wake up I have always been able to say, "There's no way I'm giving up!"

**HANDLING PRAISE:** I take a great deal of pride in awards and in having people notice what I do. But I still am my most critical evaluator. I don't need people to tell me whether I have been successful or not. I am a lot harder on myself than the public is.

**PRIVACY:** I am a very private person—and that may seem like a conflict because I am pretty visible in the community and elsewhere. But remember that when I chose this profession, it wasn't such a public one. I didn't choose coaching because there were going to be thousands of people there and I was going to get media coverage. I coached when there was no one in the gym and no one cared. And I really enjoyed doing it. It is hard to keep my life out of the glare of the media. Being scrutinized makes you somewhat cynical in some ways. And it probably makes me seek privacy even more.

**GROWING OLDER:** Getting older doesn't really bother me, except that many people think coaching is for young people. I know that I'm not too old to coach. There seems to be a different standard for women than for men. People don't talk about Bobby Knight or Lute Olson being old. People don't ask them, "When are you going to quit?" I have been asked that question more and more since I have gotten older.

It would be disappointing and unfulfilling if I weren't able to go to practice everyday and work with young people. I don't have a timetable for knowing when I will want to quit coaching. I think I will know when the time comes. And I'm not there yet.

# WILHELMINA DELCO

"*If we continue to delve into our leaders' past lives, we are going to discourage bright people from seeking public office.*"

*Wilhelmina Delco, former representative (D–Austin), Texas House of Representatives. Photo by Barton Wilder Custom Images © 2000.*

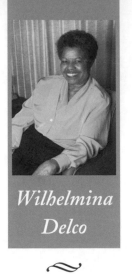

*Wilhelmina Delco*

B. 1929,
CHICAGO, ILLINOIS
CURRENT HOME:
AUSTIN, TEXAS

Although raised in Chicago and educated at historically black Fisk University in Nashville, Tennessee, Wilhelmina Delco moved with her husband, Exalton, and four children to Austin, Texas, in 1957 so that Exalton could earn his doctorate in zoology from the University of Texas. It was in Austin, during her children's public school years, that Wilhelmina decided that education for black children needed to improve. So she began making a name for herself in public service—beginning as PTA president in the early 1960s and continuing through six years on the Austin school board and twenty years in the Texas legislature. During those twenty-seven continuous years in office, Wilhelmina became a seasoned and powerful public official. She retired in 1995 from the Texas House of Representatives, where she had focused primarily on education and issues of special concern to women, children, and minorities.

In racially charged 1968, two days after the assassination of Dr. Martin Luther King, Wilhelmina made history by becoming the first African American to be elected to the Austin Independent School District Board. During her six years on the school board, she helped lead a divided city through the throes of desegregation. Her life was threatened more than once. She was also a member of the founding board of Austin Community College.

When she won a seat in the Texas legislature in 1974 without a runoff, the victory was both a personal one and one for all black people. She had become the first African American elected to the House from Travis County. She served as chair of the prestigious House Committee on Higher Education, and in 1991 her prominence led to a historic appointment as the first woman speaker pro tempore of the House of Representatives. Although she served on twenty different committees in the House, ranging from business and commerce to science and technology, she maintained her interest and influence in education. Her proudest accomplishment in the legislature came when she gained historically black Prairie View A&M University a significant share of the Permanent University Fund, a development that changed its inadequate facilities into those of a high-quality, thriving, modern institution.

Wilhelmina's consistent dedication to education has gained her a national reputation in the field of higher education. Since leaving public office, she continues to serve on various state and national boards in the field of education, and is an adjunct professor at the University of Texas at Austin.

She was the eldest of five children. They were raised by their mother in a Chicago housing project after their parents divorced when Wilhelmina was twelve. Her mother was politically active in local Democratic circles in Chicago and was among the first African American probation officers in the country. All five siblings earned college degrees. "If I misbehaved, fifty people would tell my mother," she says of her Chicago upbringing.

She met Exalton, a Texan, at Fisk University, and they married in 1950. Family has always been a top priority in their marriage. Both of their mothers, for the sixteen years preceding their recent deaths, lived with the couple. The Delcos' three daughters and all nine grandchildren live in Austin and share regularly in their lives. Wilhelmina and Exalton also have a son living in Portland, Oregon.

**AUTHOR'S NOTE**  *If a typical day in Wilhelmina's retirement resembles today, then she hasn't slowed down much. When I arrive for our interview, she is on the phone with local media representatives who have called to ask her opinion about a controversy involving the black community.*

*Although clearly agitated by their inferences, Wilhelmina switches gears and soon is laughing about being seen as a "wisewoman" by the baby boom generation. "I was booming before the babies," she quips. And her self-described "gift of gab" takes over.*

*Her home reflects Wilhelmina's priorities: family, public service, and practicality with money. She and Del have lived in the same modest East Austin house for almost forty years. Pictures of the nine grandkids in their yearly new Christmas outfits made by "Granna" stand alongside the picture of Wilhelmina and Del posing with President Clinton at the White House. Our interview is interrupted more than once by yet another phone call from the media.*

*As I walk out the front door, taped interview in hand, a camera team from the local television station walks in. Wilhelmina's day is not slowing down yet.*

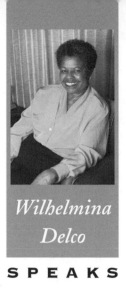

*Wilhelmina Delco*

## SPEAKS

**MENTORS**: I came from a political family. As I was growing up, all of our dinner conversations were about current events. (And we had the same kind of dinner conversations with our kids while they were growing up.) So as a kid I was interested in what was going on in the world. That trait was what made me run for the school board when I was thirty-nine.

From my mother I learned perseverance. I learned that if you stick with something that is really important, you can do it. From my father I inherited my ability to speak in public. He had the gift of gab, and he could talk about anything. I am the same way.

**MONEY:** Mother always told us that we weren't poor. We just never had any money. (Laughs.) When you stop to think about it, that is an extraordinary philosophy. Being poor is a state of mind. Lack of money is just the absence of a resource that you can earn and recover. What you do with your money is more important than how much you have. My mother was a huge influence on my life. I learned most of my values and principles from her.

**PRINCIPLES I LIVE BY:**

- Keeping your word is important.
- Personal integrity is important.
- People are more important than issues.

I genuinely like people. People who disagree agreeably can work together. That means that you don't stoop to attack each other's culture, race, history, economics, or politics. It is important to separate principle from personality.

- Treat people the way you want to be treated. I ask myself two things: "Would I like to see something I've done become a headline in the *Dallas Morning News*?" and "Would I like to hear about myself something I have said about somebody else?"
- Be sensitive about the impact you have on other people's lives. Make a positive difference.
- We are never too old to learn and to change our minds.
- No matter how hard you try, you can't re-do yesterday. You can kill yourself on "what-ifs" and "if-onlys." Those are destroying words.
- Develop a sense of humor. If, amid adversity, you can't turn around and laugh, you will destroy yourself.
- Put your money where your real interests are. Turn the rhetoric that you espouse into reality. Nothing worries me more than people who say they "love children," but they don't want to spend any money or time on them. They *love* children in the abstract, but they don't *like* them.

**MENTORING:** When I was in public office, I would go to schools and talk to the kids about aspiring to seek public office when they grew up. I would say, "I hope that you will be there someday making the laws. And when you go back to your school, people will be proud to say that they went to school with you. You will have people saying they are pleased with what you did because it made a positive difference in their lives."

Kids used to be inspired by the thought of public office. But now they say, "How much do you make?" "What were all the awful things that happened?" And ultimately the bottom line gets to be, "Ms. Delco, what is a nice lady like you doing mixed up with a bunch of crooks?"

**POLITICS:** The perception is that holding public office isn't an honorable thing. But a democracy cannot sustain itself if decent people aren't willing to serve in public office.

Just look at politics now. People don't talk about principles. They talk about personality. I have a real problem with someone who attacks my husband, my children, or my family, simply because that person has a problem with me. Attacking candidates' private lives is destroying politics today.

There are no perfect people. If you go far enough back in most people's lives, there is something they wish they hadn't done. But I don't think that keeps them from being successful at whatever their agenda is. I think we ought to judge people by what they do in the role we have assigned them, rather than what they do otherwise.

What they do in the privacy of their own lives and homes does not often carry over into how they perform as leaders. We would have had very little leadership in this country in the past three hundred years if we had judged our leaders on their personal lives. If we continue to delve into our leaders' past lives, we are going to discourage bright people from seeking public office.

**VOTING:** I have never missed voting in an election as long as I can remember. I can't imagine walking in to vote on issues or candidates that I know nothing about. I have been a lifelong Democrat, but one of the things I am learning is to look more carefully at candidates. That's not to say I will ever vote for a Republican, but there are a whole lot of Democrats I will no longer vote for. I think you learn by being involved.

Too many voters go to the polls without really educating themselves about what the candidates stand for. The whole thing now spins on perception. As an educated voter, you must look at how candidates have prepared themselves, what their agenda is, what they propose to do, whether you feel they can legitimately do the job, whether you agree with the way they do the job once in office, whether you support the ultimate goal of what they are doing—not whether they are tall or short, fat or thin, good-looking, bad-looking, white or black. You need to concentrate on issues.

**STANDING UP FOR WHAT YOU BELIEVE:** I have always been driven by issues. I ran for the school board because I saw inequities in Austin schools and I wanted to change things so that my kids would get a fair shake.

And later I ran for state office because the Texas legislature declared that equalizing public school funding would be its priority next session. And I knew that we needed more money for schools in Austin.

My experience had been my active participation in groups such as the League of Women Voters and the Juvenile Court Advisory Board. Almost everything I have ever done has been because I felt somebody needed to be there for children.

At that time the community was beginning to realize somebody black needed to be on the school board. And I was one of the few black people who *could* be there because I did not have a full-time job outside of my home. Many volunteer organizations meet in the daytime. When you work on one cause, people ask you to work on another. So I was well networked.

I was elected to the school board two days after Martin Luther King was assassinated. I believe that his death was a very important reason for my victory. I was elected in a citywide election, not just a single-member district, which means that I had support from both the white and the black community.

Being on the school board gave me name identification and visibility in the Greater Austin community. A federal government team representing the Department of Health, Education, and Welfare came to Austin in August 1968 to deal with the district's noncompliance with desegregation. The desegregation question put the school board in the limelight, and my picture was on the television every night. I was on the news every day with a microphone stuck in front of my face. "What are you going to do? How do your people feel about this issue?" they asked me. That was a whole new experience for me, and suddenly I became networked into all sorts of issues and projects involving desegregation because they were all related.

**NETWORKING:** Curiosity was what drove me to become well networked. I actually enjoy attending meetings, and I always stay until the end because that way I get all the information. Although I bring all the papers back, I know good and well that most of what I will retain is what I heard at the meeting.

And, of course, over time, if you have been at all the meetings, you are asked to run for office. I probably have held an office in every organization with "education" in its name. (Laughs.)

**COMMUNICATING:** When I ran for the school board in 1968, someone said, "Why are you running? You're not going to change those people's minds. There are six of them and one of you." And I said, "I may not be able to change their minds, but what I can do is deny them the opportunity to say they didn't know."

It was on the school board that I learned how important it is to communicate well so that everyone leaves the meeting with the same understanding. One of my fellow school board members was conservative, to put it charitably. She was very proud of her Mississippi heritage. She was a nice woman basically, but we differed profoundly in terms of philosophy and convictions. I learned quickly that if both of us left a meeting smiling after discussing an issue, then one of us had misunderstood. (Laughs.) I learned then that before the meeting adjourned, I should repeat aloud the decision that had been made, and then ask if there was any dissension or equivocation. When everyone was satisfied, I made sure the decision was reflected in the minutes.

**ADVOCATING FOR AFRICAN AMERICANS:** On the school board my proudest accomplishment was raising the level of inclusion. I saw as my role telling people about situations that they didn't really know about. The Department of Health, Education, and Welfare and I both raised a lot of awareness. I think it was important at that time to have had somebody on the school board to articulate the concerns of the black community.

One of my proudest accomplishments in the legislature was expanding the Permanent University Fund to get more money for Texas's historically black colleges. Black colleges had been the stepchildren of higher education in Texas.

After desegregation of white colleges and universities, the state felt that if blacks didn't like what Prairie View or Texas Southern (both historically black colleges) offered, then the viable option was to attend formerly white-only institutions. But I felt strongly that black students should have the same educational choices available in a setting that was comfortable and familiar to them—the same opportunity that white students had who chose an all-female university over a coed university, for example. I was proud that I was able to get that constitutional amendment passed and it is there forever and ever, amen. And just as important was providing the funding that would bring those historically black colleges up to the level of formerly white institutions.

**EDUCATING MINORITIES:** HBCUs—Historically Black Colleges and Universities—are important because part of education is to focus on role models. If all the models you see on the campus, all the examples you see of success, all of the levels of comparison are of something that does not represent who you are and where you come from, then you can never achieve that definition of success. Before, the only way that we, as minorities, could become successful was to become as close to white as we could.

It's also true of women's universities. When women go to college with a woman president, and they see women as heads of the departments, and women doing the research, they can say, "Hey, I don't have to be a man, or to emulate a man, to be successful."

**BEING DIFFERENT:** Diversity makes things interesting. When people say, "I don't see color," I don't believe them. The person I see in my mirror is a black woman. If I don't understand that I look different from you, then I have a serious problem being who I am, because there are differences between us. They are not necessarily negative differences. They aren't necessarily profound differences. But they *are* differences.

If there were an institution where fat people could be comfortable, I'd vote for it. Because I think it is ridiculous that people are perceived as failures if they don't wear size eight. Many problems in our society stem from not letting people feel good about who they are. We are always trying to change them. We are always trying to tell them, "You ought to be this or that." Maybe we don't tell them overtly, but we tell them subliminally.

**TEXAS WOMEN:** I was an outsider when I came here because I was not native to Texas. I still feel that way to an extent, and that's ironic because I have held office in Texas for twenty-six years and I have been married to a Texan for almost forty-seven years. I have lived in Texas longer than anyplace else and, of course, I feel like a Texan.

**SETTING PRIORITIES:** I am proud of the changes I was able to make in public office in Texas. But now that I am a private Texas citizen, I am starting to establish priorities about what I realistically can do well and what I end up doing if I spread myself too thinly. That's hard because I am so used to feeling as if I am supposed to respond to people who voted for me. Sometimes over those years I ended up speaking where I didn't want to speak, going where I didn't want to go, and doing things I didn't really want to do.

Now, when people ask me what I do in my spare time, I joke sometimes and say, "I stand in front of the mirror and practice saying 'no.' " Because evidently I am not saying it right. I am nowhere near mastering the skill of saying "no."

**MARRIAGE:** Part of learning to say "no" is so I will have more time with my husband, Exalton. For the first time since we got married, he and I have the freedom to spend lots of time together and to travel. I think that my having a sustainable, wonderful marriage is a great accomplishment. I lucked out. Actually, I had good judgment.

Exalton is a wonderful person. Through those twenty-six years of my public office, a lot of people saw him as "Mr. Wilhelmina Delco," although he has a Ph.D. and he was an academician. He has always earned the living, but he took a back seat to my public life. (I never made more than $521 a month as a legislator.) Now in retirement, Exalton is on various community boards, and he has done all sorts of things that are helping him to be fulfilled. That makes me happy.

**NURTURING YOURSELF:** Now that my life is not totally taken up by public and family obligations, I am learning to nurture myself as well.

I like books that I can finish in one sitting. Reading relaxes me. It takes me away from whatever problems I have. Beverly King, a black author, writes black historical romance novels, and I am enjoying reading those. I am learning some fascinating things. She writes about the underground railway, and about people who were involved in immediate post-slavery situations, and about people who lived in all-black towns.

I continue to sew for my grandkids. I love making their Christmas and Easter outfits every year.

I am allowing myself some luxuries now. I don't buy the cheap shoes anymore, even if they are not on sale. I have just begun having a standing appointment every month to get a manicure and a pedicure. Until now, the last manicure I had that I paid for was for my wedding day!

But, of course, I didn't mind those small personal sacrifices during my busy days in office, taking care of aging parents, and raising kids. I have a few regrets, but I'm proud of how most things turned out.

**SEIZING OPPORTUNITIES:** Now all three of my girls have master's degrees and are professional women. They are married and have healthy children. They are positive, contributing people.

I have always told them, "If you want the world to change, get in there and start changing it!"

You can't blame other people for what happens if you haven't made a sincere effort to change things yourself.

# LINDA ELLERBEE

Linda Ellerbee, broadcast journalist. Photo by Gordon Munro © 1999. Courtesy of Linda Ellerbee.

> "*I am Texan enough that I refer to half of my relatives as 'sister' or 'brother,' even if they are really aunts and uncles. I even have an 'Aunt Sister.*"

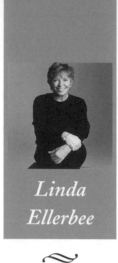

B.1944,
**BRYAN, TEXAS**
CURRENT HOMES:
**NEW YORK CITY AND
THE BERKSHIRE MOUNTAINS
OF MASSACHUSETTS**

*Linda
Ellerbee*

Linda Ellerbee has earned a reputation as a highly respected and outspoken journalist. She has received all of television's highest honors, including several Emmy, Peabody, Cable ACE, and Columbia duPont awards. Her success as a network news correspondent, anchor, writer, and producer, and her frustration with the mentality of commercial television news, led her to quit the networks to establish an independent company, Lucky Duck Productions, in 1987, with her life partner, Rolfe Tessem.

Lucky Duck is an award-winning and critically acclaimed television production company renowned for producing children's programming, prime-time specials, documentaries, and limited-run series for broadcast- and cable-television networks. Ten years after *Nick News* first aired, it is the most popular children's news program on television and one of the highest-acclaimed children's programs of any kind. It is known for the respectful and direct way it speaks to children about the important issues of our time. *Nick News* has won every award traditionally associated with adult programming, including two Emmys and three Peabody Awards (one for Linda and the *Nick News* coverage of the Clinton investigation) and a Columbia duPont Award.

Linda won the Emmy in 1986 for best writing for the ABC prime-time historical series *Our World. NBC News Overnight*, a pioneering late-night news program that she wrote and anchored in the 1980s, was cited by the Columbia duPont Awards as "the best written and most intelligent news program ever."

Her 1988 book about television, *And So It Goes,* stayed on the *New York Times* bestseller list for five months and is still used as a textbook in more than a hundred colleges across the country. Her 1991 best-seller, *Move On,* continues to be popular with women readers who appreciate her candid stories about being a working single mother, a child of the 1960s, and a woman trying to find some balance in her life. Linda's first foray into books for kids was an eight-part book series entitled *Get Real,* which was initiated in 2000 and directed toward middle school children. The series won her raves among younger readers.

The only child of Ray and Hallie Smith, Linda Jane attended public school in Houston, dropped out of Vanderbilt University in Nashville, was married and divorced four times, and has two children from her second marriage. Vanessa and Josh were born in 1969 and 1970. Today Vanessa is lead guitarist and lead singer in a rock band in Seattle, and Josh works in television production.

Linda was fired in 1972 from the Associated Press in Dallas after writing a letter to a friend—making fun of her boss, the Dallas City Council, and the Vietnam War. Intending to send it only to her friend, the young reporter punched the wrong button on the wire machine and sent the letter out across AP's nationwide wire service. Unlike her Dallas boss, the manager of CBS-TV in Houston thought the letter was funny and hired her. Soon afterward, while still twenty-eight years old, she was hired by WCBS in New York to cover hard news, and after two years she became a network correspondent.

Although she and Rolfe live in New York City during the week, their home is an old house in the Berkshire Mountains of western Massachusetts, where they spend most weekends. Linda has survived alcoholism, breast cancer, chemotherapy, and a double mastectomy. She also quit smoking, which, she maintains, "was harder than any of the other things."

Today she says, "My health is good. My children are happy and interesting. I feel good about myself. I am in love with a good man. I take time away from my work to smell the flowers. This is a real good time."

**AUTHOR'S NOTE** *"I don't feel wise. Can you lead with that?" Linda says in her raspy voice as we end our telephone interview. "Write: 'Linda Ellerbee says she doesn't feel wise . . . and probably isn't.'" Then we both laugh.*

*In reality, she has stuffed a lot of life into her fifty-six years, and she can spout out gem after gem of wisdom in an hour and a half when she puts her mind to it.*

*She is sitting back in her chair in her New York office with her cowboy boots on the desk, looking out on the Hudson River. "I am watching a boat and a ship go down the river and the sun is sparkling off the water, and even the Hudson, which I know to be dirty, is beautiful right now. I need to see beauty every day."*

*I am happy to report that Linda has, indeed, seen the year 2000, still sees beauty at every turn, and is eagerly anticipating the future.*

*Linda Ellerbee*

# SPEAKS

**TEXAS WOMEN:** Without question, my Texas upbringing has affected the way I have lived my life.

Even at a time when women were supposed to be meek and quiet, I think most Texas women weren't good at that. My family certainly had women who spoke their minds. Most of us somehow are colored by the place where we grew up. I have never once thought of myself as a New Yorker. I am a Texan who happens to live in New York right now. And I surely expect to end my days back in Texas—probably in Austin.

I attribute to my Texas upbringing the fact that I own a company with over fifty employees. I'm sitting here in my Manhattan office in my jeans with my cowboy boots up on my desk. My boots have those steel tips on the end. Someone said once, "What are those little steel tips for?" And I said, "Crowd control." When I was covering political conventions, or a riot or mob scene, I always wore cowboy boots. Nothing is more useful in a crowd than a good pair of cowboy boots.

I still say "y'all." I never did try to get rid of my Texas accent. I never wanted to. I'm still "fixin'" to do things. And I still "carry" people to the grocery store. And I am Texan enough that I refer to half of my relatives as "sister" or "brother," even if they are really aunts and uncles. I even have an "Aunt Sister." And I have an awful lot of people I call "uncle" or "aunt" who aren't even related to us.

I have to watch what I eat, but I have one very clear rule: the minute I cross the state line into Texas, all bets are off. Immediately I have to have something from the three major food groups: barbecue, Mexican food, and chicken-fried steak. (Laughs.)

**BEING DIFFERENT:** During my career, I have earned the reputation of a maverick. I'm proud that I didn't just march to somebody else's tune. My tune may have been a little off-key, and it may have been a little hard to sing, but I sang to it, and I still do.

**SELF-CONFIDENCE:** I have been called a "tough broad" and a "gutsy dame" because I portray an image of self-assurance. But to tell you the truth, I am a shy person, as are many journalists. A notebook and a pen are great shields to keep people out. I'm often frightened, but I have learned to behave as if I'm not. That has gotten me through some pretty big doors in my life.

**STANDING UP FOR WHAT YOU BELIEVE:** I think my Texas up-bringing has encouraged me to stand up for myself. If I believe that I'm right, I fight to do it my way. That's a particularly important lesson for women—particularly women my age because we were raised to subjugate our own dreams to those of our husbands or our employers.

**GUILT:** I think most women have to work on self-assurance. I am continually working on it myself. Science will probably discover an "insecure" gene in women that says, "You know you're not good enough for that! Boy, are they going to find *you* out someday." Of course, it's really all that stuff society has heaped on us. We need to be kinder to ourselves and to forgive ourselves more.

There is probably also a "guilt" gene in women. (Laughs.) We mothers never get over our guilt. Even if you are the world's most perfect mother, you are going to feel guilty. The things you didn't do are always in the back of your mind.

**MOTHERHOOD:** The most difficult thing I have ever done is to be a mother—a single mother. Most parents would say that our two main goals with children are (1) to give them a safe nest, and at the same time (2) to teach them to fly. I don't know how good I was at giving Vanessa and Josh a safe nest, but I think I was pretty good at teaching them to fly.

As adults, both are comfortable in their skins, and both are willing to take big chances and big bites out of life.

I could say that they are my proudest accomplishments. But their success as human beings is really not my doing; it's theirs. They are their own people, and what they have accomplished, they get to own. I like them as well as love them. Of course, the guilt lingers in the back of my mind that I didn't always give them enough of my time.

**MOTHERHOOD AND WORK:** In the 1970s, I was part of that first group of women allowed in television news. They said to us, in effect: "If you don't do what the big boys do, if you take time off for family or children, we'll know that women aren't serious about this work."

We felt that if we screwed up, we had screwed it up for *all women.* So I didn't call my boss and say, "Look, I won't be coming in today. I have to go to the school play."

And you know what? I was dead wrong! I should have stood up and said, "I am more than the carcass I bring to work. And my family is important. And my child is important. And I'm going to be there for my child."

Corporations don't have a long memory, but children do. I missed some important times in my children's lives. Now that they are grown, my kids have come to understand why I had to be at the political convention instead of at the school play. But nothing makes up for my not being there.

The lesson my generation had to learn was that you *can* have it all, but you can't have it all at the same moment. We need to start forgiving ourselves for not keeping up with everything all the time.

Women have the right and the need to work, but it is also true that most children want Mom at home. Those issues aren't the same for men. There is no easy answer to that.

Making choices comes at a price. None of us is really "what we do." We are "who we are," and that ought to be enough. That is certainly a feminist philosophy.

**FEMINISM:** It saddens me that the word "feminist" has been so corrupted over the years. I hate to hear a woman say, "Oh, I believe in equality, but I'm not a feminist."

If you believe in equality, you are a feminist. That is all it means. It doesn't mean hating men, or moving to the head of the table over men. It does mean throwing out all the tables, except for the round one. Frankly, it means giving back better than we got. Those were hard-fought battles. And the battles are far from over.

**POLITICS:** It is hugely important for women to keep their mouths open in politics—to run for office, to vote, to get out there and fight for those laws. Young women today don't remember that just a few years ago, want ads in newspapers were listed "Help Wanted Men" and "Help Wanted Women." All the secretarial, cleaning, and nursing jobs were in one category, and all the higher-paying jobs were in the other. They forget that it was only a short time ago that women couldn't go to the bank to borrow money without a man co-signing. Women had to stand up and fight for themselves in every state in the union to get the most basic human rights. Young women need to be vigilant to ensure that these rights aren't slowly eroded away.

**ADVOCATING FOR CHILDREN:** Girls, in particular, need to be encouraged to exercise their "choice muscles." The intention of our TV show *Nick News* is to give kids—both girls and boys—the power to choose. If you give girls power when they are young, they'll have it all their lives. It's like the Nike ad says: "If you let me play . . ."

*Nick News* is not about raising a nation of news junkies. It's about raising a nation of rowdy citizens. We try to make the constitution come to life for them. We do stories about issues. School uniforms: good idea or bad idea? We try to give both sides our best shot. Then we just look at the camera and ask kids: "What do you think? Is 'school uniforms' a first amendment issue? How does that apply to the First Amendment?"

I think *Nick News* might be my best and most meaningful work yet. Encouraging kids to think for themselves is essential. I hope they will remember to follow through as adults in asserting their opinions, and help make meaningful changes.

**SPEAKING OUT:** It's the duty of every citizen to keep her mouth open. It's not only a duty. It's damned useful. Speaking out can even save your life.

Most of us were raised in a culture that told women to be silent. That's one reason that modern medicine is way behind in understanding breast cancer. We were being encouraged to die politely, quite frankly. If we hadn't stopped whispering about this disease, we wouldn't even be as far along as we are. Our society has only just now started putting real money into studying breast cancer. And the only reason that is happening is that women got real noisy about it.

**ADVERSITY:** Everybody has bad experiences in life. Nobody gets away free. But every bad experience—whether your child gets hurt, you lose a job, or you get breast cancer—makes you come away just being grateful for the air you breathe. And then, boy, does the sun shine sweetly!

**FAITH:** I am very much aware that I am connected to all things living. I am here, walking, talking, moving around, and having a pretty great life, by the grace of God. I could be dead, I could be in a gutter drunk, I could be a battered wife. But I'm not. Life is good, and I would be a fool to think that I did that all on my own. I lost my faith as a young adult, and now that I am older, I have found it again.

**CANCER:** Since my cancer, I have never had the guts to ask God to let me live a long life. I was forty-seven when I was diagnosed. First I asked God, "Just let me see fifty." And now I am almost sixty. Then I sort of gently said, "It would be wonderful if I could see the year 2000." Now that I have seen that, I'll ask for something else small. But I don't say, "Let me live to be ninety." I try to say, "Let me live today."

When an Austin friend was dying of breast cancer, she called to say good-bye. I was crying, and she said to me: "Look, I don't know how much time I have, but I know that when I get up in the morning, I have today. The same as anybody else. And that is all anybody has—the now."

The word "now" is written large in my brain. It's probably too late for me to become a surgeon. But it's not too late to learn a new language, or live in another country. It's not too late for me to learn new ways, to seek change.

**CHANGE:** Change is like an unexpected guest. On holidays in my family, we set a place at the table for that unexpected guest. And you would be surprised at how often someone shows up.

And in a larger sense, I try to set a place for the unexpected guest in my life. You need to be ready so that when something like cancer happens, you can fight it, and your life doesn't fall apart—or if you get fired from your job late in life, or if your husband leaves you after twenty-five years.

Sometimes we do well to *choose* change. Choosing change gets harder as we get older. I see change as a form of hope. To risk change is to believe in tomorrow. And it always helps if you meet change with a good dose of humor.

**HUMOR:** I have found that a good time to laugh is anytime you can. I've always believed that women have the best senses of humor in the world—probably because they have to. Real humor—real joy—comes only after we've known real pain.

**LOVING A YOUNGER MAN:** Having been through lots of pain, I know that I am now the luckiest woman in the world. I didn't find the great love of my life until I was forty-two years old. I had to kiss a lot of frogs first.

Rolfe and I celebrated fifteen years of togetherness in September 2001. He is eight years younger, we own a company together, and we live together. And he is the love of my life. I think the two reasons we have lasted are that I'm smarter than I was at age twenty and that Rolfe and I never got married.

There is a lot to say for being in love with a younger man. Every woman should try it. (Laughs.) His being younger has been wonderful for me because the men my age were not raised to see women as equal partners. He was raised by a strong woman eight years later, and the women's movement had already begun. He was raised to see women as equal partners and be comfortable with that.

**NURTURING YOURSELF:** Another source of pure joy for me is to be surrounded by beauty. I need daily doses of it. These days I feel most alive when I am outdoors either backpacking or rafting rivers—something I have discovered just recently in my life.

I started hiking after I got breast cancer. It was wonderful for me because each time I got to the top of a hill I didn't think I could climb, I would look around and think: Well, if I can conquer this hill, what other hills in my life can I climb?

Since then I have made outdoor adventure a priority, whether it's running rivers through the Grand Canyon and Alaska, hiking in the desert or in the woods of New England, or lying in a field of wildflowers in Baja California. I need to experience that beauty as much as I need food, water, and air. I also need to be in contact with good friends.

**FRIENDSHIP:** Let me tell you about the Birthday Club. I belong to a group of about twenty-five women in Houston. Some of us go back to the first grade together. We all went to public high school together. After high school we scattered. Some moved back to Houston after college, but many moved away. Around the time we turned forty, somebody threw a birthday party for one of us and everybody came. And we decided we had missed one another. Another had a birthday the following month, so there was another birthday party. And then another one. It got to be called the Birthday Club.

These women are such a source of inspiration for me. We have learned so much, and some of us have become closer than we were when we were children because we know more. We have such great conversations.

Recently one of the women died of cancer. Her husband had left her the year before, and she didn't have an easy time of it. It was our group of women who became the whole support system for her. She was never alone in the hospital. There was always somebody there to take care of her besides a physician and a nurse. When she went home, someone from the group was always there. They loved her, they cared for her, and they buried her. They are the steel magnolias. I don't know if women everywhere are like that, but I do know that Texas women are.

**GETTING OLDER:** We steel magnolias hope to grow old together, but "getting old" is a different matter. If you don't want to get old, don't mellow. (That's not my line. I stole it from Woody Allen—and he may have stolen it from someone else.)

I don't want to be a meek, mild little old lady. My rights have not diminished as I have aged. And I'm not going to put up with it. I'm always going to insist on being treated with dignity. I'm not going to get complacent and say, "Well, you know, I fought for women's rights back when I was coming into the marketplace, but, gee, now things are okay for me, so I'm going to back off." Uh-uh. That won't work. There are still battles—big or little—to be fought in all our lives. Mellowing out really won't help you a lot.

The network bosses used to expect women in broadcast journalism to retire when we reached a certain age. And early on, some women did that. But that's not the case any longer. Now there are too many of us, and they have found out that we won't go gently or quietly into that good night. Barbara Walters is there leading the way, and the rest of us are right behind her.

One more thing about not mellowing: Okay, so maybe it's too late for me to become a brain surgeon, but I still hold out the hope that one day I will wake up and be able to carry a tune. (Laughs.)

# JULIET VILLARREAL GARCÍA

*"As a professional, I had to learn that it's okay to ask for help. . . . I now know the value of getting good minds together to think . . . [and to] move mountains."*

## Juliet Villarreal García

B. 1949,
**BROWNSVILLE, TEXAS**
CURRENT HOME:
**BROWNSVILLE, TEXAS**

At age thirty-nine, Juliet García became the first Mexican American woman to become president of a college or university in the United States when she was named president of Texas Southmost College in 1986. In 1991 she became president of the University of Texas at Brownsville. She graduated high school at age sixteen, married at nineteen, and had two children thirteen months apart while working on her bachelor's and master's degrees in speech and English at the University of Houston—all by the time she was twenty-two. Restless with teaching at the junior college level, she went on to get her Ph.D. in communications and linguistics from the University of Texas at Austin at age twenty-seven. She has completed postdoctoral studies at Harvard and MIT.

As president of the University of Texas at Brownsville (UTB/TSC), Juliet V. García is known for her aggressive pursuit of educational opportunities for young people and for thinking "outside of the box." She has sculpted a unique partnership between a university, UT at Brownsville, and a community college, Texas Southmost College, to provide a seamless four-year educational program designed to meet the needs of students in the lower Rio Grande Valley. The program is a national model, allowing some students to enter on the college level while others take remedial courses to catch up, with the goal of achieving university-level courses when they are ready.

Under her leadership, the predominantly Hispanic student body has swelled to ten thousand, making it the fastest-growing university in the University of Texas System. Since 1992 student graduation rates have increased 105 percent for bachelor's candidates and 184 percent for master's candidates. The university-college partnership has added eleven new baccalaureate degrees and nine new master's degrees. And today, according to *Hispanic Outlook in Higher Education,* UTB/TSC produces more Hispanic baccalaureate math majors than any other university in the nation.

Her innovative approach to education has led the university to achieve an international presence because of its groundbreaking "biliteracy" program, which goes beyond simple bilingualism. Biliteracy ensures that students of all nationalities can speak, read, and write both Spanish and English fluently, coupled with a command of the technical terms needed to practice their professions. The important second component of biliteracy training provides that students are taught how to function in a different cultural environment—all with the aim of making them more marketable in today's global economy.

The Continuing Education Division of UTB offers one of the largest Elderhostel programs in the state of Texas and is acclaimed as one of the best in the nation.

Because of her leadership and innovative approach to Hispanic education, Juliet has been listed among the top one hundred Hispanics in the United States by *Hispanic Business* magazine. She has been chair of the board of the American Council on Education and presently serves on numerous boards and councils, including the White House Initiative on Education Excellence for Hispanic Americans and the prestigious Carnegie Foundation for the Advancement of Teaching. She is chair of the Advisory Committee to Congress on Student Financial Assistance. In October 2000 Juliet was installed in the Texas Women's Hall of Fame as the recipient of their education award.

Although neither of her parents went to college, they stressed education and bilingualism for her and her two brothers. The children spoke Spanish to their father and English to their mother. Their mother died when Juliet was nine, and her father raised his three children while working as a customs broker for an airline company.

Juliet married her brother's friend Oscar, whom she had known since childhood. He is six years older than she. As husband and wife, Juliet and Oscar have made a strong team for more than thirty years. Although Oscar attended college, he never completed a degree. Instead he supported his wife and took a major role in raising their two children while Juliet finished her graduate degrees and taught subsequently on the university level before becoming president of UTB. Oscar owns a feed and seed store in Brownsville. Their son, Oscar David, holds a master's degree in commercialization of science and technology, and their daughter, Paulita, holds a degree in business. Both are married. Juliet and Oscar's oldest granddaughter is named Julieta, after her grandmother.

**AUTHOR'S NOTE**   *Juliet García is a hard woman to track down because her life is a blur, sometimes even to her, she admits. She has been in Austin today on university business, and tomorrow morning she is off to Washington, D.C., to meet with the Presidential Commission on Educational Excellence for Hispanic Americans. At the end of the week she will be back in Brownsville meeting with her faculty and speaking to students. A typical work week.*

*Our interview takes place in a quiet corner in the downtown hotel where she is staying. At the end of a long workday, her business suit is still crisp, her eyes sparkle, and her laugh is genuine as she talks about her life and work. Her enthusiasm for both is contagious!*

*I come away from the evening still thinking about some of her sage advice: "Work on something important. It doesn't have to be important to the world. It just has to be important to you."*

*Juliet Villarreal García*

**SPEAKS**

**ASKING FOR HELP:** As a professional, I had to learn that it's okay to ask for help. When I was younger, I had always practiced the philosophy "If you have a B and you want an A, you just have to stay up later and study harder. It is up to you to do everything by yourself."

My first task as college president was to balance the deficit budget. I needed to cut $1.2 million. So I sat in my office for two nights and tried to work it out. I couldn't figure it out. On the third night I called in some folks and said, "I need help to think through this." And of course, we worked through it. So now, whenever I have a task, I know the value of getting good minds together to think. I have found that you can move mountains when you have an army marching along with you.

**PERSEVERING:** In order to grow our university, our faculty and staff and I have been running very fast for several years now, and we get tired. Folks often tell me, "You ought to slow it down. You are going to burn people out."

It is a great challenge for me to keep that fire hot among our faculty and staff and to keep my own energy from flagging. We simply prop each other up. Sometimes I burn out myself for a couple of days, but I can't afford to lose the momentum because our community is like a tidal wave of need coming toward us. The community never loses its enthusiasm. The high school graduates are eager to start college, and there are so many adults who are taking the opportunity we offer to get a college education. Who am I to say, "It's time to slow it down"?

**MARRIAGE:** While I am in the fire fighting off the demons, my husband, Oscar, has always been there as my greatest supporter and my best critic. He has always been the one to see five or ten years into the future. He tells me things like, "I know it's hard, but this is happening for some reason. This is preparation for the next stage." Sometimes after hearing me give a speech, he might say, "You are talking to folks who don't understand where you are coming from. Bring it down a couple of notches." Oscar owns an old-fashioned feed and seed store—one of those wonderful ones where you can get a baby duck or a baby chick or cattle feed or a saddle, and you can't leave without buying something. He is my touch with reality.

Without his encouragement I don't believe I would have ever gone to graduate school. While I was still an undergraduate at the University of Houston, he said one evening: "School is easy for you. Why don't you keep going?" So I had our first baby and I began my master's degree. Thirteen months later we had another baby. (Don't believe anyone who says that you can't get pregnant if you are nursing a baby.) (Laughs.)

**FAMILY:** For example, when our babies were little and I was in graduate school, it was his idea to make a family rule: no studying on Sunday. It was the smartest thing we could have done because all day Sunday we would play. Our Sundays were always wonderful days of adventure. We would do everything in Austin that didn't cost money, and go places where people didn't frown on babies making noise or a mess. On Monday I would be refreshed and I would hit work again.

**GRANDMOTHERHOOD:** Until a few years ago, work was what made me feel most alive. But since my grandchildren came along, I confess that they excite me the most.

Before grandchildren, I thought that life went like this: you raise your babies, you pray that they will turn out okay, that they will get married to good people, that they will get out of college. And then you can say, "We did it. It worked!"

But now I find that grandchildren are the dessert. And it's good stuff! (Laughs.) Becoming a grandmother re-spirits the soul better than anything else I have ever experienced.

**PROUDEST ACCOMPLISHMENTS:** Besides being proud of my family, I am proud to have survived in my role as president! (Laughs.) In the university environment, you have lots of smart people, lots of people wanting their own way, and often lots of intrigue. The hardest task for a president is to orchestrate everyone around the same focus, to get the genuine commitment of everyone, and to maintain that momentum.

I am proud of the quality of the programs we have built. For example, our nursing students pass the state boards with higher grades than the state average (not average or below average as people often expect border schools to do). One secret of our nursing school is including the whole family in orientation so that the family members learn about the heavy demands their student will have to meet over the next two years. Some are families who have had no reference point about college until now because theirs is a first-generation college student. We help students form support groups among themselves for study and to help them through personal and family crises. When they experience a family death or divorce, their support group is there to help them cope. The personal nurturing our nursing students receive epitomizes what we are attempting to do university-wide with all of our programs.

**BILITERACY:** I am immensely proud of our biliteracy program. Students of all cultures get the chance to become fluent in Spanish and English, as well as learning to deal well in both the Hispanic and Anglo cultures. They have the option to take much of their advanced coursework in either English or Spanish. These special courses, along with the traditional language courses, allow them to hone their skills in both languages and within their field of study.

Imagine the opportunities available on the global market to a new engineer who is certified as biliterate, compared to a new engineer who is monolingual and monocultural. Now imagine the future physicists and chemists and historians who are biliterate. If we put biliteracy to work in Texas, our state could be doing a thriving business with Mexico and all of Central and South America.

We are attracting biliterate professors from major universities all over the country who want to put their biliteracy to work. Existing faculty who are not biliterate are encouraged to go through our intensive Spanish courses at UTB and then to an intensive training school in Guadalajara, Mexico, for two weeks.

I think the need to become biliterate is no different from the need to become computer literate. People don't understand the advantages until they have eased their way into literacy of both types. In Europe, biliteracy is not a radical idea. People grow up speaking two or more languages as a requirement in school, and they learn the ways of the cultures close to them. With those two skills, it becomes relatively easy for them to go into business in a neighboring country.

**INVESTING IN THE FUTURE:** In the United States, biliteracy seems radical to most people. In fact, being Hispanic, even if you are biliterate, is seen as a negative by most of the Anglo population. Anglos tend to see Hispanics as uneducated, low producers in the labor market, or totally unemployed. While it's true that Hispanics as a group are on the lower end of the economic ladder, their condition can be changed gradually over time by education. Our three-pronged experiment at UTB is working very well: nurture them in the lower levels of higher education until they catch up, bring them into higher education, and develop their biliteracy into marketable skills.

When I sold the notion of biliteracy to the University of Texas Board of Regents, who are all businessmen and -women, they immediately figured out the economics of it. They just sat up and listened; you could just see it click in their minds. One regent said, "You know, George Bush asked me to help him start a business in Mexico. And we were reluctant because we didn't have people we trusted (who also knew the language and the culture) to be our emissary, our accountant, our attorney. But if I got a graduate from UT at Brownsville—an M.B.A.—it would be a whole different story."

It doesn't take a group of idealists to make biliteracy work. People can push a program for biliteracy for economic reasons alone. I really don't care why people choose to invest in Hispanic education. I just know what the results will be.

**BEING ASSERTIVE:** Being assertive with the board of regents or with others in the business arena is a skill I honed in college debate. My debate partner was male, and we competed against males. It was the first time I had ever argued with men in that way, because I wasn't allowed to argue with my father. It was the best training I could have gotten for my future job because I learned how to fight and then shake hands, something women are generally not trained to do. In debate you learn how to distance yourself and not get emotional about it. That is a very important skill.

**BEING FEMALE IN A MALE BUSINESS WORLD:** Getting the attention of the board of regents is affirming, but my business dealings don't always result in such positiveness. Throughout my career, I have often experienced prejudice from men—both Hispanic and Anglo. Sometimes if I don't speak Spanish to them, Hispanic men accuse me of being *agringada,* which means I have taken on *gringo* characteristics and have left my culture.

Sometimes, the Anglo man to whom I am speaking won't even look me in the eye. Instead, he talks to the male on my team who is sitting beside me. That happens sometimes in academics when I am testifying before a committee. That personal slight from a man is hard to take because I want to think that the merit of my words should be sufficient. I have learned when to kick back at an insult and when to distance myself. Sometimes it's really hard not to kick back, but I remind myself that there are a whole lot of people—both faculty and students—who are depending on me to keep my temper in check so I can win the day for our university.

**LEARNING FROM MEN:** There are times, however, when I have used men, and their tremendous egos (laughs), to my advantage. (Ann Richards would kill me if she heard me saying this, because we have talked about it.) I sit on many boards and committees, mostly male-dominated. When I was a new member of the Federal Reserve Board, I knew nothing about banking. So after I had listened to everyone for a while, I chose the smartest guy, sat next to him, and picked his brain. I got a briefing of the highest caliber.

I do this on every new board I sit on. Those smart men love to teach "the little lady" about whatever their expertise is. It doesn't bother me to be taught by men, and I learn what I need to know.

**FEMALE NETWORKING:** Early in my career, most of my important contacts were men because more men were in positions to help. But when two powerful women helped me to become president of TSC and then of UTB, I realized that the female network is ten times as powerful.

There is a level of *confianza*—a familiarity, a rapport—among women that is lacking in our relationships with men. In a roomful of women at a budget-strategy meeting, I can drop a comment about my granddaughter into the proceedings, and no one will think less of me. In fact, such comments can build instant rapport, breaking down cumbersome layers that often keep people from learning from each other.

**MOTHERHOOD AND WORK:** Most women share one common dilemma: the guilt of not being a "perfect mother." All mothers face that problem, especially if they work away from home. Boy! I have felt it just like everyone else. And it feels really crummy.

And not being the "perfect wife" has bothered me also. I can speak to the nation with ease, but when I get in the kitchen, I get nervous and cut my finger. It's hard to be a lousy cook when you have a husband who is such a good one. (Laughs.) When you are a competitor, you kind of want to compete in everything.

**STAYING AT HOME:** My daughter got a degree in business, and she has chosen to stay at home with her kids and keep house. She asked me once, "That's okay, isn't it, Mom?" And I said, "Sweetheart, that's what most women would love to do. Of course it's okay! You have an option."

**NURTURING YOURSELF:** Whether you are a businessperson or a stay-at-home mother, it is essential to take time off and recharge your energies. I do that in several ways:

- Being with my grandchildren does wonders for me.
- Going away with my husband for three days every summer to a cool spot, away from the oppressive Texas heat. We hike and talk. That works for us.
- Keeping weekends for family activities. I won't let my weekends be interrupted by work.
- Nurturing myself spiritually by recalling what my mother taught

me: that my skills, strength, and courage are gifts from God to be used for the benefit of the common good. I have found that you have to stay centered spiritually, no matter what your method is. I also believe that angels abound.

- Re-spiriting myself mentally. That is absolutely essential. Every once in a while, I take a course at another university. I have studied at Harvard, MIT, and the London School of Business, where I have taken courses in literature and other subjects completely outside of my area of expertise.

**FRIENDSHIP:** Another way to nurture yourself is through friendship. My biggest mistake has been to let my close friendships dissolve by not nurturing them. I haven't made it a priority to call and to make time for my friends. It is easy to give all of your time to your babies and then to your work and to your husband. But somehow all women should maintain close friendships. It is very lonely not having many close girlfriends.

**IF I WERE A YOUNG WOMAN STARTING OVER:** Cultivating my friendships is one thing I would do differently. But I am pleased with most of the other decisions I have made in my life.

If I [had] followed the pattern of women today—the more usual pattern of waiting longer to get married, of having my babies later, of thinking career is first—I think I would have made a big mistake. The keel that has kept me balanced has been my marriage and my babies. I wish I could have had five kids.

It's true, having my babies so early was hard because we were poor and in school. Sometimes we didn't know how we were going to survive the week. But in retrospect, I am glad we had babies when I was young because now I am young enough to enjoy my grandbabies. Would I have gotten married later? No. Everything we have accomplished—every degree I got—came after I was married. So I don't know life without marriage. And it has worked out.

The career has been wonderful, and I will get the gold watch someday. But not having a family to fall back on would not be living.

# CARMEN LOMAS GARZA

*Above: Carmen Lomas Garza, artist. Photo by Mark Jordan © 2000.*

*Right:* Tamalada (Making Tamales). *Artist: Carmen Lomas Garza. Medium: gouache painting. Size: 20 x 27 inches. © 1987 Carmen Lomas Garza. Photo by Wolfgang Dietze. From the collection of Leonila Ramirez, Don Ramon's Restaurant, San Francisco. Courtesy of Carmen Lomas Garza.*

"*I prefer the term 'Chicano' to 'Mexican American' because of the connotation. 'Chicano' has come to mean a reclamation of our heritage; it means self-determination.*"

## Carmen
## Lomas
## Garza

B. 1948,
**KINGSVILLE, TEXAS**
CURRENT HOME:
**SAN FRANCISCO, CALIFORNIA**

~

When Carmen Lomas Garza was thirteen, she decided to become an artist, and it was when she was a college student during the 1960s that she discovered the theme that would shape her works: Chicano art. She has been a self-supporting artist since age thirty-three (1981) and is recognized throughout the country as a leader in the Chicano art movement. Most of her works are paintings, but she also concentrates on Day of the Dead *ofrenda* installations, lithography prints, and paper and metal cutouts.

Carmen labels her work "Chicano" art because she discovered her own style and theme as a college student during the political Raza movement of the 1960s. The Raza movement occurred when young Mexican Americans began to revolt against the discriminatory treatment they had endured as children and which they had seen their parents suffer as adults. The young militants adopted the word "Chicano" to replace terms used by others to describe their ethnicity. However, instead of following the militant political style of many Chicano male artists, Carmen wanted to portray the positive everyday experiences that give validation to Mexican American family life. Carmen's works most often tell stories of traditional family scenes fondly remembered from her childhood—from making tamales to dancing to Tejano music.

Because her works tell stories, she is considered a "narrative" artist. Some critics also label her a "primitive artist," some a "folk artist," and some a "naïve artist." To refute these labels, she explains: "There are no primitive cultures left in the world, I am formally trained as a studio artist, and I am not following strictly in the footsteps of my 'folk.'" Stylistically, she was influenced by children's art, which she studied in college for her degree in art education. She was influenced also by her mother, who painted cards for Lotería, a Mexican game akin to bingo. "I want my work to be direct, simple, and easy to read but still be considered fine art," Carmen says.

Carmen grew up the second of five children in Kingsville, Texas, a small community not far from the border with Mexico. She holds a Bachelor of Science degree from Texas A&I (now Texas A&M) University in Kingsville, where she studied art education and studio art. She holds a master's degree in education from Antioch Graduate School–Juarez/Lincoln Center and a master of arts degree from San Francisco State University, where she concentrated on lithography and painting in oil and gouache (opaque watercolor).

She has had several one-person shows in museums in the United States, including the Smithsonian Institution in Washington, D.C., the Whitney Museum of American Art in New York City, and the Laguna Gloria Art Museum in Austin, where a thousand people attended the opening day of her exhibit in 1991. She was commissioned to create a permanent installation for the San Francisco International Airport, which opened in 2000. The piece is a sixteen-by-twenty-four-foot copper cutout depicting a mariachi dancer.

In collaboration with Children's Book Press of San Francisco, Carmen has published four books for children, featuring both her art and her narrative: *Family Pictures/Cuadros de Familia* (1990), *In My Family/En mi familia* (1996), *Magic Windows/Ventanas Mágicas* (1999), and an instructional book to accompany *Magic Windows/Ventanas Mágicas*, which demonstrates how to make paper cutouts. All four books portray the childhood of a Mexican American girl, and the narrative in each tells the stories behind the pictures.

Her books have earned numerous awards, including the Pura Belpré Award for illustration, the Tomás Rivera Mexican-American Children's Book Award, and the International Reading Association Notable Book Award.

A book of her paintings, *A Piece of My Heart/Pedacito de mi Corazón*, was published in association with the Laguna Gloria Art Museum to accompany her solo exhibition in 1991.

While her work affirms the Mexican American culture, it naturally appeals to all cultures. An art reviewer once called Carmen Lomas Garza's work "as culturally affirming for those who grew up in similar circumstances as it is culturally expanding for those who did not."

**AUTHOR'S NOTE** *It was 1991 during her solo exhibit at Laguna Gloria Art Museum that I discovered Carmen Lomas Garza's work. The exhibit had drawn a thousand people the first day, but I visited the old villa on the lake one quiet Wednesday afternoon, so I had the place almost to myself. I walked from room to room, absorbing every painting in quiet reflection. When I left, I took with me a warm glow and a fascination for Carmen's art that I would never forget. At the time, I couldn't pinpoint the reason why Carmen's paintings had held me spellbound.*

*Today, as I speak with her, I understand better why I was drawn to her paintings and to the spirit that pervades them. Carmen is as honest in person as she is in her artwork, and her stories are as compelling to hear as they are to look at.*

*Perhaps I relate because I grew up among ten siblings, in an atmosphere not unlike that of Carmen's childhood. Perhaps it is because of the years I spent in San Antonio working alongside Mexican American friends who invited me into their rich culture and family life.*

*Or maybe I relate solely because of Carmen's genius, her ability to bring outsiders like me into the richness of her culture and make us feel a part of it all.*

## *Carmen Lomas Garza*

# SPEAKS

**WHAT MAKES ME FEEL ALIVE:** My greatest reward is to see a Mexican American family—three or four generations—as they study one of my paintings at a museum or an exhibition. They are all pointing to the painting and talking about their own experiences in the Mexican American culture. That scenario is the best feedback that I can get because Chicano viewers are the most important critics. The newspaper critics pale in comparison.

**CHICANO ART:** My main goal as a Chicano artist has always been to address the whole family—men, women, and children—and to bring about an appreciation of the values we have in our own culture. I tend to use my mother or my grandmother as the central figures in most of my paintings, probably because they were the main nurturers in my family. Women are typically at the center of most of the family activities I depict, but the men are also there. Both of my parents were instrumental in raising and loving us, as was my grandfather.

Children especially seem to relate to my work because it is easy to understand. Because of my own experiences growing up in the public schools and the damage that discrimination did, I want to make sure that Mexican American children today grow up feeling proud of their culture, of their heritage. So when a museum hosts an exhibit of my work, I keep the children in mind by insisting that children's activities are included. I usually insist that the exhibition opening be scheduled for a Sunday afternoon so that whole families can attend and meet the artist.

Of course, my viewers are not solely Chicano. My art attracts ethnically diverse audiences as well. When I get good feedback from people of other cultures, I see it as a celebration of our similarities. I think other cultures relate to it because family life is universal.

**GROWING UP CHICANA IN TEXAS:** When I was a child, our family life was very nurturing and active. We were always celebrating holidays, and our mother was the one who created those events for us, with the help of our grandmother. But once we got into public school, the world became a difficult place. If we spoke Spanish at school we were punished, and when we spoke English we were ridiculed for our accent and made to feel ashamed. The education system was punishing me for speaking two languages. By the time I graduated from high school, I was confused, depressed, introverted, and quite angry.

Racism became a focal point in my college years. We Mexican Americans had seen our parents and grandparents suffer from discrimination. As college students, we decided not to tolerate it anymore. We joined the new Chicano movement of the late 1960s, and I began the slow process of self-healing through my art. During my art training at the university, I had done all the different styles that were required (abstract art, still life, etc.), and I was pretty good. But those styles were not satisfying. That art was not coming from my soul.

My own style, which I decided to call Chicano art, was criticized by the faculty and Anglo students as being too colorful, too folksy, too primitive, not universal, not pop art, not avant-garde. They failed to see that the art I was creating functioned in the same way as the *salvia* (aloe vera) plant when its cool liquid is applied to a burn or an abrasion. My art was helping me to heal the wounds inflicted by all the years of discrimination and racism.

**EDUCATION:** I am very, very fortunate in that both of my parents wanted the three girls in my family (as well as my two brothers) to get a higher education. (In the Mexican American culture, daughters weren't always encouraged to go to college.) My mother had never gotten the opportunity to go to college, and both parents saw education as being crucial to a better life. They felt that my ability as an artist could help me make a living as an art teacher.

**PREJUDICE:** But it was as a student teacher in art that I experienced the most biting prejudice of my life. Although 80 percent of the high school students in that small South Texas town were either Mexican or Mexican American, they were not allowed to speak Spanish. I got in trouble with the administration for allowing the Chicano students to listen to Tejano music while they worked (instead of the steady diet of country-western music the few Anglo students in the class were insisting on). I also got in trouble for explaining the art assignment in Spanish to a student who couldn't understand English. The Anglo students had complained to the administration about me because I was bending rules to help Chicano students succeed. And I had to stop bending rules or I would be dismissed from student teaching.

A few weeks into the school semester, the Mexican American students decided to stage a walkout because they felt their rights as Chicanos were being violated in numerous ways. For example, they wanted the right to speak Spanish to their friends at school, to study more about their own heritage, and basically to celebrate their Mexican American culture. Although I had nothing to do with the walkout, the supervisor for student teachers saw me talking to the students at lunch and assumed that I had instigated the protest. I was not allowed to continue my student teaching at that school, and I was told that if I tried to talk to the administration about it, the other Chicano student teachers would be dismissed also. It was a hard slap in the face for me, but the real tragedy was that all of the eighteen-year-old Mexican American boys who had walked out of class that day were expelled from school and were immediately drafted into the military. By the time the rest of their classmates reached graduation day, those Chicano boys were fighting in Vietnam.

All of those boys lost their innocence. Some lost their arms and legs, and some lost their lives. That's when I decided to dedicate my life to baring the values of Chicano culture in my art. I wanted the world to understand the values held dear by those Chicano boys who died in war simply because they had wanted to be able to practice their civil rights at school.

**CHICANO HERITAGE:** I prefer the term "Chicano" to "Mexican American" because of the connotation. "Chicano" has come to mean a reclamation of our heritage; it means self-determination. My people are quite often seen as aliens in the United States, but my roots go back ten thousand years in the area where I was raised that is now thought of as South Texas. Texas is where the bones of our ancestors are buried, so we have every right to be there. That is our home.

Most Anglo Texans think that Texas history began in 1836 with the battle of the Alamo—as if nothing existed before that. Back then my ancestors, the mestizos (a mixture of the Spanish and the Texas Indian), were working on the ranches (*ranchos*) that the Spaniards had established. The lifestyle of the people—the indigenous people of South Texas and Northern Mexico—fit the harshness of the semiarid region. My people had been able to survive, with a rich culture intact.

**TEJANAS:** Our culture today reflects that survival instinct, and you can see it in the Mexican American woman of Texas—the Tejana. I find Tejanas to be different from the Mexican American women in California, in that Tejanas are much friendlier, more fun-loving, ready to party, and more celebrative. I think we inherited those qualities from our Tejana ancestors, who, through their camaraderie, had learned to survive the harsh physical environment of South Texas.

**TEXAS:** When I move back to Texas, it will probably be to Austin, and not just because I have siblings there. The climate is not quite so harsh as around Kingsville, and the Austin spring is so delicious with the magnolias and all the flowers. It gives me such great joy to listen to the mockingbird. Every time I hear a mockingbird in California, it reminds me of my other home.

**SENSE OF PLACE:** Texas is my home, but I also feel a great sense of community here in San Francisco. I am certainly not a reclusive artist. I do my best work when I am in my own community among my friends.

Once I spent a month alone at a retreat where I had the luxury of spending all of my time creating art. But instead of being ecstatic about the time alone, I learned that I need my community to be happy and productive. I missed my husband and friends, and I missed visiting all of my favorite places, the Galería de la Raza (the Mexican Museum), and shopping in the *mercados* of my neighborhood. Being isolated made me aware that I should not take my community for granted.

**DANCE:** I also missed my dance group. When I was forty-seven, I discovered Mexica (popularly known as Aztec dancing). This form of ceremonial dancing has been very spiritually and emotionally uplifting for me, as well as being good for my body.

Mexica has allowed me to learn much more about my indigenous heritage and about how important dance was to the spiritual life of those ancient people. It has opened up a new type of spirituality for me. Mexica has to do with the natural elements: Mother Earth, the sun, animals, and the respect that one should give to all of those elements in our lives.

**CATHOLICISM:** Spiritually, I am much more fulfilled by Mexica than by Catholicism, the religion of my childhood. I am no longer an active Catholic; in fact, I have a love-hate relationship with the Catholic Church. I love the teachings of Jesus, but I don't agree with a lot of the requirements the Church imposes on people. I have a difficult time forgiving the Church for the destruction it did to the indigenous people in the Americas. For example, when the Europeans arrived in Mexico in the early 1500s, they burned almost all of the books written by the indigenous people. That book burning, in effect, erased all the records of that culture.

At this point in my life, I am not interested in going back to the male-dominated religion of my childhood, but I am still very much drawn to the family altar—the *ofrenda*—in the home, which celebrates family history and its ancestors. My father built our home altar from wood, and my mother maintains it with family photos, with icons of importance to us, and with artistic decorations. It is a special place in their home in Kingsville.

**DAY OF THE DEAD:** The *ofrenda* has become one of the important segments of my artwork, especially as it welcomes the visiting souls of our ancestors on Día de los Muertos, the Day of the Dead celebration. Día de los Muertos extends Mexican beliefs in regard to the afterlife beyond what the Catholic Church teaches. Honoring my ancestors is an important part of my belief system. It is important to me to fashion from raw materials (not to buy already made from Mexico) as many of the items in the *ofrendas* as I can. So I make the paper cutouts, paper flowers, skull masks, portraits, and altar cloths. If I'm not able to use real fruit in the installation, I make fruit from papier-mâché.

**MARRIAGE:** My depiction of family events and celebrations in my art-work makes it obvious that family is important to me. However, I made the choice not to have children because I knew I couldn't be both a de-voted parent *and* an artist. By the time I met my husband, Jerry Avila Carpenter, when I was thirty-three, I knew very clearly what I needed in a mate and what I would not tolerate. Jerry likes my art and my being an artist. If he were not supportive of my career, mixing marriage and an art career would be very difficult. We have been together almost twenty years.

**THE BUSINESS OF ART:** I wish I could spend 100 percent of my work-ing time just creating art in the studio, but I also have to manage my career. The business of art takes a lot of effort and money, as I have to put a lot of money back into the business for materials, space, office supplies, computer, etc. The business side is something I have had to learn, but the payback is that I have control over the marketing and distribution of my art.

If I am working intently on an art piece, I am in the studio every day (a ten-minute drive from my office at home). But sometimes it is several weeks before I can make it back to my studio because I am so busy work-ing on proposals, books, memo writing, bookkeeping, taxes, or whatever. Half of my time is spent here in the office at home.

I tell young artists that the sooner they learn to deal with the business side of art, the more control they will have over their careers. When I was in my early twenties, I learned a lot about running an art business from two male artist friends in South Texas who owned a gallery and framing shop. They taught me about materials and about exhibiting, installing, and presenting the artwork.

**LEARNING NEW THINGS:** But my initial art education was only a beginning; an artist's development never stops. I am still learning new techniques—mostly through my own experimentation with various ma-terials.

As I get older, I am doing bigger pieces. I have gone from the small paintings of my earlier career to my present three-by-four-foot paint-ings, partly because painting large images is easier than painting small ones. When I was a young artist, I didn't have a lot of materials or storage space, so I kept my paintings small. Framing was also less expensive with small paintings. Today I can afford more materials and bigger framing, but I usually limit my works to the three-by-four-foot format for several reasons: I can carry that size fairly easily in my arms, the works will fit into my station wagon, and storage space in San Francisco is at a premium.

**MENOPAUSE:** My art career almost came to a standstill in my late forties, when I experienced some of the most difficult years of my life. I was going through my passage, but I didn't realize what my problem was. At the same time I was going through those physical changes, my career was shooting up. I had trouble keeping my life together because menopause had hit me so hard.

I had every symptom: hot flashes, insomnia, indigestion, bone aches, sinus problems. I felt like I had the flu all the time. I was lethargic and depressed. I couldn't work and I didn't want to go out. I didn't want to relate to people. The most frightening of all, though, was that I didn't feel like carrying on my art business. I wanted to work only here in the house; I didn't go to the studio. My doctor thought I was having "stage fright"—the most ridiculous thing I had ever heard. (Laughs.) He dismissed the idea of menopause because I was too young, he thought. I was lucky to have a lot of support from my husband. Finally I found a new doctor and I began hormone replacement therapy.

I think that every woman should talk to older friends and family members to find out how menopause affected them. My friends were great sources of support. I also began reading and researching on my own, as well as talking to my new gynecologist.

When I look back, I realize that most of my forties were affected by menopause. It was as if I had gone through a type of death. But I think I came out of those rough years with a greater appreciation for life.

**LOOKING TOWARD THE FUTURE:** Now that I am on this side of menopause and also am more experienced in the business of art, I am planning more aggressively to get art projects funded and to create exhibitions. Instead of reacting to requests, I am asserting myself to make things happen.

A recent solo exhibition of my paintings and paper cutouts was organized by the San Jose Museum of Art, and it will travel for eighteen months to several states, including California, Texas, Florida, and New Mexico.

By the time this book is published, my Web site should be well established: www.carmenlomasgarza.com.

**NURTURING YOURSELF:** Part of being a productive artist is making sure that I nurture myself along the way. I balance my professional life by spending time with my husband and my friends—going out to eat and having people over for dinner. My husband and I like to walk in public parks regularly, and we go out *salsa* dancing as often as we can. I spend time with my family in Texas by talking on the phone and by going to visit during the holidays. I do my Mexica dancing regularly for exercise and for the spiritual and emotional uplift it gives me.

I believe in treating yourself to the best. That includes buying yourself a really good Christmas present and treating yourself to flowers, massages, good food, and fun times. You should buy nice clothes if you can afford it; your body is your most important possession.

One of my new philosophies comes from the Dalai Lama of Tibet: "Is what I am doing (or about to do) making me a better human being? Am I bettering other people's lives as well as my own?" From now on, I will try to apply that thought to every aspect of my life.

> " *Success*
>
> *is the*
>
> *greatest*
>
> *revenge.* "

*Glenna Goodacre,
sculptor, works on
maquette of the Irish
Famine Monument
in her studio in Santa
Fe. Photo by Summer
Pierce © 2000.*

*Vietnam Women's Memorial, Washington, D.C. Sculptor:
Glenna Goodacre. © 1993 Vietnam Women's Memorial Project,
Inc. Photo by Greg Staley Photos. Courtesy of Glenna Goodacre.*

*Glenna
Goodacre*

B. 1939,
LUBBOCK, TEXAS
CURRENT HOME:
SANTA FE, NEW MEXICO

Glenna Goodacre is one of the women artists who have made it big in the "man's world" of art. Her name has become synonymous with at least two of her best-known works: the Vietnam Women's Memorial on the Mall in Washington, D.C., dedicated November 11, 1993, and the U.S. golden dollar coin featuring the image of Sacagawea, issued in February 2000. The Vietnam Women's Memorial honors American women soldiers who served in the Vietnam War, and the dollar coin honors the Shoshone teenage mother who accompanied explorers Lewis and Clark to the Pacific Ocean in 1805.

Glenna's career in the visual arts spans four decades, and she has concentrated on sculpting for more than thirty years. She specializes in expressive, sensitive portraits, and in children in action. Her commissioned bronze portrait figures and busts are in public collections in ten states in the United States, and hundreds of her pieces are in private collections all over the world. Among her works in Texas are *Park Place*, a seven-piece sculpture on the grounds of Texas Tech University in Lubbock, and *Philosophers' Rock* at Barton Springs pool in Austin.

Glenna has won numerous awards from the National Sculpture Society, Allied Artists of America, Knickerbocker Artists, and the National Academy of Design. She was elected a member of the National Academy of Design in 1994.

She grew up Glenna Maxey in Lubbock, in a typically conservative West Texas family. Her mother, Mabel, was a homemaker with interior design skills, and her father, Homer, was a building contractor. Both had college degrees.

Instead of attending Texas Tech University like the rest of her family,

Glenna majored in art at Colorado College in Colorado Springs. The only sculpture class she ever took turned out to be a disaster when she broke her leg skiing. She made a D in the course because she didn't get the chance to complete her work. Her professor told her not to try sculpture again, as she had no future in it—and Glenna believed him.

For the next ten years as a young housewife and mother in Lubbock, she limited her artwork to painting and drawing. Then, determined to make art a profession, Glenna scraped together $2,000 in 1967 and spent six weeks studying painting and drawing at the Art Students League in New York City. While there, she never ventured down to the sculpting department, still convinced that her art skills did not include sculpture.

Her drawings had caught the eye of an art dealer, Forrest Fenn, the owner of a small foundry in Lubbock. He gave Glenna a lump of wax and challenged her to sculpt something. She set the lump aside for six months, but one day she sat down at the kitchen table and sculpted her first piece: a seven-inch miniature of her five-and-a-half-year-old daughter, Jill, in a ballerina costume. "I think I used a bobby pin, a paring knife, and a toothpick," she recalls, smiling. When Forrest presented her with the finished bronze, both he and Glenna knew that she had a future in sculpting. Today Glenna keeps that first miniature on her studio desk while she works on bigger-than-life-size figures.

At the insistence of Fenn, she progressed quickly from miniatures of children to life-size commissioned pieces of West Texas dignitaries and heroes. Glenna moved with her family to Boulder, Colorado, in 1970, and Forrest and Peggy Fenn moved to Santa Fe. The couple opened Fenn Gallery, which became the main outlet for the sculptures Glenna was producing in Boulder. After a divorce in 1983, Glenna moved from Boulder to Santa Fe.

Her creativity also extends to designing houses. During her first fourteen years in Santa Fe, Glenna built or remodeled seven houses and studios, living or working in each until she designed one she liked better. "Designing and building houses is my hobby," she said. "But the last house I built is so wonderful, I think I may finally stop building."

Glenna has two children, Tim and Jill. Tim and wife, Denise, live with their two children in Boulder, and Jill and husband, Harry Connick, Jr., and their two children live in Connecticut. Glenna married Mike Schmidt, a Dallas attorney, in 1995. "I really have it all," she said. "Of course, it has taken a lot of work and a lot of juggling to get here."

**AUTHOR'S NOTE**  *One can almost breathe in the creativity amidst the smell of wet clay inside Glenna's spacious, sunlit studio. This is the most recent of several studios she has occupied in Santa Fe, and she says it will be her last. She has finally designed the perfect one. When she bought the building from another artist a few years ago, it was a huge barnlike room with fifteen-foot ceilings. A re-designer by nature, Glenna added a whole wall of windows, a huge fireplace, and another room for cast-making.*

*Various works-in-progress are usually stationed throughout the expanse of the main room. On my first visit, works included a seven-foot-tall figure of Ronald Reagan awaiting a finished face, an unfinished bust of Greer Garson, and life-size figures of an old man and a dog, part of the Park Place work being cast in the next room. In a corner by itself was a twenty-five-figure maquette (a miniature wax study) of the Irish Famine Monument for Philadelphia. The maquette was the tiny beginning of the project that would become Glenna's largest work to date—the work-in-progress that would fill her whole studio a year later, leaving no room for other works.*

*Glenna's West Texas gregariousness sets a congenial tone for her staff and makes for a productive but relaxed atmosphere. While Glenna sits across her big pine desk from me, her three staff members are in constant motion around the studio—answering phones, dealing with delivery people, building clay forms around armatures, working on plastic casts of the finished sculptures, and petting Rio, the studio Labrador retriever, as he wanders from room to room.*

*"This is why I love peace and quiet when I get home in the evenings,"* Glenna says. *"The action and noise never stop here in the studio."*

*Glenna Goodacre*

## SPEAKS

**SUCCESS FROM FAILURE:** "Success Is the Greatest Revenge." That was my title for a commencement speech at Colorado College a few years ago. I had been nervous about what to say, since I was returning to the roots of my worst experience in the sculpture world. From the podium I was looking out at historians, philosophers, and mathematicians—minds that were way out of my realm. But I gave them a good laugh when I said, "Right here at Colorado College I got a D in sculpture." You can learn from a problematic time in your life and eventually use it to your benefit. It took me ten years to overcome the fear of sculpting foisted on me by that professor. Now I can laugh about it.

**HUMOR:** In fact, my three staff members and I are always laughing about things. It is important to have a good sense of humor in this business. Sometime over a couple of glasses of wine I should talk about all the funny things that have happened in my career—all the nude models, for instance. That subject alone is hysterical.

**BEING FEMALE IN A MALE ART WORLD:** It helps to laugh when I recall all the hurdles I've faced—and gotten over—in the art world. Being accepted as a female was one of the biggest ones. For years I wasn't accepted into art shows because I was just "one of those girls" in the eyes of most art dealers. In a man's world, sculptures of women and children are seen as weak and "namby-pamby."

In truth, I do sculpt a lot of men—like that big Indian out in the yard in front of the studio and the larger-than-life Ronald Reagan that I did in 1998 for the Reagan Presidential Library in Los Angeles. Earlier in my career, I was commissioned to sculpt several military generals. Those generals probably helped me in the man's world. But I lean toward the figures of women and children. There are still only a handful of truly successful women artists, and I feel very fortunate to be one of them.

**REALISM VS. ABSTRACT:** I have always been out of the mainstream of art because my style has always been realism. When I started college in 1957, everything (in the art world) was abstract. I couldn't have cared less about abstract art, but I did far-out kinds of pieces just to get a grade. Then I would sit in the corner and do my exact little drawings and paintings because that was what spoke to me. I considered becoming a medical illustrator because of the exact nature of medical drawings.

**PREPARING FOR AN ART CAREER:** After college, I married and had children—the accepted path of the day that all my friends were taking. When my kids were little in the 1960s, they played on the green shag carpet around my easel while I painted. My priorities were being a wife and mother first and an artist last. But I longed to have a *real* career in art. I remember feeling angry because I wasn't getting to spend enough uninterrupted time painting and then feeling guilty because when I was painting, I might be neglecting my children. I painted things to gratify myself, but I also did a lot of "crap craft," as I called it, because it was a money-making thing. I did pastel portraits of my friends' kids for a fee, and I could make $250 from a big commissioned oil painting!

And I found another way to make money as a young mother; I became an FHA-approved house contractor, a business I had learned from my dad. I built a lot of houses—Plan 18: three bedrooms, kitchen, den, fireplace, double-car garage with fake brick front for $18,500. (Laughs.) That's when you decorated in avocado green and harvest gold. And you did a lot of big-print wallpaper and shag green carpet that you raked.

But I had a strong urge to get out of Lubbock—not because of the town itself but because I wanted to step beyond feeling like "little Glenna—Homer and Melba's baby doing her craft thing." In Lubbock painting was synonymous with decoupage and macramé.

My view of an art career changed drastically when I spent those six weeks in New York City at the Art Students League. I was with two other Lubbock ladies, and we stayed at the Barbizon Plaza Hotel. Like a sponge, I soaked up all I could learn in the classes, the museums and galleries. But just as important was the attitude I learned from the people I met. It was the first time I had been with people who viewed art as their "profession." That was really an eye-opener. I came back a changed woman.

I didn't take sculpting classes at the league or anywhere else. I've never had any formal training in sculpture. I have learned mostly by doing: mashing the clay. Of course, I had had all the years of training in anatomy and physiology and all the drawing, which had prepared me for sculpture.

**LEARNING NEW THINGS:** I'm constantly learning, either from my own mistakes and successes or by studying other artists. Mike and I travel to art museums all over the world. Recently we spent several days in the Hermitage and in the Russian Museum in St. Petersburg. That was a marvelous learning experience! And Christmas in Paris—four hours one morning in the Louvre and then several hours in the Musee d'Orsay.

Of course, I go back to Italy a lot to see the big boys—Mike (Michelangelo) and Leo (da Vinci)—those guys. I go back to learn, but also to be humbled. It is important to get away from my own studio so I can walk back in here and say: "My God, that man is way too short! Why didn't I see that before? And that eye is a half-inch higher than the other one. That looks terrible!"

**IF I WERE A YOUNG WOMAN STARTING OVER:** I have often thought that if I had gone to art school instead of college, I might be ahead of where I am now. I might have had proper training in building an armature, mixing clay, casting a bronze—all the things I hire others to do for me now. I sometimes wonder where I would be if I had studied sculpting right out of college instead of spending ten years painting and drawing before my sculpting began.

But I don't think I'd change anything now. I did everything in sequence (going to college, marrying, having kids, starting my career)—and I'm pleased with how everything has turned out.

**MENTORS:** When I consider my mentors, I include Forrest Fenn on the list because he really taught me the technical aspects of working three-dimensionally. He takes full credit for my career, and we both laugh about it. (Laughs.) He would give me advice and I would go do what I wanted to do. Forrest is retired now and has sold his gallery in Santa Fe to Nedra Matteucci. We are really good friends to this day.

While I was growing up, my parents had tremendous influence on my artistic development. Mother and Daddy both were creative, and they recognized my artistic talents. Besides the good art education I got in the public schools back then, I was also taking private lessons from artists my parents found for me around Lubbock.

Much later, I met the best art professor—and also the hardest one—I ever had. He was an old man from the East named Frank Gervasi, and he was a big influence on my life. When I began my courses in New York, I thought I was really hot stuff because I could compose things well and get my drawings to look like something. I was painting a geranium and Mr. Gervasi walked up behind me. I was expecting him to say how wonderful and great I was, but instead he said, "Well, it's pretty bad. You can work on it a while longer and make it worse." (Laughs.) I learned a lot about art from him, and he was the one who gave me the courage to enter the associations and competitive shows in New York City.

When I told him that I was determined to become a professional artist, he gave me this advice: "You'll need to divorce your husband, put your kids in an orphanage, and go off and paint." So I did that—twenty years later. (Laughs.)

**DIVORCE:** I was married twenty-three years, and I really hadn't planned on getting divorced. But when divorce did happen, it turned out to be a big beginning. I moved to Santa Fe, and a whole new world opened up to me. The children were grown and gone. Relying totally on myself was exhilarating.

**THE SECOND TIME AROUND:** I certainly never planned to remarry, but I'm glad I did. I work here in Santa Fe and Mike works in Dallas, and we honeymoon every weekend. It works out beautifully. We travel a lot together. He goes to art shows with me and I go to lawyer meetings with him. Our living arrangement keeps our relationship fresh.

**SENSE OF PLACE:** Mike and I both have roots in Santa Fe because our West Texas families both had vacation cabins on the Pecos River. We met here in Santa Fe a few years ago.

When I moved to Santa Fe at age forty-four, it was like coming home. I belong here. In Santa Fe, art is not a hobby; it's a profession. And gender doesn't matter.

**MONEY:** I'm really fortunate. I get to do what I love, and I am making a good living from it.

My father, a great businessman, taught me that you can borrow money to make money. I never had a business course, but I have always done well with money.

I remember being scared to death when I walked into the bank in 1967 to ask the president for a $2,000 loan so I could study in New York. That $2,000 was really the beginning of my professional career.

**SCULPTING VERSUS "ART":** Ever since I got hooked on sculpting, I have been drawn to the three-dimensional. But a lot of people still regard sculpting as a "craft" rather than a "fine art." I am tickled at some people's response when they see my drawings and paintings side by side. A typical reaction is: "I didn't know you were an *artist,* too!"

Art shows used to have two categories: "artists" and "sculptors." It was as if sculptors were the bastards of the art world. Now art show directors practice a little more political correctness, but paintings and sculptures are still often separated. Some people's definition of "sculpture" is "that thing you bump into when you step back to look at a painting." (Laughs.)

**TIME MANAGEMENT:** I keep regular studio hours—usually nine to five. After a full day up on a ladder with my arms up, I am physically tired. If I'm working on a miniature, I might take the piece home, but not very often. My staff also leaves at five. I don't work on the weekends unless I'm really, really pushing, and that's not often. Sometimes I take a little longer at lunch if there's someone I'm enjoying talking to.

**CREATIVITY:** The most frequently asked question is "How long does it take you to do a piece?" My pat answer is "I never clock in hours. And I am always thinking about one piece while I am working on another."

It is more interesting to work on several pieces at the same time. When I work too long on one piece, I get all bogged down to the point that I literally can't see it anymore. When I was doing Ronald Reagan for the presidential library, I ended up cutting his face off and starting over. That happens quite often.

**VIETNAM WOMEN'S MEMORIAL:** I am a control person; I like to be in charge. I got a big lesson in tolerance while creating the Vietnam Women's Memorial because I was forced to give up control of my own creation to the Washington bureaucrats for about six months while they tried to redesign it. For about a year I found myself raging and roaring around because I was so frustrated with the bureaucratic process. During that time I started calling myself "the Big Bitch of the West." In the end, it all came around, and I am proud of the results. I guess most of all I am proud to have done a sculpture that means so much to so many people.

**IRISH FAMINE MONUMENT:** My current project is one that I hope will mean a lot to another whole segment of society—the Irish immigrants to the United States. The Irish Famine Monument—my largest piece yet—will consume all of the coming year for both my staff and me. It commemorates the Irish immigration to the United States, brought on by what is commonly known as the Potato Famine. It was commissioned by an Irish society in Philadelphia, and it will be dedicated there on the banks of the Delaware in 2002. As usual, this piece is taking much more of my time than I had anticipated. The armature (the foam structure inside the sculpture that supports the clay) looks like a giant white iceberg in here, and it's filling the whole studio. It's pretty scary to look at the physical expanse of this impending project!

**THE SACAGAWEA DOLLAR COIN:** While I was waiting for the Irish project to fund, I won a competition to do the sculpture of Sacagawea on the new golden dollar. That coin has been a roaring success since it came out in 2000. The U.S. Mint has struck 750 million by now, and we still don't see them in circulation because people are hoarding them. Of course, eventually the coin will start circulating because it will become a regular part of our money system. People will get used to the idea and start using them. It has been wonderful for me to have a sculpture of such national prominence—one that everyone will be familiar with because they will be carrying it around in their pockets.

**GETTING OLDER:** Since I've gotten older, and probably because of my successful career, I have gained a self-confidence that I didn't have as a young woman. I have been to the White House on several occasions for dedications of my works (the Vietnam Women's Memorial and the dollar coin). I can go up and say, "Mr. President, how are you today? Good morning, Mrs. Clinton." I feel at ease talking to just about anybody. Other things I notice about myself as I get older:

- I seem to be working harder and challenging myself more. When I began sculpting at age thirty, I was doing miniatures. And now most of my figures are bigger than life, and my compositions are getting more complicated. Park Place has seven figures. The Irish Famine Monument is twenty-eight feet long and has twenty-five figures!
- Even though I have lots of friends whom I like to spend time with, the older I get, the more I treasure my time alone. After a typical day at the studio with people coming in and out, and three phone lines ringing, I go home and revitalize myself with quiet time. I rarely turn on the TV. I love the silence. I read most of the time— authors such as Grisham and Clancy—escape literature. I live on top of a hill in a house in another part of Santa Fe, and I like to hear the wind in the trees.
- I am tending toward less and less detail in sculpture. I am now fighting the tendency to work a piece to death. Knowing when to stop is the hardest thing for me. I could get every line and every wrinkle just so, but then the piece becomes boring. I don't like the detail to distract from the whole.

  When I was doing the Vietnam piece, Sarah, my chief assistant, had been working on the shoelaces of the boots. She had them just perfect. Every time someone came in to see it, they would say, "Gosh, it's so real. Just look at those shoelaces." Well, after they had gone, I'd go mess up the shoelaces. I don't want people to look at the shoelaces. I want them to look at what the piece is trying to say— the feeling of it.

**LOOKING TOWARD THE FUTURE:** There is no such thing as retirement in my line of work. I just keep going because I stay so busy, I guess. As long as arthritis doesn't make it impossible, I'll keep sculpting forever.

However, someday I may come down off the ladder and quit doing such huge pieces that require oil-based clay. Then I can go back to the old style of water-based clay that is more spontaneous than the oil-based kind. (It's the kind you used for grade school art projects.) Water-based clay is just plain old pottery clay—really sticky—and it's hell on your hands. It is hard to control because it dries and cracks and falls apart. It would be impossible to use pottery clay on a big sculpture because you have to keep the piece wet by spraying it with water and covering it with plastic cloths.

I became enamored with pottery clay a couple of years ago when Mike and I were in the Russian Museum in St. Petersburg. I found a new hero—a Russian sculptor named Paul Troubetzkoy, who died the year I was born. The spontaneity and lack of detail in his work—part of which was possible because he used pottery clay—fascinate me. Every wrinkle is not defined, but you know the wrinkles are there. Each piece looks like he squished it all together in about fifteen minutes. This guy Troubetzkoy has really gotten to me. I'm really excited about the possibilities for my future work.

**KAY BAILEY HUTCHISON**

*Kay Bailey Hutchison (R–Texas), U.S. Senate. Photo by Senate Photography Studio. Courtesy of Kay Bailey Hutchison.*

"*Through those difficult times, I learned that merely possessing intelligence and talent is not enough to be truly successful. You have to persevere.*"

## Kay Bailey Hutchison

B. 1943,
GALVESTON, TEXAS
CURRENT HOME:
DALLAS, TEXAS

Kay Bailey Hutchison (R-Texas) is the first woman to represent Texas in the U.S. Senate, winning by the largest margin of votes ever received in the United States against a sitting incumbent senator. That was in 1993, when she defeated Senator Bob Krueger to fill the unexpired term of Democrat Lloyd Bentsen. The morning after that election, she woke up to the newspaper headline "Former University of Texas Longhorn Cheerleader Elected."

That headline was just one instance in which she has faced bias and a double standard. During that first year in the Senate, she was indicted and then acquitted of charges widely seen at the time as politically motivated. According to the respected *Almanac of American Politics,* "It was a rotten prosecution from the beginning."

Later that same year Kay was elected to her first full, six-year Senate term by 23 percentage points, the largest margin by which a Republican had ever won in Texas. She has been responsible for several important federal laws, including the antistalking bill and homemaker IRA legislation. She has been a national leader on tax issues and spearheaded congressional efforts to repeal the marriage penalty tax. She established the U.S. southern border as a federal priority, dramatically increasing the size of the U.S. Border Patrol and securing hundreds of millions in federal assistance to improve conditions in the *colonias.* She devised the welfare-funding formula that broke the impasse on welfare reform.

In the Senate, her typical day begins at 5:45 with a morning walk outdoors or on the treadmill and ends usually at midnight, after she has finished the office work she has brought home with her.

Senator Hutchison has been celebrated as one of Texas's one hundred most influential women of the twentieth century. She grew up in La Marque, near Houston, the middle child and only girl of three siblings, each five years apart. Her mother was a homemaker and her father was in real estate and insurance. Her older brother is retired in Houston, and the younger is a restaurant owner and newspaper food columnist in Weslaco. She maintains close ties with both her high school and her college friends.

Kay graduated from the University of Texas at Austin and the UT Law School. For two years she worked as a news reporter for KPRC-TV in Houston, covering the state legislature in Austin, and she then moved to Washington, D.C., for a stint as press secretary to fellow Texan Anne Armstrong, co-chair of the Republican National Committee.

In 1972, at age twenty-nine, she was elected to the Texas House of Representatives, where she served two terms. President Gerald Ford appointed her to the National Transportation Safety Board in 1976. Two years later, when she was thirty-five, Kay moved to Dallas and married a former Texas House colleague, attorney Ray Hutchison.

For twelve years she left political life, except for an unsuccessful bid for the U.S. House of Representatives in 1982. During those years she concentrated on business pursuits, including serving as senior vice president and general counsel of RepublicBank Corp., the largest bank holding company in Texas. Kay cofounded Fidelity National Bank of Dallas and owned McCraw Candies, a manufacturing company with national distribution. In 1990, at age forty-seven, she reentered politics by winning a breakthrough race for Texas state treasurer, defying a generally Democratic trend for statewide office in that election. As state treasurer, she increased returns on Texas investments to a historic $1 billion annually, convinced the legislature to limit state debt, and stopped a growing effort for a state income tax.

In 2000, she coordinated the effort of the nine female U.S. senators to write *Nine and Counting*, which draws a road map for women as they try to break barriers in politics, business, and other fields. The brainchild of Senators Hutchison and Barbara Mikulski (D-Maryland), the book became a national best-seller. Proceeds of book sales were dedicated to the Girl Scouts of America.

Kay attributes her fighting spirit to her Texas roots, which go back to her great-great-grandparents, Anna Maria and Charles S. Taylor, who settled in Nacogdoches. Charles signed the Texas Declaration of Independence and

Anna Maria was one of the thousands of Texans—mostly women—who fled for their lives from the Mexican Army in 1836, an event known as the Runaway Scrape. She is here today because her great-great-grandmother survived that scrape, though all four of her living children died from the rigors of that time. Anna Maria and Charles had nine more children.

**AUTHOR'S NOTE** *"Representing a big state like Texas involves a crisis a day or sometimes a crisis an hour," Kay tells me by phone from her Senate office in Washington. She has already taken care of a crisis this morning, and she has only twenty minutes until she needs to get in the car and be driven across Washington, D.C., to a luncheon where she is the guest speaker. But she seems surprisingly relaxed.*

*Twenty minutes into the interview, she says, "I'm leaving now, and I'll call you back when I get in the car." A few minutes later, my phone rings and we talk another twenty-five minutes until she gets to the luncheon site. "I'll call you in an hour and a half, on my way back from my luncheon speech," she promises.*

*True to her word, she resumes our interview via her car phone, as her driver takes her back across D.C. When she arrives in the parking lot of the Russell Senate Office Building, she sits in the car another twenty minutes so she can finish answering my questions in peace.*

*A typical day for a U.S. senator . . .*

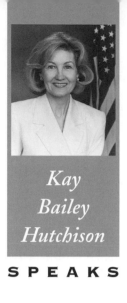

_Kay_
_Bailey_
_Hutchison_

**S P E A K S**

**FAMILY:** I think that family forms the basis of what is most permanent in life. If your family is solid, it gives you the strength to deal with the ups and downs you experience in other parts of your life.

My parents were my first and most important mentors. They spent their time nurturing our family, and they gave my brothers and me a wonderful childhood. I learned my work ethic from my dad. He worked hard, long hours, but he also spent lots of time with us. He was always there to help with my school projects, and he was supportive of anything I wanted to do. He didn't ever push me to do certain things, but when I decided to run for the Texas legislature at age twenty-nine, he was there to help me.

My mother stayed at home with us and made our lives secure. It seems that she was always carpooling, taking my friends and me to ballet class and elsewhere. She was a great support to me throughout my life. Mother got her first cancer when I was graduating from law school, but she didn't tell me because she wanted me to focus on my last exams and then the state bar exam. She lived with me for a month to help me while I studied for the bar, all the while knowing that she had cancer, but not telling me.

**DEALING WITH AGING PARENTS:** Mother finally died of a brain tumor thirty-one years later. My dad had died ten years earlier. I'm happy I had both of my parents for a relatively long time, and I'm glad that I took lots of time to be with my mother in the final years of her life.

During her last bout with cancer in 1997–1998, I sometimes canceled things and just stayed with her. She was a very strong person and she never complained. It was a tough experience.

**TEXAS WOMEN:** Mother was a good example of what I think of as a strong Texas woman. I wouldn't want to say that Texas women are different from all other women, but I would say that there is a Texas trait of spirit, grit, determination, a can-do attitude.

In the early days of Texas, women were a great part of the effort for Texas independence. Although mostly behind the scenes, they also fought for hearth and home. If their men were at San Jacinto, they were at home with guns pointing out the windows. They were ranching women who did everything the men did, and they were willing to live in a harsh place.

I have a letter written by my other great-great-grandmother, Martha Hall Sharp. She was the daughter of the governor of Tennessee, and she had moved with her husband to Texas. She had come from relatively easy, genteel living to this stark land. She didn't know anyone. But her letter was not one of complaint. She wrote to her family back in Tennessee: "Out in this new country, I see no one but strangers, but they are the kindest people I have ever met with. The society is as good as in any portion of Tennessee." This was in 1849, just after Texas became a state. She saw the positives of life in this new land; she was upbeat and happy. That's the kind of stock from which we come.

**MENTORS:** It is a strong Texas woman, Anne Armstrong, who has been my main mentor throughout my professional life. Anne is fifteen years older than I. When I was twenty-seven, I left the television station to be her press secretary in Washington, D.C. She taught me a lot and has been a major part of my life ever since. Anne has been the chairman of every campaign I've ever had. She is a natural at knowing when to stand your ground and when you need to compromise. From her I've learned the importance of good judgment. She has been there through some of my roughest times.

**LEARNING FROM SETBACKS:** I don't know of any successful person who hasn't had setbacks, both in their professional and personal lives. The people who succeed in life are those who have drawn the lessons from their setbacks to become stronger and better. Through those difficult times, I learned that merely possessing intelligence and talent is not enough to be truly successful. You have to persevere.

**PERSEVERANCE:** Perseverance is the operative principle of my day-to-day life. Somewhere along the way it was ingrained in me to "go the extra mile"; "don't take 'no' for an answer"; "keep working on getting things done, even if people tell you that you can't do it."

Since the day I decided to go to law school, being female has put obstacles in front of me. But I've never felt that anything was insurmountable. I feel that I have had to work harder to prove myself, and I have had setbacks that have made it even more difficult. But in the end, it has probably made me stronger. If I had had an easier life, I might not be where I am today.

I think that having to persevere so much in your life toughens you for the injustices you encounter. You learn not to take things personally. When I got out of law school in 1967, the major law firms in Houston would not hire a woman. For over two months, I looked for a job. Rather than giving up, I decided to take a different route and, really on a lark, I became a television news reporter. That profession led me in a different direction, one that was probably better in the long run.

When I was being unjustly prosecuted during my first year as U.S. senator, I just tried to do my job and not feel hampered with the adversity. I let the lawyers and my husband—who was a huge support—handle the legal things. I tried not to think about the consequences if the justice system didn't work. I just had an abiding faith that it would.

**ADVERSITY:** In my earlier years, I wouldn't have thought I could live through the experience of being indicted. But I find that when you are confronted with something that horrendous, you find the reserves to deal with it. I knew that the indictment was political. (The Democrats wanted their Senate seat back and hoped I'd plea-bargain not to run for reelection.) I was fortunate enough to have had an honest judge, and that made the difference. I got a fair hearing, and the people of Texas waited to make judgments because the charges were so out of character for me. In the end I was vindicated.

**PROUDEST ACCOMPLISHMENTS:** My proudest accomplishments are the results of my work in public service.

*In the Texas House of Representatives:*

• Getting fair treatment for rape victims in Texas, and as a result, other states followed suit. Back in the early 1970s, most states had no laws to treat rape victims with dignity or even fairness. In fact, usually the rape victim was the one on trial. I cosponsored that landmark legislation with Sarah Weddington, a Democrat.

• Passing the first mass transit bill for the State of Texas. It was the beginning of both Houston's and San Antonio's transit systems.

• Passing a bill to authorize historical commissions in every county in Texas to preserve Texas heritage.

*In the U.S. Senate:*

• Creating a homemaker IRA in 1997. Before that, homemakers did not have the full tax benefits of setting aside retirement savings, with the law restricting their tax-deferred savings to $250 a year, compared with $2,000 a year for those who work outside the home. Many women who had no outside job skills because they had devoted their lives to raising children were finding themselves bereft after losing their husbands through death or divorce. They had no retirement security. Now, my legislation creates equity in tax treatment for savings, regardless if one works outside the home or not. If both spouses start, at age twenty-five, to put aside $2,000 a year, they will have close to a million dollars in a nest egg when they retire at age sixty-five. If the homemaker loses her husband, she will have a substantial nest egg in her own name.

• Passing the antistalking law in 1997. My bill makes it illegal to stalk someone across state lines or on federal property. Together with individual state antistalking laws in at least forty-eight states, my provision offers security to the potential victims of stalkers.

• Working to strengthen our national defense. I have led the effort in Congress to establish a new post–Cold War national security strategy, based on our vital interests. As a global superpower, we've found ourselves unfocused in the application of military power. We're diminishing our strength and harming our military readiness. I am doing everything I can to prevent that.

- Breaking the logjam on welfare reform by devising the formula to which states could agree.
- Passing marriage tax penalty relief in the U.S. Congress.

**TEAMWORK:** Making progress in the Senate takes a lot of teamwork. I must work with people of different philosophies, and even with colleagues who may have opposed me on another issue. Team sports, where men have typically had more experience, prepare one for working with people, whether or not you get along well. It's not whether you like someone, it's whether you can come together as a team and produce something.

**ADVOCATING FOR WOMEN:** One example of my teamworking effort has been with the other women in Congress. Although representing women is not our first responsibility in lawmaking, we have made it a point to address some issues that are particularly important to American women—issues such as the homemaker IRA and breast cancer research. Men aren't against these issues, but they tend not to think about them because they haven't had the same experiences as women.

I came face-to-face with a problem unique to women when I got married. When I was a young single working woman, I had started an IRA. When I got married, they said, "Oh, now you can't have an IRA." And I said, "Wait, this isn't right!" And I vowed to do something about it. When I became a senator, I wrote the homemaker IRA bill and the Hutchison-Mikulski bill became law.

**MARRIAGE:** Marrying at age thirty-five allowed me to know who I was. My husband and I got to know each other as mature adults, and therefore we accepted each other in that context. He is ten years older than I. I think many of the hardships of marriage occur when people get married young and then they change. Sometimes the changes are compatible, but many times they are not.

I like Benjamin Franklin's advice about marriage: "Keep your eyes wide open before marriage, half shut afterwards."

**NURTURING YOURSELF:** I admit that I haven't found an ideal balance between my professional and personal lives yet. I am spending long hours every day still trying to solve all the problems of the world. However, I do try to walk two or three miles at 6 A.M. most mornings, whether I am in Washington or in Dallas. And that helps a lot. In Dallas I have two neighbors with whom I walk around my neighborhood, and in D.C. I usually walk with a fellow senator down the Mall where the Smithsonian Institution is. That's how I keep my sanity.

Reading a good book helps me recharge my energy; it is like taking a vacation. If I had a "perfect" vacation, it would be going to a place where I could sleep and eat and walk and read. I love historical novels and biographies; *The Rise of Theodore Roosevelt* is one of my favorite books. I have read some Margaret Thatcher biographies and a lot about Winston Churchill. I also love books like *Shogun, Winds of War,* and *War and Remembrance.*

It has become a luxury just to do normal things—things such as being at home in my Dallas neighborhood with my friends, going out to eat in blue jeans, not wearing makeup. That doesn't happen very often.

**GETTING OLDER:** I used to enjoy social functions, and I loved going to parties. But I don't anymore. Now my enjoyment is being able to stay home because I rarely get to be there.

I like the maturity that experience brings. Maturity makes your judgment better. I feel secure in my decision-making, and I love what I am doing with my life.

Now that I'm older, I think that I have fewer ups and downs. Life is more even-keeled. When you are younger you get so excited when something good happens, and you get very down when something bad happens. I seem to have come to the point where I'm never *really* excited about anything and I'm never *really* down about anything.

**LOOKING TOWARD THE FUTURE:** This is such an exciting time to be a woman in America. Women are becoming equals in our system. We are able to reach our full potential more here than in any other country in the world. I think the generations of women behind us are going to be full participants in society, and I'm excited about it. We are going to see women breaking that glass ceiling all over the place!

# BARBARA JACKET

"When I see kids who have potential that they aren't developing, I raise hell with them; I push them to do what they are capable of."

*Barbara Jacket, U.S. Olympic coach. Photo by Summer Pierce © 2000.*

**Barbara Jacket**

B. 1934,
**PORT ARTHUR, TEXAS**
CURRENT HOME:
**PRAIRIE VIEW, TEXAS**

∿

Barbara Jacket knows sports. She started her sports career in 1944 as the only ten-year-old on the high school softball team at Lincoln School in Port Arthur, Texas. Her career climaxed as head coach for the U.S. Women's Track and Field Team in the 1992 Olympic Games in Barcelona, Spain. BJ, as she is known to her friends, was only the second black female to become head coach for a U.S. team in the Olympics—twenty years after her college coach, Dr. Laura Jackson, had become the first.

Along the way, she had been head coach for seven U.S. track teams competing in international games in every corner of the world. She recalls coaching the U.S. team during the World Championships in Rome in 1987. The famous sprinter Florence Griffith Joyner, "FloJo," was on the relay team.

BJ has been honored many times both regionally and nationally as "Coach of the Year." During her twenty-five years as head women's track coach at Prairie View A&M University in Texas, her Lady Panthers claimed more than twenty national championships. Five of her Prairie View track stars became Olympic qualifiers, and she turned out fifty-seven all-American athletes. She was head of the Athletic Department at Prairie View from 1990 to 1995—the only full-time female athletic director ever in the Southwest Athletic Conference.

In 1972, as a result of the new Title IX national legislation that bans sex discrimination in schools, Prairie View began offering scholarships for women's sports, and the AIAW (Association for Intercollegiate Athletics for Women) came into being.* Two years later, the Lady Panthers won the first of their twenty national championships in the AIAW (the National Collegiate Athletic Association [NCAA] did not include women in those days). BJ's 1974 championship team was made up of only five players, and they beat teams such as the University of California at Los Angeles and the University of Oregon to win the title. She claims that title as her greatest lifetime achievement.

She was inducted into the International Women's Sports Hall of Fame in 1995, joining such sports greats as Wilma Rudolph, Chris Evert, and Martina Navratilova. BJ graduated from Tuskegee Institute in Alabama with a degree in physical education in 1958, and she earned her master of science degree while teaching and coaching at Prairie View in 1968.

Today BJ serves on the Division I Men's and Women's NCAA Track and Field Committee, for which she is the area director for cross-country. She still teaches physical education at Prairie View, where she is preparing her students to become coaches.

Looking ahead, BJ says, "When I retire, I'll continue to help coach the track team, I'll go fishing, and I want to write a book about my life."

**AUTHOR'S NOTE** *Within ten minutes of meeting Barbara Jacket, I feel that we have known each other more than just these few minutes. My guess is that I am not the only one to feel that way around BJ. I feel like a family member as she leads me unceremoniously through the back door and into the coziness of her well-lived-in house in a middle-class Prairie View neighborhood. We settle at the kitchen table for our interview, where she falls into an easy banter, her voice husky and coachlike. BJ likes to laugh, and her tears also come easily when she reflects on the stark yet powerful upbringing her mother provided for her and her brother (her sister lived with a relative).*

*I want to see her accolades testifying to her illustrious career in sports, so BJ leads me to a corner of her den, where dusty trophies and medals appear to take a back seat in her priorities. Soon it becomes obvious that the mementos she is most proud of are well placed around her living room—plaques and small gifts from her former college athletes. Beaming, BJ points out words engraved on each gift, personal expressions of that athlete's gratitude for the immense influence BJ has had on her life.*

*Title IX of the Educational Amendments of 1972 is the landmark legislation that bans sex discrimination in schools, whether it be in academics or athletics. Title IX states: "No person in the U.S. shall, on the basis of sex, be excluded from participation in, or denied the benefits of, or be subjected to discrimination under any educational program or activity receiving federal aid."

## Barbara Jacket

### SPEAKS

**POVERTY:** When I was a kid, I didn't know that we were poor because we always had something to eat. Now when I look back, I realize we were survivors. We lived in one room—my brother, my mama, and I. Mama cooked full-course meals on a two-burner hot plate. She worked at the hospital, and my brother and I went to school. My mama and I slept in the bed and my brother slept on the floor. When a family moved out and we were able to spread out to three rooms, we thought we were in heaven!

Then my mama got her own bed, and my brother and I slept on a hideaway bed. He slept at the head or the foot, and I slept vice versa. I learned a lot about life in those early years. Maybe the hardship helped make me the competitor I am today.

**COMPETITION:** I was born wanting to compete. It was in my blood. As a child, if we were spittin' for the line, I wanted to spit the farthest. If we were pitching pennies, I wanted to pitch the farthest.

Today I watch all the sports on TV. I'm always mad when football season is over, 'cause then I have to watch basketball. (Laughs.) When I watch track meets on TV, I have my stopwatch in my hand so I can time the relay splits.

As an adult, I have had to learn to stifle that competitiveness a bit—especially when I play cards. I almost lost all my friends, until I learned to play cards for fun and not for blood. (Laughs.)

**GROWING UP WITH BOYS:** I'm sure my competitive nature was nurtured as I grew up playing with the guys in the neighborhood. My uncle used to call my mom and say, "Go over there and get that girl off the YMCA football field. She's the only girl out there!" I had no breasts when I was ten or eleven, and I thought nothing of playing "shirts and skins" with the guys. I was just one of them.

In the summertime the boys and I would crab all day until we had two croker [burlap] sacks full of big blue crabs. We even competed at crabbin'.

**ADVOCATING FOR THE UNDERDOG:** My competitive nature showed up in another area as well. When I was young I liked to fight. I'd fight for my sister, I'd fight for my cousin, I'd fight for everybody. After my freshman year at Tuskegee, I came home for the summer. My brother was six feet three inches tall and weighed over two hundred pounds, but he was always a softy. He came in the house and said that somebody wanted to jump on him. I said, "Let's go!" So we went back to the corner where they were supposed to be jumpin' on him. I told those guys: "If you *ever* touch him, you'll have *me* to deal with." And that was the end of it. (Laughs.)

**PREJUDICE:** But my fearlessness sometimes put me in graver danger than what I faced from fighting the kid on the corner. In Port Arthur, as in most other places in the 1950s and 1960s, there were signs at the drinking fountain in Woolworth's: "Colored" and "White." Being mischievous children, sometimes we would walk in the store and say, "Let's see how that white water tastes." We'd taste it and say, "It doesn't taste any different to me!"

When I tell that story to white people today, they usually laugh. But when I mention it to black people—especially those in the South—they get chills because they all know I could have been killed over that mischievous act—even though I was just a kid.

When I was in college in the 1950s at Tuskegee in Alabama, there was one black restaurant. We couldn't eat in white restaurants. We had to sit upstairs at the movies. In 1957, my sophomore year at Tuskegee, we rode buses to Montgomery and marched back to Tuskegee town with Martin Luther King. White people owned most of the shops in Tuskegee town, and we Tuskegee students boycotted those stores, and the businesses failed. We were successful in shutting down the whole town!

When we traveled to out-of-town venues as college athletes in the 1950s, black people weren't allowed to stay at Holiday Inns and all. Sometimes there were small black hotels that we could stay in. Sometimes we stayed in campus dorms. In Alabama and Mississippi, blacks had to walk on the opposite side of the street from whites. It wasn't quite that bad in Texas, but even as late as 1966 in Prairie View we still couldn't go into the cafes. We had to tell them what we wanted at the back door, even though they had a black cook. The cook fixed your hamburger and you got it to go.

As children in Port Arthur, we weren't aware that prejudice was unnatural. We thought that's how it was supposed to be. But after we got older, we realized that we should have rights.

As I look back at those years, I realize that in some instances, I have welcomed the change. But in other instances, I have not. When we were segregated, we had teachers who cared. Our black teachers insisted that we learn. In integrated schools now, when a black student acts a fool, the teacher ignores him and teaches to those who are listening. But before integration, if you acted a fool, the teacher got you, the principal got you, and then your mom got you when you got home.

For a while after integration, whites wouldn't come to Prairie View to college. But they finally found out that our color doesn't rub off on them. (Laughs.) And now we have several white students at Prairie View.

**REMEMBERING YOUR ROOTS:** I've got a lot of white friends and I get along with everybody. But I get along because I don't forget where I came from. You see, a lot of people want to forget. If I forget that I came from the west side of Port Arthur (the black side of town), then I'm lost. I like going back to Port Arthur and being with my old friends. It was in Port Arthur that I received my most important mentoring, and where I began setting the stage for my career.

**GROWING UP IN SPORTS:** When I was ten years old, the high school basketball and track coach, Ms. Guidry, heard that I could throw a softball from center field to the catcher. So, although I was just ten, she made me the catcher on the high school team—the Royalettes—and the next day we traveled to Prairie View to the state championship tournament. The high school sewing teacher had one night to alter my uniform so it would fit a ten-year-old.

Later, in high school, I played basketball under Ms. Guidry. Although there was no integration yet, Ms. Guidry got permission once for us to play a team from the white high school. We beat them in their own gym, and our ego got a real boost! (Laughs.)

Now kids are used to playing on integrated teams, and they take it all for granted. It's not unusual today to see girls playing on the same teams as boys. During my lifetime I have seen tremendous advances not only for blacks in sports but also for women.

**WOMEN'S SPORTS THEN AND NOW:** When I came to Prairie View in 1964, I began by coaching swimming. Two years later I organized a women's track team. That was before Title IX, before gender equity. The college hadn't had a women's track team up to that time, and they didn't want to give me any money for a team. When they built the gym in 1964, they didn't include dressing facilities for women. They weren't even thinking about the possibility of women's sports back then. The Title IX legislation came about in 1972, and suddenly we were allowed scholarships and facilities for women's sports.

**ACADEMICS:** Especially now that women have such a good opportunity in sports, I am disappointed when unmarried female athletes become pregnant and have to give up school and their careers. To me, their education should come first, athletics second, and their social life last. But you can't stop ladies from falling in love with men, and you sure can't stop them from being promiscuous. Often, the man gets his degree and moves on, and the woman is stuck with the child.

**COACHING:** So as a coach and teacher, I have always insisted on self-discipline both on the field and in the classroom. And I have encouraged self-discipline in the other areas of their lives as well.

I am fussy with my athletes. I call it "raisin' hell." (Laughs.) When I see kids who have potential that they aren't developing, I raise hell with them; I push them to do what they are capable of.

It helps to use humor when you are pushing people to their limit. When the athletes thought they were dying out there on the track, I would start singing, "What a difference a day makes—twenty-four little hours." But they appreciate all that hard coaching later on. Lots of my students send me letters, and many come back to tell me how I influenced their lives. Those are the times I am glad I have been a coach and a teacher.

**TEACHING:** Although I am known as a coach, teaching is the most important thing that I do. I never wanted my job to depend on how well my students could jump or throw, or how fast they could run. That's why I stayed at Prairie View, because here I can do both. I have had chances to coach at other universities, but those jobs didn't involve teaching.

As a teacher, I have been able to help the young black males as well as the females. Of course, the males give you the hardest time. I like those challenges.

I have always tried to teach my students about life out in the real world—that it's not easy out there, and that they are going to have some ups and downs. I let them know that the world doesn't owe them anything—that they have to go out there and get it for themselves, but that they shouldn't be afraid to ask for help.

I tell them, "Work hard! Don't expect to get something for nothing. Anything worth having doesn't come easy. Just because the boss is above you, you don't need to feel inferior to him. But you are always going to have a boss somewhere, and you've got to cope with that reality. You can't buck the system."

I love teaching because I can really touch the lives of students. I always smile when they come back and tell me, "You told me it wasn't going to be easy, but I'm doing okay." And I say, "When I was kickin' your ass, I was kickin' it for something—for you to be successful!"

**PROUDEST ACCOMPLISHMENTS:** I had several high school teachers who led me in the right direction. But if it hadn't been for sports, I could not have gone to college because my mama had no money to send me.

So graduating from college was one of the great achievements of my life. I sometimes think I persevered to graduation just to prove to people back home that I could do it. I especially remember the old lady who we rented our one room from. She disapproved of things I did as I was growing up, such as playing ball with the boys. She would sit on her porch and say about me, "She won't ever be anybody." I remember crying about it and telling my friend, "I'm going to make her out a liar. I'm going to *be* somebody!" When I was at Tuskegee, I mailed newspaper articles to her about my athletic successes there. I never heard from her. I don't know if she even remembered saying that I would never be anybody.

But the most gratifying event of my career—my greatest accomplishment—came in 1974 when the team I was coaching won its first national championship. That win was a stepping-stone to the rest of my career. I would never have gone on to international coaching without that initial championship. Of course, my Prairie View teams won many more national championships after that.

**COACHING IN THE OLYMPICS:** I was proud to be named head coach for the 1992 U.S. Olympic Women's Track and Field team, and I'm glad I got to do it—once. The pressure was unbelievable—something I don't ever want to feel again! You see, if things go bad, it is looked on as the head coach's fault. If things go well, it's looked on as the athlete's doing.

In 1964 when I started the team at Prairie View, I had no idea that I could ever reach the apex of coaching—the Olympics. But then my program developed through the 1970s, and we started winning national championships. That's when I began getting coaching positions in international competition, and in the mid-1980s I was named head coach for the Pan American Games and the world championships. Those positions were prerequisites to becoming the Olympic coach. I looked around then and realized, "The Olympics are reachable!"

Coaching elite athletes in the Olympics is much different from coaching your own team. Elite athletes have their own agendas. You have to work around personalities. Most of the athletes bring their personal coaches, and the Olympic head coach oversees everything and puts the relay teams together. I had six assistant coaches to help with other events.

Of course I wanted to do the best I could and get the best we could out of the athletes. But when they finished running the last event, the four-by-four relay, I said, "This is it! Been there, done that. Don't want to do it again." The team won four gold, four silver, and two bronze medals.

Coaching elite athletes becomes a business—one that is all about money for the athletes' futures. They are concerned with getting sponsorships and the commercial success that goes along with it all. That cold business aspect makes high-level coaching much less fun than coaching your own team and seeing it develop.

**PRINCIPLES I LIVE BY:** As I have guided my own teams and students through their own development, I have tried to instill the values that are most important to me:

- Be grateful for what you have. Sometimes when I talk about the past, I get full [of emotion] because I feel so blessed. I don't take anything for granted. I have a sign in my office that reads: "It's a sin to be ungrateful."
- Live to the fullest.
- Nothing is promised to you.
- Remember that tomorrow is another day. Just because bad things happen to you on Wednesday, the sun might shine for you on Thursday.
- Trust in God. I have learned to put all my troubles in God's hands.

**ENJOYING LIFE:** I had some ups and downs comin' up, but most things went the right way for me. My good days outnumber all my bad days. I feel good about my life today. I don't do anything I don't want to do.

I swim, walk, and ride a bike for exercise these days, and I don't seem ever to run out of energy. I am rarely sick. I get seven or eight hours of sleep a night. I eat everything bad—like pork chops and chitlins. But it doesn't seem to have slowed me down much!

"*I have not allowed myself to be intimidated by men. I have always felt comfortable being 'one of the guys.*'"

*Edith Irby Jones, M.D. Photo by Summer Pierce © 2000.*

## Edith Irby Jones

B. 1927,
CONWAY, ARKANSAS
CURRENT HOME:
HOUSTON, TEXAS

Edith Irby Jones was the first African American—male or female—to be admitted to a white medical school south of the Mason-Dixon Line. She first heard of her acceptance to the University of Arkansas Medical School in 1948 when a *Time* magazine reporter called for an interview. When she graduated in 1952, the news appeared in 160 newspapers all over the United States. A ceremony took place at the medical school in 1985 to unveil and hang her portrait in the entrance hall.

In 1985 she was elected the first female president of the National Medical Association, a predominantly black organization founded over a hundred years ago. Before 1894 when the NMA was founded, black physicians were not allowed to treat their patients in hospital settings.

As late as 1985, only 3 percent of American physicians were black. At one time Edith was one of only three black female physicians in Houston. She has conducted her private internal medicine practice in Houston since 1962. In addition to seeing her own patients, she is a clinical assistant professor at both Baylor College of Medicine and the University of Texas School of Medicine. She was named Internist of the Year in 1988 by the American Society of Internal Medicine.

Edith was the daughter of sharecroppers. Her father was thrown from a horse and died when she was three, and when she was six her older sister died of typhoid at age thirteen. Both of these traumatic experiences contributed to her early decision to become a physician.

She started formal schooling when she was ten. Before that, she learned at home with her mother and had read most of the encyclopedia, as well as the works of Shakespeare, Milton, and Robert Louis Stevenson. She was allowed to name both of her younger brothers, Robert and Louis.

Edith grew up in Hot Springs, Arkansas, a resort town, where, at age fourteen, she began her own transcription and typing business during after-school hours to help support her family. She typed 120 words a minute on a mechanical typewriter, and she took shorthand. Her clients were the professional guests who were in town for the therapeutic baths.

Edith received a bachelor of science degree in chemistry, biology, and physics from Knoxville College in Tennessee, where she earned her tuition by typing for the college president. She attended graduate school in clinical psychology at Northwestern in Chicago before entering medical school. She paid for medical school by working and through scholarships provided by the black community.

She and Dr. J. B. Jones, a university professor, were married in 1949, and they raised three children, Gary, Myra, and Keith. J.B. died in 1990.

In addition to spending long hours practicing medicine, Edith is active in the community. She entertains often at home for various groups. One week the party could be for her grandson's Little League team, and the next week, for a group of her elderly patients. She serves on various community boards and advisory councils and has staff privileges at six Houston hospitals.

**AUTHOR'S NOTE** *Edith's thirty-eight-year-old daughter, Myra, greets my daughter Summer and me at the door of her childhood home—a two-story rambling 1960s-style home in an affluent neighborhood of Houston—the house where her mother still lives. Myra, a lively, beautiful attorney and dancer with long braided hair, lives in Martha's Vineyard, but she has come for the weekend to see her mother receive a prestigious award—one of many in her mother's long career. That ceremony took place last night. Today Myra has been assigned the task of entertaining us until her mother can make it home from giving yet another speech. Myra seems a natural at entertaining her mother's friends. I suspect that she has had a lot of practice.*

*Over an hour later, Edith walks in the door, and Myra disappears, no doubt grateful for a reprieve. Like her daughter, Edith exudes energy and natural beauty more befitting a woman fifteen years younger. I am delighted just listening to the melody in her voice and the lilt of her Southern accent. There is no doubt that this woman loves her life and what she does.*

*During the spirited interview Edith's ten-year-old grandson, Kenneth, drops by for cookies and a hug. He lives in the neighborhood and bikes to his grandmother's house often. Today he is in his baseball uniform. His team has just lost a Little League game, and he knows he can expect kind words from his grandmother.*

## Edith Irby Jones

**SPEAKS**

### PRINCIPLES I LIVE BY:

- If I give of myself, my blessings will equal more than what I have given.

  One Sunday when I was five years old, they were taking up a collection in church. I had a little red pocketbook filled with pennies. My father said, "Go ahead and put your money in." But I objected. So he said, "If you give your money to God, you will get multiples—more than what you put in." I believed him and went up and put my money on the table. I stood there and waited for my multiples to come back. But after a while, when nothing happened, I went back to my seat. When I told my papa that the minister didn't give me back my money in multiples, my papa explained that my multiples would not come from that table, but they would come from other situations. Since that day, it has been the philosophy of my life.
- I am responsible for what happens to me because I make choices.
- I am what I think myself to be. If I hold only good thoughts about myself, I become what I want to be. I have not perfected it, but I would like to have *only* good thoughts.
- If I respect every person I deal with, that person feels the respect, and she or he becomes a better person. Sooner or later, that person catches on and spreads respect to the next person. And it goes around and around.

**MENTORING:** Because mentors have been so important in my life, I have made sure I am available to mentor others. If someone needs my help, I always say yes. If they really need money, I give them mine. If they need time, my time is theirs. If they need an expert outside of my field, I can tap somebody in my network who can provide that service. Most people just need the encouragement to realize that with the right tools they can accomplish whatever they really want to do. I try to provide those tools.

**MENTORS:** I have had a myriad of mentors throughout my life. Some of my earliest mentors were a white physician's family who treated me as if I were a member of their family, providing me with special dresses for school programs and hiring me (at age eight) to be an everyday babysitter for their eighteen-month-old. The grandmother, in particular, spent lots of time talking with me. She convinced me that I was smart enough to become whatever I wanted, and she encouraged me to become a doctor like her son. So, even as a child, I set that goal for myself.

Then there were people in my church who carried me to conventions and seminars and exposed me to things that I might never have seen. I probably had fewer material possessions than anyone else in the community, but I was rich in attention. The church members helped me realize that I was different, that I had special talents, and that I had a mission to share these talents with others. In high school, I thought for a while of becoming a missionary to a foreign country. Of course, later I learned that being a missionary didn't necessarily mean that I even had to get out of my own yard. I could minister to people across the fence.

Another mentor, my high school English teacher, expected us to read all of the classics, to know grammar and to use it. From her I learned that it is not acceptable to express oneself in idioms. Even now, I rarely use slang because it makes me feel guilty.

**ADVERSITY:** My mother was one of my greatest mentors. Although not highly educated, she was wise. Because I was small, she realized that I might have trouble making people take me seriously. I weighed only ninety-six pounds when I graduated from medical school, and my mother said, "Edith, you are short, but don't let your size deter you from doing what you need to do. If someone tries to obstruct you, do not raise your foot to kick him. Otherwise you'll lose your momentum, and you'll get to your destination later than you had planned—or you might not get there at all."

So I usually don't fight back. I try not to dislike people or to condemn them. I just assume I don't understand them and I put space between myself and them, so that I don't get their vibrations.

**BEING AFRICAN AMERICAN:** As the only black medical student at the University of Arkansas in 1948, I was required to eat in a room by myself and use a separate rest room from the other female students. But soon many of my classmates began eating and studying with me, and generally looking out for me. They remain some of my best friends today.

Medical school was a pleasant experience, but of course I didn't escape racism outside of school. My mother had taught me not to internalize other people's prejudices. A racial slur can be either ignored or addressed appropriately, but you must get over it and move on.

**MOTHERHOOD AND WORK:** I tried to teach my children the same lessons about living that I had learned from my mother. Although no one has suggested that I get a medal in mothering [smiles], I think I did well, and I enjoyed raising them. I am very proud of them and their lives as adults.

Having a solo practice allowed me to keep my children close to me in a back office until they started school. My secretary brought her children to the office, and together we shared "mothering" tasks. When they were older, I arranged my appointments so that I could see the children off to school and be there for their school activities. In the evenings, I came home and had dinner with them. If I needed to go back to the hospital, I waited until after they had gone to bed.

I tell young women doctors that if they really want to be mothers *and* physicians, they should go into private practice so that they can have more control of their schedules.

**WOMEN IN MEDICINE:** Until recently, most women physicians have not been as assertive in the professional arena as I have been. As their numbers increase, they are becoming more assertive, and they are joining in on the fellowship with male doctors and becoming more involved in leadership roles.

Perhaps the reason I have been so assertive is that I had to fight so hard to become a doctor. It was tough being one of the handful of women in medical school fifty years ago. There were only three women in our class. Men felt that women should not be granted the opportunity to go into medicine because "women should stay at home and rear the children." They believed that educational resources would be wasted on women because they expected women to drop out of medicine early in their careers to raise families.

**MEN:** Men are men, no matter what race, what color. They have been taught by society that they are superior. However, I have not allowed myself to be intimidated by men. I have always felt comfortable being "one of the guys."

**CAREERS:** I can't imagine wanting to retire. I enjoy the camaraderie of the other doctors, the challenge of difficult cases, and I enjoy my patients. I stay in medicine because it is so much fun!

Because I have been so happy in my own career, I advised my children: "Find something that you enjoy doing and do it well. Don't work for money. Instead, work for the good that you can do for others, and you will be doing much for yourself as well. The money you make will be all that you need." They seem to be following that advice. Material things are not the first concern of their being.

**MARRIAGE:** My career developed and has been successful largely because of my late husband, J.B. He was a college professor and my personal speechwriter. Over the years he had learned how I thought, and he would put it down in my language, not his. He would take care of the details of my trips, as well as the children's needs at home, while I was away at seminars and conferences.

J.B. was my coach, although I don't think he recognized that fact. He was nine years older than I was. I learned from him how to have confrontations without getting emotionally involved. When I married him, I thought he had all the answers, and when he died I still thought he had all the answers. I just wondered why he had taken them with him. (Laughs.)

**WIDOWHOOD:** That was nine years ago, and I still miss him. I miss having someone to talk to when I get home—someone to talk to about the good things that went on that day or the things that rubbed me the wrong way. I miss seeking his advice. I learned so much from him.

One aspect of widowhood is that you have more time to spend on other pursuits. When J.B. died, I got even more involved in my professional and volunteer activities because I had more time to give. The children were raised and the house was built. The office was running well.

You can approach widowhood in two ways: You can say, "Oh, poor me! Here I am alone, with nobody to help me deal with all of the day-to-day problems." Or you can find someone to fix the roof, mow the lawn, or do whatever you can't do, or don't want to do. And you can go on living.

I certainly have not gone around moping. But I would much rather have him here with me.

**FAITH:** My faith has helped me move through overwhelming situations in my life, such as losing my husband. I grew up Baptist, but as I have matured, I have been exposed to many other religious philosophies, and I realize that there are many different ways to reach the Spiritual Being. When I allow myself to tap into that force which I call God, I have power to do what is necessary.

When people asked me before I started medical school, "Aren't you afraid to go to the University of Arkansas? You know there is adversity for blacks. You know there are lynchings in Arkansas and Mississippi?" I said, "I'm okay." I wasn't afraid. I felt at ease. I felt comfortable. I felt that there was nothing that could harm me.

**PRAYER:** When I pray, I don't beg God to change a situation. Instead, I get quiet and I concentrate until I feel at one with the universe. Then it seems that I can pull energy from the universe to deal with the situation at hand. I find answers to whatever it is I am trying to figure out—whether the problem is finding my lost car keys or how to solve a difficult medical case.

**CAREER CHALLENGES:** Because I have been in medicine almost fifty years, I have seen most of the rarer medical problems at least five times.

Even though medicine has changed, I stay abreast of what is technologically expedient for my patients—what the advances are, what the experiments have been, what the clinical studies have shown. I attend seminars and continuing education programs, and I teach at both the University of Texas and Baylor College of Medicine. It has been a continuing learning process. We don't do things today the way I started out doing them in 1952. I have even forgotten some things I used to do. When I finished medical school, we had two antibiotics—penicillin and tetracycline. We have so many now that it would be impossible to attempt to remember the names of them.

**LOOKING FORWARD TO THE FUTURE:** The world is so fascinating now. I am grateful that I have lived to see the miracles of science and medicine. I look forward to having advanced care for the diseases we don't yet understand. I know the best is yet to be.

## NINFA LAURENZO

*Ninfa Laurenzo, restaurant entrepreneur. Photo by Al-Fin © 1997. Courtesy of Fina Flores/Alfredo Pérez.*

"*You cannot put a fence between yourself and those who work for you. You have to form a team and be a part of that team yourself. I call them 'friends,' not 'employees.'*"

## Ninfa Laurenzo

B. 1924,
**HARLINGEN, TEXAS**
D. 2001,
**HOUSTON, TEXAS**

She was desperate to feed and support her children after her husband died, leaving the forty-five-year-old mother with five children, ages six to twenty-one. The family tortilla and pizza factory wasn't profitable enough to make ends meet. So in 1973, at age forty-nine, Ninfa Laurenzo mortgaged her two-story house and some land for $10,000, and she got a $3,000 loan from a family friend. Ninfa and the children cleared a place in the little warehouse they owned and opened a ten-table restaurant near the wharves in Houston.

Her three older children waited tables, washed dishes, and tended the cash register. Ninfa brought pots and pans from her kitchen at home, and combining her family's two heritages, Italian and Mexican, she invented recipes no one had ever tasted.

"We had only $16 in the cash register when we opened for business," said Ninfa. "At the end of the day we had $186!" From the first day, customers in that busy industrial area lined up to sample Ninfa's homestyle cooking.

After a year, gross sales approached $100,000. Overhead was low since none of the Laurenzos received paychecks, and most of the earnings went back into the business. Ninfa's became a trendy place to eat. National celebrities sat at tables next to ship channel workers.

Within ten years, her family operation had expanded to fifty-one diversified restaurants in several states, and the business had become a multimillion-dollar corporation. Today the largest Ninfa's in Houston seats a thousand people. The original Ninfa's at 2704 Navigation, now expanded to 175 chairs, is still a popular spot in Houston.

During the first twenty-three years of its existence, the family business rode the roller coaster of the Texas economy—sometimes flush, sometimes lean with the times. In 1996, after expanding too quickly, the company was forced into involuntary Chapter 11 bankruptcy by a long-term supplier. Serrano's Cafe and Cantina corporation bought the Ninfa's chain. Although disappointed with having to sell, Ninfa said, "I teamed up with a nice group of people—Serrano's."

Ninfa and her two younger sons, Tom and Gino, played an active role in the new corporation. Until shortly before her death, Ninfa continued her daily quality inspections of the restaurants carrying her name. All five of the Laurenzo children are college graduates and manage their own restaurants.

When she was away from the restaurants, Ninfa spent most of her time with family, which had grown to include eighteen grandchildren. Family was the most important element in her life, she maintained. Ninfa and her twin sister were the youngest of twelve children. Her parents instilled in her both love of family and her work ethic, she said.

The matriarch was known throughout Houston as "Mama Ninfa." She served on numerous boards, both in Texas and nationally, and on several presidential advisory councils under George Bush.

"Most of my education has been life," Ninfa said. "Life has taught me a lot. If you work at what you love every day, you will be successful."

Ninfa underwent a mastectomy for breast cancer in 2000 and was recognized for her work to increase breast-cancer awareness. She died of bone cancer on June 17, 2001, at her home in Houston.

**AUTHOR'S NOTE**   *It is a sizzling summer day in Austin, and Ninfa has arranged to meet me at noon in the newest restaurant to bear her name. Her two youngest sons, Tom and Gino, have recently moved to Austin to open a colorful Ninfa's Mexican Restaurant on Austin's popular West Sixth Street, next to Katz's Deli and Bar.*

*Ninfa arrives driving her Lincoln Town Car. "I like a big car because I'm kind of a big woman." With her is her longtime assistant and housekeeper, Angel Rosa Acosta, a small, pleasant, brightly dressed woman whose gray hair is pulled back in a bun. Ninfa's niece, an artist, is driving up from Mexico to stage an exhibition at the new restaurant this evening. Ninfa and Angel have driven from Houston to be here for the exhibition, and to inspect the newest Ninfa's Mexican Restaurant.*

*As we talk in the foyer, the coolest place in the house, the new restaurant fills with the lunch crowd. All the tables are full, and patrons crowd the foyer, waiting to be seated. We continue our interview amid the noise. Many smile broadly and wave as they recognize the legendary Mama Ninfa.*

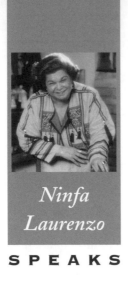

*Ninfa
Laurenzo*

## SPEAKS

**WRITING YOUR OWN JOB DESCRIPTION:** I was born to be a business person. When I was in high school, I put a beauty shop in my home. I would work after school and on weekends so I could have some money to help my parents.

In our culture you are brought up with the attitude that you must help and share with your parents. It was a wonderful time. So early on I learned what it was to have a little business of my own and be able to make decisions independently. I wasn't meant to be a teacher like my twin sister. I was meant to be in business. I always felt it.

**PERSEVERING:** The only time in my life when I felt I couldn't go on was after my husband passed away in 1969, when he was only forty-seven. Within the next two years, both of my parents passed away. I was sad for a long time, but it never killed my spirit.

It was 1973, and I had no money, as the tortilla factory that my husband and I had owned was not profitable enough. I had to support my kids. I asked myself, "What am I going to do? God, help me!" I had no one else to turn to.

It is a long, beautiful story. I went to Mexico City and I prayed. One morning after I came back, I woke up and called one of my sons. "You know what?" I said. "I am going to open up a taco stand. If nothing else, at least we will have food on the table for the kids."

When you don't have much collateral, it is difficult to approach banks for a loan. So finally I mortgaged our home, and the ball started rolling.

Nineteen days after we started the first Ninfa's, we had a fire. It was terrifying seeing the flames going up and all our dreams going away. My family house that stands next door on the corner almost caught fire. What a terrible evening that was. All the kids were crying.

We went in the house after the fire was out and we cried and cried. Then finally I said, "Look, let's all say a prayer and then go look at the damage." We decided to salvage the disaster because the walls were still standing. My daughter-in-law is artistic. She painted the tables and chairs and painted flowers on them. The boys and I cleaned the kitchen and painted walls. We worked day and night and finished it in ten days. The little ones went to school during the day while the big kids and a few neighbors performed the miracle! We opened our refurbished restaurant ten days later.

So we have been on a few emotional roller coasters with this business through the years. I learned that you just have to stay strong. You have to be able to turn around and say, "Today is another new day."

Through it all, I have continued to keep a positive attitude about business. I have always gone on with the strength I get from God—and with good common sense.

**GROWING A BUSINESS:** My kids and I learned early on how great it was to make our customers and our employees happy. We didn't worry about how much money we were going to make. That wasn't the attitude. We were surviving, you see.

I have always dealt with my employees as if they were my family. I spread my love to them. They feel as if this is their business, too. That philosophy doesn't translate through a cold computer. In this business, we are dealing with human beings who come in as our guests and who want to be entertained. I tell my employees, "Smile. There is no reason not to smile."

I try to create an atmosphere that makes employees happy to come in, to stay, and to work. You cannot put a fence between yourself and those who work for you. You have to form a team and be a part of that team yourself. I call them "friends," not "employees." One of our mottoes is "We are cooking with love."

We grew the company with that attitude of love. Some of my employees have been with the organization since I opened the door in 1973. I have people who have been with me for twenty-five, twenty-four, twenty-one, and nineteen years. That speaks for the loyalty they have developed because they are working with people who are for real. Of course you need computers to run a business. But you cannot empty the business of all human warmth. That loving attitude shows up in the food.

The company who bought Ninfa's has new management ways and new ideas. And that's fine. They can take care of the business end. As long as I stay with the company, I can take care of human resources.

**RESPECTING OTHERS:** I walk into the kitchen in one of our restaurants and say, "Buenos días, mis muñecas. How is everybody?" (I call them my dolls, you know?) You've got to make everybody feel like they are very important. They are part of the whole organization that makes the restaurants go. So therefore they should be treated with kindness and love.

**FAJITAS:** I was the person who introduced fajitas into the market for the first time—down at 2704 Navigation Blvd. Nobody knew what fajitas were. Now fajitas are sold all over the world.

I took the idea from a cooking tradition in the northern part of Mexico. My parents cooked beef skirts at home, and they called them *arracheras.* They would broil them either on coals or in the oven. And that's how come I knew them. But my kids and I cut them up in strips and put them into large tacos. We figured, "Well, we are going to call these 'tacos al carbon.'" Later on we served them on a platter, and people would fill their own tacos. That is how fajitas, as we know them today, were born.

**RUBBING ELBOWS WITH THE FAMOUS:** We have had different presidents, governors, actors, and actresses visit the original Ninfa's on Navigation. Sometimes people come in from the airport with their suitcases. I remember one time years ago, I was at the cash register and Rock Hudson looked through the window. He showed me a small suitcase and said, "Can I bring this in?" I nodded. "Sure, bring it in." He went in and met his friends who were waiting for him.

**COOKING:** Within our recipes at Ninfa's, there is always a little Italian influence. It can be in the cheeses or in the way it's cooked. We use a lot of olive oil in our foods. I suppose that it is a throwback from the culture combination of Italian and Mexican in our family. My husband, Tommy, was Italian-American.

**SHARING YOUR WEALTH:** When I owned Ninfa's, we spent a lot of time on civic causes. For example, Ninfa's helped the M. D. Anderson Cancer Hospital for years. We always did the parties at our restaurant for the children who do the Christmas cards—or we would take the food to the hospital. Barbara Bush and I have done that together.

I have always considered that if you have something, you need to share with others.

**MENTORING:** I get the chance to speak to young people often. They say, "You know what, Mama Ninfa? You inspired me. Now I've got a business and it's going well."

It is wonderful to be able to make other human beings realize that they have the strength, they have the youth, they have what it takes to be successful.

I tell people: "Don't get down on yourself. Go into the area that you love, and do it with all your love, and you will be successful. If you work at it every day, honey, you will be successful."

**SEIZING OPPORTUNITIES:** I would encourage young people to plan for their future, to stay on the right road, to educate themselves. They need to set their goals, plan way ahead, and go for it. They can do it.

**MENTORS:** My siblings and I grew up in the era before television—all we had was a radio. Our parents loved to talk to us. They had a wonderful friendship, which they spread to all of us.

We were taught manners. We were taught to say "Gracias" and to be respectful. They instilled in us the habit of saying "good morning, good afternoon, *buenos noches,*" and such niceties.

**ENJOYING LIFE:** This morning Angel, my longtime assistant and housekeeper, and I walked into the elevator at the Marriott. Angel said "good morning" to the gentleman who came into the elevator. He never responded. Six more people got into the elevator from different floors as we came down from the fifteenth floor. Nobody said "good morning."

When we walked out of the elevator, both of us were thinking the same thing: "What a bunch of angry Americans. What is the matter with us? Why do we get up with such a negative attitude that we can't say 'good morning' to another human being?"

Saying "good morning" starts my day. We walked away and we said to each other, "Isn't it a shame that some people don't feel like we do? We get up in the morning and say, 'Thank you, Lord, for another day.'"

Honey, I enjoy life so much that, even at this age, I am planning a cruise next year to Europe. I don't stop planning. The day I stop planning is the day I will have given up on myself. And I don't want to do that.

**TRAVEL:** I was born to travel. I have been to the Far East, all over Europe, to the Holy Land, to Jordan, to Egypt, South Africa, Central Africa, Hong Kong. You name it, I've been there.

In my later years I have come to like cruises because you can get in, unload your stuff, and you are ready to relax and enjoy the trip. I have been on cruises to the Caribbean, to South America, Alaska, the Far East.

My advice on packing: pack light. Have repeats. Always keep blouses clean. I like polyester for traveling because it doesn't wrinkle and you can wash it. If the weather is going to be hot, you have to take cottons. Usually I don't like to travel to hot places. I try to go in a cool time of the year.

I can sleep anywhere. I think that if you have a clean conscience and you have faith, there is no need to stay awake.

**GETTING OLDER:** I have had to slow down a little because the aging process has set in. But it's nothing. I can tolerate that. I have a livelihood, health, and family.

**FAMILY:** The Latino culture teaches you a great love of family. That love is instilled early and grows with you. The way we love other human beings comes from the fact that we are brought up so close to our family, and we learn to spread the love to others. I am not saying that other cultures don't have strong families. I can speak only for the Latino culture.

I don't understand people who are glad when their children turn eighteen so they won't have to support them anymore. I have never felt that way. I have always been happy to have the chance to share my life with these people—my children. And my children have become my wonderful friends.

**TEACHING THE WORK ETHIC:** My children learned the work ethic by watching their father and me work in the tortilla factory. They used to work in the factory for a few hours on Saturday. Their father would teach them what the business was all about.

When I opened up the first Ninfa's on Navigation, Tom was my first dishwasher. He was about fourteen. Then he turned out to be the best cook on the line because he could read those tickets fast. He worked and attended college at the same time. He studied at night and he made the Dean's List. He has a degree in finance. All of my children have degrees. I borrowed money from lots of different places so they could go to college.

**WIDOWHOOD:** Roland, my oldest, graduated from the Naval Academy in May 1969, after his dad had died in January. I had to go through the graduation by myself. I remember sitting in the stadium in Annapolis with tears in my eyes, thinking how my husband would have enjoyed his son's graduation. I have been a mom and a pop for almost thirty years. But most of it has been wonderful.

**MOTHERHOOD:** I worked hard as a single mother. Sometimes I wouldn't sleep. I would prepare their uniforms for school, sometimes until 3 A.M. Sometimes I would go twenty-four hours without sleep. You do what you have to do.

Being a parent has been the greatest reward of my life. Sometimes at banquets, one of my sons will get up and say, "Mama is the best!" That is gratifying. It makes me feel that I have done the right thing by these people.

**PROUDEST ACCOMPLISHMENTS:** In addition to being proud of my children, I am proud of some honors I have received. In 1986 I was called by the White House to be an ambassador of goodwill to Puerto Rico to receive the pope.

Another high point in my life was standing at the podium at the Republican National Convention in New Orleans to second the nomination for George Bush as the presidential candidate. It was a breathtaking experience for me—a Mexican American woman who began her career by making pizzas and tortillas down there in the Second Ward in Houston. I am proud to be a role model for my people.

**TEXAS:** There is an attitude in Texas that makes you feel that you can do anything you want to do. I admire so many women who have come out of Texas and done well. I like the image Texas brings to mind—that of bigness, of strength, of goodness.

People from Rhode Island, where my husband came from, thought Texas was full of cowboys and horses, but of course that's not true. We are for real.

**BEING MEXICAN AMERICAN:** I call my culture Mexican American— not Hispanic, Latino, Chicano, Tejano, etc. You are born here, but you are of Mexican extraction. How beautiful—you have the best of two worlds.

## AMY FREEMAN LEE

*Amy Freeman Lee, educator and lecturer. Photo by Parish Photography, San Antonio © 1999. Courtesy of Amy Freeman Lee.*

"*You can find redneck philosophy anywhere, not just in Texas. And you can find sophistication and cultivation in Texas just as well as anywhere else.*"

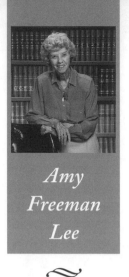

## Amy Freeman Lee

B. 1914,
SAN ANTONIO, TEXAS
CURRENT HOME:
SAN ANTONIO, TEXAS

Amy Freeman Lee epitomizes a passion for excellence: excellence not bounded by a single area of expertise but by an eclectic array of many critical areas of our time. Her career has spanned more than fifty years, during which time she has served successfully in the fields of architecture, art, civic affairs, criticism, education, humane ethics, lecturing, and writing. In these fields, Amy has filled the roles of artist, critic, lecturer, teacher, trustee, and writer.

Amy was raised by her maternal grandmother from age four, after her mother died in the influenza epidemic. She credits her grandmother for providing the atmosphere that encouraged her to become an appreciator and practitioner of the arts.

"My grandmother was a tiny French matriarch who ran a very tight ship. The focus of her life was totally on me. From the very beginning, I studied painting, music, dancing, and elocution."

Following in the tradition of her Texas pioneer ranching family, Amy became an expert equestrian at an early age, and she bred, trained, and showed horses all over the United States.

Throughout World War II, in spite of being classified 4-F because of an injury to her back sustained while riding, she volunteered and served as a member of the Army Air Forces Aircraft Warning Corps.

While San Antonio has remained her home since her teenage years, her multifaceted career has not only covered all fifty states but also has assumed international proportions.

She is a noted critic and judge in all forms of fine art and poetry. Her paintings and sculptures have been exhibited all over the world and are included in many private and public collections.

Amy is a sought-after lecturer. She has served as a faculty member at San Antonio Art Institute, Our Lady of the Lake University, Trinity University, and Incarnate Word College, all in San Antonio.

She is past chair of the board of the Wilhelm Schole in Houston, founder-president of the Texas Watercolor Society, and trustee and secretary of the Humane Society of the United States.

She was elected to the Texas Women's Hall of Fame in 1984, was appointed by the Supreme Court of Texas to serve on the Grievance Oversight Committee and the Commission for Lawyer Discipline, and was appointed by the governor of Texas to the Texas Commission for the Humanities.

Amy maintains a busy schedule of lecturing, painting, and writing and finds joy in working in the education of young children.

**AUTHOR'S NOTE** *While teaching high school in San Antonio during the late 1970s, I listened to Dr. Amy Freeman Lee's weekly radio editorials on KTSA as I drove to work. Amy's polished presentation and authoritative voice drew me into her thoughts on philosophy, education, art, literature, and a myriad of other subjects.*

*I never met her during my years in the Alamo City, but now, twenty years later, I am back in San Antonio to interview her. From her spacious high-rise condominium tucked in a quiet corner of an affluent San Antonio neighborhood, Amy has a view of her historic part of town. Animated, she recounts the people and ideas that have driven her life for almost ninety years. She laughs often and easily.*

*"I walk with a stoop because I fell from a horse when I was a girl and broke my back," she mentions matter-of-factly as she slides behind the wheel of her car to drive me to lunch. That ailment hasn't stopped Amy all these years from driving herself from one commitment to the next around the state of Texas.*

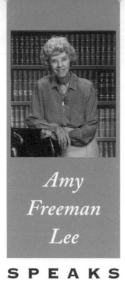

## *Amy Freeman Lee*

# S P E A K S

**PRINCIPLES I LIVE BY:** My Grandmother Freeman, who reared me, taught me the values that are basic to human life: personal responsibility, conscientiousness, courtesy, and caring.

**FAITH:** I think the essence of God is unselfish love and creativity.

I am a nondenominational theist who believes that life has a purpose: the opportunity to refine our soul. In the process, one is merely an instrument that, like all good instruments, must stay in tune with the Creative Spirit.

My belief is based on three basic principles of theism: a transcendent entity which we call God or the Creative Spirit, the immortality of the individual soul, and the existence and operation of free will. As humans, we have the power of free will, but we also have the inescapable personal responsibility that accompanies it.

My faith is supported by four pillars: selfless love, prayer, respect for all faiths while following one's own, and knowledge that as part of the divine creation we are all one.

I find spiritual comfort in prayer, in the company of dear friends, in the beauty of nature, in the essence of the arts, and in the devotion of animals.

I am not part of an organized denomination. I respect everybody's choice of faith, which is the most private and most beautiful part of life. It is a manifestation of ignorance and arrogance to believe that one possesses the only right way to worship. That concept has caused prodigious prejudice and violence in the world.

I am not a scholar of comparative religion, but I am a student of it. I'm drawn to Buddhism because of its central concept that God created all of the cosmos and that every part is equally sacred. Another aspect of organized religions that has offended me is the idea that humankind is paramount and all else is secondary.

I am very drawn to Hicksite Quakerism, the original Quakerism that originated in England with George Fox. Hicksite Quakers (named after Elias Hicks) worship in a meetinghouse and engage in meditation. They are a small group in the world, but they have enormous influence because they really live their faith. While they are born pacifists, they will serve in wartime other than in the capacity to kill.

**PRAYER:** Prayer plays a central role in my attempt to enact my faith.

No doubt prayer means different things to different people. In my life, prayer has been my attempt to communicate the essence of myself to God—to the Creative Spirit—and prayer is as direct a communication as one can have. I try to remember not to use prayer solely as an attempt to ask favors, but also to express appreciation for my blessings. The fact that prayer is integral in my life bespeaks the influence of my grandmother.

I find spiritual comfort in prayer, in the company of dear friends, in the beauty of nature, in the essence of the arts, and in the devotion of animals.

I was asked recently by a minister's wife who was being polite, "And Dr. Lee, where do you worship?" I said, "Everywhere." She seemed shocked, didn't say anything, and walked on. But it is true. I pray wherever I am.

**CREATIVITY:** To observe God at work, one merely has to be cognizant of the innumerable forms of creativity that are extant in daily life. Robert Graves said that his symbol of creativity was the White Goddess. He believed that you cannot command her nor make her stay longer than she wishes. So when she comes, you had better drop everything else because you don't know when she is going to return. That is a way of saying that inspiration is evanescent and mystical.

Of all the literary pursuits, the writing of poetry is the most challenging. Putting the right word in the right place at the right time is a fascinating demand. All poetry should be read aloud to get the phonics and the rhythm. Poetry is not the only aesthetic love in my life. Painting has occupied a large part of my heart, since I started art lessons when I was seven.

Poetry and painting provide a wonderful balance because if you get tired of one, you can move into the other. In painting you have silence, and in poetry you have sound.

**LOVE:** Speaking of love, if I were limited to just one piece of advice to the present and coming generations, I would implore them to master the ability to love. I mean love in the traditional, classic sense—the ability to forget oneself and to learn to sacrifice. Many choose not to care because it makes one vulnerable and causes hurt. However, love remains the only means not only to personal happiness but also to general survival.

Being "in love" is one of life's greatest paradoxes because it is not only a glorious, exalted interlude but also an exceedingly dangerous one during which you lose the ability to be objective. You simply do not see reality. Chemistry is, indeed, a volatile and potentially destructive force.

**FRIENDSHIP:** One of the most rewarding forms of love is friendship. Through friendships we find the source of extended family, which is a precious gift indeed. We are all products of our childhood, especially our first five to ten years. The experiences from that time leave us with some scars as well as polish. Perhaps friendships are based partially on finding someone with matching scars.

**MENTORS:** Among my friends, I have two major mentors: Dr. Marilyn Wilhelm, who founded the Wilhelm Schole in Houston, and Mr. Paul Irwin, president of the Humane Society of the United States. I respect not only their intellectual capabilities but also the fact that they both make a witness of what they believe.

Dr. Wilhelm is a distinguished educator who has devoted her whole life to the education of young children. Through her incomparable creativity she has joined that rare group of human beings who have taken the next giant step in their chosen discipline. She has reinforced my belief that we are all one and that everything is in higher hands. In addition, she has helped me to focus on selflessness and reasonableness. She is my adopted family.

Mr. Paul Irwin is a Methodist minister who gave up the pulpit to broaden his ministry through work with the Humane Society of the United States. He has taught me to be patient while striving for progress in the humane movement. His wise leadership has had a profound global influence in our treatment of all sentient beings and the planet.

I did not realize that someday the tables would be turned and that I would be called on to enact the role of mentor.

**EDUCATING CHILDREN:** When I turned sixty-five, I found out that I had spent my whole life at the wrong end of the stick. All my teaching had been done at the university level. Young children entered my life for the first time through the doors of the Wilhelm Schole (*schole* is a Greek word meaning "a lifetime love of learning") in Houston, and they changed my life. To experience what they can learn at an early age, to hear their fresh and enchanting remarks, and to feel their love is more than a gift; it's a grace!

I am absolutely convinced that the first few grades are what count. If fundamentals are not taught in kindergarten and in the first three grades, it is highly unlikely that students will ever catch up.

At the Wilhelm Schole, the children are from all walks of life and from all different kinds of families. The students advance according to their potential. For example, in math you may have a six-year-old child sitting next to one who is eleven. The other salient characteristics of the school are the practice of having the older children teaching the younger ones and of making the arts integral to the curriculum.

**ANIMALS:** Because one of the greatest joys in my life is the companionship of animals, I am delighted that the Wilhelm Schole imbues the students with the concept of "reverence for life"—all life. If I get to heaven and my dogs are not there, I am going to ask for my money back!

By instinct, intuition, emotion, I have been devoted to the "humane movement" all of my life. I have always had a passionately deep feeling about all creatures.

As a member of the board of the Humane Society of the United States for twenty-eight years, I have had the privilege of working directly on behalf of animal welfare.

The Humane Society's slogan is "It's their world, too," because we are all here together on the planet as interrelated entities. The Humane Society is pursuing a reasonable approach to try to persuade people, especially children, never to be brutal, cruel, or violent, but to be compassionate. We teach not only how to care for animals but also why we must do so as part of our responsibility as stewards. We work through education, legislation, and, when necessary, through litigation.

So far in my life, my greatest challenge has been helping to get our foot in the door of the animal laboratory scientists' world in an effort to reduce cruelty.

If you could x-ray my spirit you would find the humane movement as the core of myself.

Although I am a native Texan and have chosen to live my life here, I do not agree with two typical Texas activities: blood sports and rodeos. Both are primitive and destructive influences, and I have stood against them both in private and public ways. To be specific, it is impossible to comply with the official rules of the Rodeo Cowboy Association governing every rodeo event without being cruel. I'll debate anybody anywhere on this point.

I do not seek friendships with people who engage in blood sports because I know that we aren't going to get along. Don't misunderstand me; if your family is starving and you go out and kill a deer to feed your family, that's different. I'm talking about killing for fun and for what is called "sport."

**STANDING UP FOR WHAT YOU BELIEVE:** I find it emotionally difficult to handle animal cruelty in a reasonable manner. I used to react with anger, hate, and retribution, which are all the wrong ways. A number of people who influenced me taught me that I could create change more effectively by being objective instead of subjective.

**WHAT MAKES ME FEEL ALIVE:** As an advocate of animal welfare, I have had many opportunities to speak to a wide variety of audiences over a period of many years. Audiences have always fascinated me because every audience is different and presents a significant challenge. Perhaps this accounts for the fact that I feel most alive when I'm addressing an audience.

**PUBLIC SPEAKING:** I never write down my speeches because I want to look at the audience when I talk and because I do not like to be read to in public. I want it to be a direct communication. I take only skeleton notes with me when I give a speech. Having only notes gives me the independence to use whatever words seem best for the particular audience I find in front of me.

**INDEPENDENCE:** Perhaps that bent for freedom of expression comes partially from the strong desire I had for independence when I was growing up—a desire that was sometimes thwarted when I was a child. After my mother's early death, I was reared in an extremely protective atmosphere.

If I were a young woman starting out to build my life today, I would fight for independence at a very early age so that I would never fear doing anything alone. This desire is distinct from the universal human experience of loneliness. Although we all die from a variety of causes, in the end it is loneliness that is the real face of death.

**FEAR OF FLYING:** I am sorry to say that there is one aspect of independence that I have never mastered—that of being unafraid to fly in a plane. My fear began as a young woman when I witnessed a university classmate's fatal crash as she took a flying lesson.

It is a major limitation for me. There is no reasonable reason not to fly, not only because it is the safest way to travel but also because when it's your time to die, you will do so wherever you are.

I realize that I travel in the most dangerous way—by car. But if a trip requires flying, I won't go. Let me tell you what that does to you: you can't go anywhere. If I want to go to Europe, I have a four-and-a-half-day drive to catch the *QE2*. Since I believe in reincarnation, I think that God is going to send me back as a fighter pilot next time.

**TEXAS:** This time around I think I am glad to have lived in Texas—for many reasons. I like the people, although, frankly, I have found that people everywhere are alike. For example, you can find redneck philosophy anywhere, not just in Texas. And you can find sophistication and cultivation in Texas just as well as anywhere else.

I like the Texas climate, the long summer days, and the topography, because I need a lot of light and space. I love the Hill Country outside of San Antonio and several scenic areas out in West Texas, including the Big Bend country and the Fort Davis Mountains by the McDonald Observatory. The McDonald Observatory is a spiritual experience.

**LIGHT:** I had a summer home in Maine for thirty years. About the end of the third week of October, it began to get really dark by 3:30 P.M., and I always had to leave because that darkness was depressing. I began to realize just how much I loved the sunlight and long days. I could live in the land of the midnight sun. In Maine in the summertime I could paint until 9 o'clock at night without any artificial light.

No doubt the major reason I have such a need for and admiration of light is because light is the symbol of purification, ascension, and enlightenment.

**SAN ANTONIO:** In addition to my love of Texas, there is a very big part of my heart devoted to San Antonio.

I like San Antonio for several reasons. We have always been tri-cultural—Anglo-, African-, and Latin American, and we have lived together, if not perfectly, at least without violence. Yes, there have been some terrible prejudices, but we continue to eradicate them.

San Antonio has enormous local color. We are rich in the combination of the West and the South and the Spanish Colonial. Texas is a microcosm of the world because so many different cultures are represented in our population.

**BEING DIFFERENT:** I have always said, "The reason I decided to spend my life in San Antonio is that it is hospitable to eccentrics." And so I have been happy here. We have some absolutely fabulous eccentrics who have provided color and texture to our tapestry.

**LOOKING TOWARD THE FUTURE:** In spite of the status quo of the world—the wars, the hatreds, the brutality, cruelty, and violence, I have high hopes for the future, including that of Texas.

We are at the end of the Newtonian-Cartesian era. We are now aware that the universe is more than physical, and that the so-called lower creatures are not mere mechanisms. When translated, this means that we are beginning to turn away from materialism. For the first time, we admit that we have ecological problems and that in order to survive, we must solve them. Also, for the first time, we have adopted a global point of view.

We have made the world one through our technology, but now we must match this technology with spirituality. The humane movement devoted to the "reverence for life" and the need for a sustainable future are beginning to grow.

Thanks to recent brain research, we now know that the left side of the brain is devoted to facts and the right side is devoted to feeling. Both sides of the brain must be in balance for us to function on a truly human level. We are beginning to understand, if not enact, that caring is the name of the game.

**SETTING PRIORITIES:** Regardless of where one lives, there are immutable principles to be followed. As I have grown older, I have found the need to eliminate trivia from my life. The key is to learn how to evaluate objectively. Why waste time attending large parties and enduring the noise level and the inane conversation? You realize that there is just so much time and energy and that you must learn to allocate them to areas of substance and significance.

**NURTURING YOURSELF:** Being careful about how you spend your time and energy are important to self-nurturing. I give the following advice: work hard, but don't forget to take time off to dance. It is wise to practice moderation and reasonableness in order to achieve a proper balance. The enactment of duty and responsibility comes first, but there must also be time to play. A glass of French champagne once in a while never hurt anyone.

**WHAT REALLY MATTERS IN LIFE:** I have found that what really matters in life is to be able to give and receive love, to be blessed with good health and safe passage, to be in love with one's chosen discipline, and to have caring family and friends. All else, including competition, power, publicity, possessions, and fame are unimportant. I have been especially blessed that God has spared me the temptations of extreme affluence and the dangers of fame.

At my age, I am trying to stay off the front page and out of the obituary column!

**SARAH McCLENDON**

*Sarah McClendon, journalist. Photo by Summer Pierce © 2000.*

"*I am told that I should be careful about criticizing the CIA—that I might get bumped off.... If you hear that I committed suicide, I didn't!*"

## Sarah McClendon

B. 1910,
TYLER, TEXAS
CURRENT HOME:
WASHINGTON, D.C.

In 1944, when Lieutenant Sarah McClendon became pregnant at the age of thirty-four, her husband left. To complicate matters, she received a compulsory honorable discharge from the army because of her "condition."

Determined to make a living for herself and her child, Sarah went to work, relying on her journalism degree from the University of Missouri. She reclaimed her birth surname, McClendon. When Sally was nine days old, Sarah landed a job as reporter for a Washington, D.C., news bureau and began covering Franklin D. Roosevelt at the White House.

In 1946 she opened McClendon News Service in Washington. Today, in her nineties, Sarah continues her one-woman operation, including service to both large and small newspapers throughout the country. In addition, she works as an analyst and lecturer and appears on countless radio and television broadcasts.

Having covered every president since FDR, Sarah is the most senior member of the White House Press Corps. Her longtime friend, veteran UPI correspondent (now retired) Helen Thomas, calls Sarah's reporting "courageous and bold." By now a Washington institution, she is known around the capital city as simply "Sarah" by one and all.

She takes it as a compliment when longtime friend broadcast journalist Sam Donaldson says she has been a thorn in the side of every president since FDR.

Comedian Mark Russell has called her the "Mother Superior of Washington journalism."

President Kennedy once boasted laughingly, "I'm not scared of Sarah McClendon! But, then she's not scared of me, either."

Sarah's 1996 book, *Mr. President, Mr. President!: My Fifty Years of Covering the White House*, received first place for biography from the National Federation of Press Women.

Raised in Tyler, Texas, Sarah was the last of nine children in the McClendon family, all idealistic, politically active, and committed to public service. Her father was postmaster and her mother a suffragette.

Sarah, the only one of her siblings to become a journalist, began her career at the *Tyler Courier-Times*. Early in her career, she was fired by a few newspapers for being "too aggressive."

As one of the first female journalists in D.C., Sarah fought to break down barriers for women reporters. She was the first woman to apply for membership in the National Press Club and, after a twenty-seven-year fight, finally was admitted in 1971. Later she was elected vice president of the organization.

One of Sarah's strong beliefs is "Nothing happens by accident."

---

**AUTHOR'S NOTE** *It is intimidating to consider interviewing a woman who has spent the past fifty-plus years coaxing revelations out of U.S. presidents. But Sarah turns out to be one of my easiest interviews. She loves to talk.*

*We sit in the sunlit parlor of her childhood home, built in 1878 by her aunt's husband. Sarah has come home to Tyler this July weekend for an afternoon book signing in the historic house. Vases of yellow roses grace every table around the room.*

*The event will commemorate Sarah's eighty-seventh birthday and the recent publication of her biography,* Mr. President, Mr. President. *As Sarah looks around the parlor, she observes, "The house looks wonderful. That chair is part of a five-piece suite that was two hundred years old when I was a child."*

*"May I call you Sarah?" I ask.*

*"Yes, that's my name," she says. "Everybody else calls me Sarah, including all the taxicab drivers in Washington."*

## *Sarah McClendon*

# S P E A K S

**FAITH:** I wasn't raised Catholic, but I became a Catholic as a young woman. I kept in regular contact for two years with nuns in a convent in Houston, and I tried to become one of them. But then some newspaper man kissed me and that was over. (Laughs.) Another determining factor was the underwear the nuns wear under their garments in the hot summertime down there in Houston. And I couldn't do that.

**JOURNALISM:** I'm lucky that things turned out the way they did, because journalism is the best profession anybody can have. As a journalist, you can write about anything you are big enough to investigate. And then you've got to decide *how* you are going to get the story. Sometimes it really frightens me to think, "How am I going to do this?"

I love my work and I love people. Very few people get to be as independent in their business as I am. I can decide what I am going to work on today and what I'm not going to work on. I don't have some editor telling me what to do.

I have written about all kinds of people. I work every day, but I still don't have time to write everything I know. I would like to be three people.

**WHAT MAKES ME FEEL ALIVE:** I feel alive when I have written a good story that people will read. I am producing a lot of articles these days.

I like living. I can't wait to get out of bed in the morning. I don't sleep very much. I work till one or two every morning and get up about 7 A.M.

And then I nap a lot during the day. People criticize me because every time things get quiet, I take a little nap. I sleep till somebody wakes me up or jostles me or says something nasty about me. (Laughs.)

I don't go to the White House as much as I used to, because I'm in a wheelchair these days. But I keep up with what's going on with four or five phone calls a day to the White House. They fax me. My fax is working day and night. And I don't go to the Capitol as much as I did, but I keep up with certain individuals there all the time. And I keep the television—C-Span—on all the time, as it shows what's going on on the floor.

I don't go on vacations. I don't enjoy them. I never just sit down to chat. Unless I am talking about something I am interested in or unless I am learning, I believe I am wasting my time. I like life that way.

**MOTHERHOOD:** Even as a grown woman, my daughter, Sally, doesn't understand exactly what I am doing or why I am doing it. She's like a lot of family members who don't understand why newspaper people have to work all hours. And she would just as soon that I quit working today.

Sally resented my career while she was growing up. She called herself a "political kid" because, as a child of a prominent person, she grew up in the shadow of politics. She thinks that she and other "political kids" were denied a lot of attention because of their parents' professions. I'm sorry she feels like that. And I wish she could understand. I am going to keep on working.

**RESPECT:** Respect is a thing that is hard to get and hard to keep. I've fought for it practically every day of my life. My weapons are my intelligence, my writing, my ethics, and the way I persist at finding the truth and insisting on telling it. I feel respect when someone knows what I can do and trusts me to do it. I feel it when someone treats my facts as accurate and my opinions as worth considering. I feel it when someone really listens.

**BEING DIFFERENT:** Other reporters criticize me because I have always posed questions that are different from the usual kind asked at a White House press conference. Most of the fifty-five questions allowed are all on one subject. And I come along and ask something totally different. And some reporters will say, "Well, what's she asking that for?

We're not interested in that!" But I look at the whole country to see what the people are worrying about, what they are thinking about, what their issue is for the day. I usually try to base my question for the president on what they want to hear. It's been very rewarding.

When I became a White House correspondent as a young woman, my bosses told me, "Get a different angle, a different tangent. Don't give us a duplication of the wire services." So that is how I built my news service.

I can get into a taxicab anywhere in Washington today and it's not unusual for the driver to turn around, look at me, and say, "Ma'am, I do thank you for asking those questions."

**TEXAS WOMEN:** I am a crusader and an independent thinker, which I attribute to having grown up in Texas. Throughout our history, Texas has gone through many campaigns for what we have thought was right. We are persistent. I have experienced discrimination from people in Washington, D.C., because I am Texan. I think the bias against Texas began during the Civil War.

I think Texas women are different from other women. Very much indeed. We are ourselves. We are not just copying somebody else. That independence shows up in both men and women. I think it is good for society.

**SELF-CONFIDENCE:** Believe it or not, I am naturally a timid person with a great inferiority complex. For example, it has always been hard for me to ask anyone for a salary when I deserved it or to make business arrangements. But when it comes to getting after some facts for a story, I am tenacious.

**PRINCIPLES I LIVE BY AS A JOURNALIST:**

- Exposing the truth. Quite often the facts show just the opposite of what a person claims. But I check and check my facts. The truth is hard to find.
- Being accurate.
- Being fair. I am so afraid of not being fair.
- Trying to make things better for the underdog. Sally told me recently that I can't save the world. And I said, "I'm going to keep on trying."

**HELPING THE UNDERDOG:** My life would not have meant nearly so much without the help I have been able to give to others. If life is a climb toward being the best we can be, I believe we ascend faster when we stop to help others up.

I have a reputation for helping the underdog. I have a box at home filled with letters from people all over the country who send me their problems. One woman asked me to help her find her husband. And I intend to try. If the question is too crazy, I send the letter back to the writer. But if I think I might be able to help, I put the letter in the box. When I get the chance, I pick up one at a time and address the problem.

**GETTING OLDER:** For most of my adult life, I wouldn't tell people what I planned to do or talk about myself at all. I was scared to, because when I would tell my feelings as a child, my older siblings would criticize me. I have finally come out of my shell in the past two or three years. Now I am very open about everything.

I used not to take on any close friends. But I have some wonderful women friends now. Some are much younger than I, but age doesn't mean much to me. Some people are frightened of age.

I enjoy being in my nineties. There are advantages to being old. One is that you don't have to look so many things up in files or in the dictionary. You can remember a lot of things. My memory does lapse at times. I sometimes forget names, and I can't remember every bill I've paid. However, quite often when I can't think of something, it will come to me in a few hours. I think the brain must be a marvelous computer—much better than anything anybody has invented yet.

Now that I am older, I am feeling some age discrimination. Some reporters have wanted me out of the way for years. On the other hand, some have started being real nice to me. Government officials have begun inviting me to breakfasts and other functions. They tell me that I make things more interesting.

**FRIENDSHIP:** When Liz Carpenter and I started out in Washington as young reporters, we were not friends. In fact, we were mortal enemies. We are very good friends today. Liz and I were laughing about it the other day. She had come up to D.C. from Austin and was going into the White House in her wheelchair, and I was coming out in my wheelchair.

We met at the gate and accidentally locked wheels. So we sat there at the gate and talked about forty minutes. I was saying, "It's too bad there's not a photographer around here to see this."

**TEENAGERS:** One thing I have discovered this past year: Our society treats teenagers so badly.

We need to remember that it was teenagers who won the Battle of the Bulge for us in World War II. We don't give today's teenagers enough credit for having any sense, for having courage. We sometimes baby-sit them too much and cut down the amount of courage they might otherwise have. I think we should treat them better.

**EDUCATING OUR MALES:** But we also need to educate our males better. One of society's biggest problems is men's prejudice against women. It costs us way too much money and heartache. We saw prejudice at Annapolis the first year that women were allowed into the Naval Academy. The young men were furious. They thought women would ruin everything for them. They must have learned that prejudice as boys. Mothers have a job to do in teaching their sons to accept women as equals.

**EDUCATING OUR YOUNG PEOPLE:** We need to educate the public in ways that we have not before. We should have mandatory premarital counseling. We are lucky that we don't have more divorces than we have. We treat getting married and raising children like a game of chance. Americans have always been scared of counseling. But we need to encourage people to seek advice so that they'll realize what they are going to be facing.

**REFLECTIONS FROM A HALF-CENTURY AT THE WHITE HOUSE:** *Leadership:* Of the twelve presidents I have covered, I was most interested in John F. Kennedy because he was such an effective leader. I didn't know or care anything about his private life. I didn't know anything about his bedroom scenes and don't pretend to. People say it's not too hard to be a leader when you know you have money in the bank, as he did. But he really wanted to make things better for people. I think it was a shame that he didn't live to fulfill some of those intentions.

*Rubbing elbows with First Families:* Although I didn't much like Roosevelt, I think he was probably the smartest and the most courageous president we've ever had. My father felt that Roosevelt was a dictator, and so do I.

You couldn't help but like Truman. He talked right off the cuff. He told it like it was. Truman was a marvelous and unusual man. I was recently in Independence, Missouri, to give a speech on the anniversary of the birthday of Bess Truman. Bess had more power over her husband than we give her credit for. And she was more interested in government than she was given credit for.

I am very fond of Lady Bird Johnson. She's a fine, fine person. She knew everything that was going on. She didn't always approve of everything that Lyndon did.

I think that Mrs. Roosevelt was the most capable of all the first ladies.

I am not so sold on Mamie Eisenhower because she didn't participate enough.

I like Mrs. Nixon. She did a great deal, far more than she got credit for.

Mrs. Carter did a lot of good work—casework, we call it.

Barbara Bush is a very good woman. Very nice to me. When she was entertaining the board members of the DAR [Daughters of the American Revolution] at the White House, I said to Barbara, "You know, I just discovered that I've been a member of this organization for fifty-one years." And she said, "You don't look it, kiddo!" (Laughs.)

I don't really go into first ladies very much. But I like Hillary Clinton because she is smart. A very able woman.

*War:* I often think how ineffective wars are. I have been an officer in the U.S. Army, I respect the military, and I certainly agree that our country needs a strong defense. But I also know that we get into wars because some leader has impaired judgment and a lust for power.

*Federal government:* The government belongs to the people, but a lot of people these days don't understand government. They don't understand that we need the federal government. I agree with George Washington, who said, "We have got to have some organization that supervises the states."

*Federal secrets:* There is so much secrecy in our government—secrecy against the people, a practice I adamantly oppose.

I am on the board for the Coalition on Political Assassinations. It is composed of scientists, professors, doctors, and others like me from all over the country who are investigating the assassinations of Jack and Bobby Kennedy and Martin Luther King.

Of course the government was behind the JFK assassination. I believe the words of Colonel Fletcher Prouty, the liaison between the joint chiefs of staff and the CIA during the Kennedy years. He says that shortly before JFK died, several Cabinet members were in the Oval Office one day, and Kennedy told them that during his next go-round as president, he planned to bring the troops back from Vietnam, stop the war, and tear the heart out of the CIA. Well, as soon as he said that, he was a marked man. Colonel Prouty feels that this was a coming together of not one but several groups in government. It is probable that the CIA hired the Mafia or another country to assassinate JFK.

I feel that it is absurd that this country, as big and strong as it is, has not investigated the JFK assassination adequately enough to know the truth. I think that we will find out the truth. It wouldn't be too hard for us to find the truth if it weren't being purposely kept from us.

So many deaths in Washington are written off as suicides—deaths that most likely were murders by responsible parties inside the Departments of Defense, Justice, and the CIA. I am quite sure that Vincent Foster, who used to work at the White House, was murdered because of what he had found out and what he was going to tell President Clinton. Presidents don't always know what's going on. That's one reason that press conferences are so important. Presidents learn from press conferences.

I am told that I should be careful about criticizing the CIA—that I might get bumped off. I am so outspoken that sometimes, after I have criticized the CIA before a large audience, one or another of my friends will call and say, "I want to spend the night at your house to protect you. You might get hit by the CIA tonight." And I always say, "Well, if you hear that I committed suicide, I didn't!" (Laughs.)

## DIANA NATALICIO

*Fulfilling a dream, Diana Natalicio throws the first pitch (a strike) to open an El Paso Diablos ball game. Photo by UTEP University Communications.*

*Diana Natalicio, president, University of Texas at El Paso. Photo by UTEP University Communications. Photos courtesy of Diana Natalicio.*

> "*I threw a strike and he was just blown away by that. It was the thrill of my life! . . . That was as close as I ever got to realizing my lifelong dream of being a major league baseball player.*"

*Diana*
*Natalicio*

B. 1939,
ST. LOUIS, MISSOURI
CURRENT HOME:
EL PASO, TEXAS

Diana Natalicio has been president of the University of Texas at El Paso (UTEP) since 1988. During her term, she has worked with the university's students, staff, faculty, and friends to give the university a new and unique focus: that of serving the area's majority Hispanic population.

She was born Diana Siedhoff (Natalicio is the surname of her former husband), and both sets of grandparents were German immigrants. Today her mother lives close by her in El Paso, and Diana sees her often. "I grew up in a secure, classic Midwestern atmosphere," she says. Like many of today's students at UTEP, she was the first of her family to go to college. Her parents and grandparents discouraged her from speaking German, and today she regrets that she never became fluent in that language. However, she speaks fluent Spanish, a skill that has brought her closer to the people of El Paso and has allowed her full involvement in the community. "I would feel very isolated in El Paso if I didn't speak Spanish," she says.

She earned a bachelor's degree in Spanish at St. Louis University, studied Portuguese in Brazil on a Fulbright Scholarship, and got her master's in Portuguese and her doctorate in linguistics at the University of Texas at Austin. She came to UTEP as a visiting assistant professor of linguistics at age thirty-two. Through the years she moved through the ranks, from chairman of the Department of Modern Languages to vice president for academic affairs before becoming president at age forty-nine.

In 1996 Diana was appointed by President Clinton to the National Science Board, a group composed of twenty-four of the country's top academic and industrial leaders. She served as vice chair of that board. Governor

George W. Bush installed her into the Texas Women's Hall of Fame, which recognizes women whose outstanding records of achievement have made "a significant impact upon the lives of Texans."

In the early 1980s, half of UTEP's students were Anglo, most from middle- to upper-class families. Now, after much recruitment, UTEP has become the largest Mexican American-majority institution in the United States. Of the university's fifteen thousand students, nearly 70 percent are Hispanic. In addition, fifteen hundred students cross the border from Juárez, Mexico, every day to attend UTEP classes.

The university has gained national recognition for its successful programs in such areas as environmental science and engineering. The number of minority engineering graduates is among the highest of any American university. The U.S. Department of Education recently cited UTEP as having one of three exemplary teacher-preparation programs in the nation, and *Time* magazine honored the university for its community outreach programs. In recognition of UTEP's success in creating educational opportunities for nontraditional students, the National Science Foundation has designated the university as a Model Institution for Excellence.

Since Diana became president, UTEP has nearly tripled its annual operating budget, from $65 million to $165 million. The number of doctoral programs has grown from one to eight, and annual grant and contract funding grew from $3 million to more than $55 million by 1999. UTEP offers fifty-three master's degrees and more than sixty bachelor's degrees.

In 1997 Diana received the prestigious Harold W. McGraw, Jr. Prize in Education, which is annually bestowed upon educators whose creativity and ideas spark change and who serve as effective models for educating future generations of Americans. The prize included a $25,000 honorarium, which she donated to UTEP for the establishment of an endowed scholarship for teacher education.

**AUTHOR'S NOTE**   *The young Mexican American woman behind the sales counter tells me that she attends the University of Texas at El Paso. So I ask her if she has met Diana Natalicio. Her eyes light up. "Oh yes, Dr. Natalicio is wonderful! She walks around campus, talking to students. She likes us and we like her."*

*That enthusiastic description of Diana Natalicio is my first impression of the woman I will be interviewing soon. So I'm not surprised when, as I drive Diana into Austin from the airport a few weeks later, she begins asking about my life. And later, as my interview with her unfolds, it becomes clear that this is a woman who is sincerely interested in other people's stories—not just mine and that of the girl behind the counter. Maybe that's one reason why we both like her so much.*

*Diana Natalicio*

**SPEAKS**

**BASEBALL:** I have often joked that the only job that could take me away from my job at UTEP would be that of baseball commissioner. But it has not been offered to me. (Laughs.)

As a girl, I used to dream about being a baseball player. I was an excellent pitcher because I played baseball every day as a kid with my brother and the neighborhood boys. But the hard lesson I had to learn was "If you are a girl, it doesn't matter how well you play baseball; you absolutely don't have the chance to compete on a team."

Today I practice throwing the ball in my front yard for exercise, and I like to go to the ballpark, eat a hotdog, drink a beer, and watch the Diablos, El Paso's AA team. At one game, I got to throw out the first ball, and the catcher said to me, "You aren't going to bounce it, are you?" Well, that was a challenge! I threw a strike and he was just blown away by that. It was the thrill of my life! The crowd was in the stands, the team was on the field, and I was standing there on the pitcher's mound. That was as close as I ever got to realizing my lifelong dream of being a major league baseball player.

My staff surprised me by creating a baseball card with a picture of me on the mound that day. Occasionally, I'll use my baseball card as a business card to inject some levity into a situation. When a new business contact seems a bit uppity and asks, "Do you have a card?", I say, "Sure!" And I hand him or her the baseball card. After that, the person realizes that I don't take self-importance seriously.

**GIRLS IN SPORTS:** Although baseball is still a "boys' sport," I'm glad that girls now have more opportunities to compete in most of the other sports. I'm convinced that playing sports teaches people how to lose. I have noticed that many women find it harder to cope with losing than do men, perhaps because they didn't play sports. Learning how to lose gracefully is good training and has helped me in every job I've ever had.

**WORK ETHIC:** Although I've liked all my jobs, being president of UTEP is my favorite so far. I enjoy working hard, long hours, something I learned from my father. He was the sole owner and manager of a small dairy, so quite often he worked day and night, but he never complained about it. I learned that if you work hard enough, you can make almost anything happen. For years I watched him save his little business against all odds.

**SETTING GOALS:** Emulating my father's work ethic, I learned to set goals, and stay at the task until each goal is accomplished. My proudest accomplishments are the programs the faculty and staff and I have been able to put together at UTEP over the past eleven years. We have developed UTEP into a first-rate university that serves the majority Hispanic population of our area.

When I arrived at UTEP nearly thirty years ago, the university had a profound inferiority complex as an institution. We were punishing ourselves for not being "Harvard on the border," as bumper stickers around El Paso back then humorously proclaimed. UTEP had set itself up for failure, aspiring to be something that it wasn't. Eleven years ago when I became president, we sat down and looked at who our constituents were— 85 percent from El Paso County and another 8 percent from Mexico. And we asked ourselves, "What are their needs and how can we best meet those needs? In addition to creating educational programs, how can we serve as a real resource to this region?"

We laid out an agenda to increase research funding, to add doctoral programs, and to make a name for UTEP on the national level as a university effectively serving a Hispanic population. Faculty and board members balked at first. They said, "Whoa! Don't be ridiculous. You are going to embarrass yourself and the university because we'll fall flat on our faces!"

But today, UTEP faculty and staff are writing four hundred proposals a year. We have gone from $3 million to $55 million a year in research funding. We went from one doctoral program to eight. Our university has created a niche, a unique identity in people's minds, and we are becoming visible statewide, nationally, and in Mexico.

After these successes, UTEP faculty and staff assume that if we dream big and work hard, things will happen—if the dream is grounded in our reality. The programs we offer must reflect our mission as an institution, and they must play on our institutional strengths and our regional focus.

Our campus has a lot of productive energy now. I have a deep sense of satisfaction about where we are. Not only have we worked extremely hard, we have had to be willing to take some big risks.

**TAKING RISKS:** I am a calculated risk-taker. That means that I always analyze things carefully. Then, quite often, I push myself, and this university, to the edge. No person or institution should be satisfied with where they are now. Sometimes people on my staff are a little apprehensive when I say things such as "Well, let's just go ahead and raise $50 million!" But I haven't been disappointed yet.

It was in Brazil, where I was living as a Fulbright scholar, that I learned to take risks. The first week after I arrived, I didn't open my mouth much because I didn't want to embarrass myself by saying something in Portuguese that wasn't right. Then I told myself, "You are going to be here a year. If you don't start talking, it is going to be a very long and lonely year!" And so I began to risk a little bit. And people didn't fall over laughing or scream in pain because I made a grammatical error. Pretty soon it was I who was laughing at myself.

**HUMOR:** Learning to laugh at myself turned out to be extremely important. It is powerful to be able to joke about yourself, to stand up and say, "I blew it. I made a mistake!"

Many women need to learn that lesson. I have noticed that women tend to be more guarded in public situations than do men. Women need to use humor more—to take what comes along and play with it a little bit. Use humor well and you can disarm people. You can level the playing field. Humor is one of the greatest appeals of women like Ann Richards.

**TEXAS WOMEN:** Their ability to use humor is certainly a part of why so many Texas women stand out on the national scene. I have lived in Texas nearly forty years now, and I have traveled a lot in my work, so I think I can say with some authority that Texas women are less reserved—and seem to be more self-confident—than women in most other places. Maybe people who live in expansive space feel free to express themselves. For example, I sense that women who grow up on ranches are a lot more self-sufficient. Maybe it has to do with spending a lot of time outdoors, with no space limits. Perhaps when you live in a crowded place you learn to be more quiet.

**TEXAS:** Since I have lived in El Paso, I have developed a need for space that I never had before. I live in the desert, and when I find myself in a forest or a large city, I feel closed in. I need to see the horizon. When I am back in the Midwest where I was born, I miss the light and open space. Missouri is beautiful, but I don't think I would ever be happy there again. I just feel like I need more room.

Sunlight is extremely important to me. The light in El Paso and in nearby New Mexico is beautiful. I love the colors of the desert—the sunset and the odd way in which rocks on a mountain face change colors during the course of a day. I can understand why artists come here to paint.

**SOLITUDE:** It is to the desert and the nearby mountains that I go for what I call "solitary recreation." Although I love my work, I get overstimulated easily because I deal with so many people in so many different settings. I feel as if I'm on stage a lot. So I try to carve out time to go hiking and cross-country skiing in the New Mexico mountains a couple of hours north of El Paso. It allows me to take my mind off of work. I find peace and spiritual fulfillment in just sitting and staring at a beautiful vista and thinking about how it was all put together.

Sometimes when I'm hiking, I take a book along, and when I get to a comfortable place, I sit and read for a while. When I get back home, I realize that because I have stopped the activity and agitation, things have settled into their proper places in my brain. I guess that's what is called "peace of mind."

**EL PASO:** But after enough "solitude recreation," I am always ready to come back to El Paso because I love the city and the people so much. El Paso is a border city, so there is a lot of blending of cultures and peoples. The population is 70 percent Hispanic, and we have a good number of Asians and African-Americans, as well as Anglos. Most El Pasoans don't seem to judge each other by color or by ethnicity. I like that attitude. I feel a strong sense of teamwork in the community. People are respectful of each other.

Because the Hispanic people are the majority here, they seem to set the tone. They are incredibly warm, generous, and family-oriented. As an Anglo in El Paso, I feel accepted and appreciated by the Hispanic population, and I return that respect. I work hard to support and advocate the Hispanic heritage at UTEP and in the community.

**MEXICO:** Texas is beginning to acknowledge the importance of Mexico to our state's future. Business and government leaders are beginning to recognize Mexico's assets rather than viewing that country as a liability south of our border. The truth is that Mexico has a young, talented population that could be a real asset for all of us.

As part of the university's agenda, I have begun work on one of my dreams: to create what I am calling the "Ellis Island of the Southwest." I envision an immigration history center in El Paso to commemorate, celebrate, and validate the arrival of a large and growing segment of our population in the United States. Our society has celebrated the immigration from Europe, and the contributions those settlers have made in the United States, but we haven't celebrated immigration from Mexico.

El Paso, "the Pass of the North," has been the pathway for immigration from Mexico for more than four hundred years. For centuries, people have been coming through the mountain pass created by the Rio Grande. At Ellis Island, the ships' manifests carefully recorded immigrants' arrivals. But the names of immigrants coming across the Rio Grande are, in many cases, not recorded except in family memories. And so the challenge is to build a grassroots immigration history museum where the descendants of Mexican immigrants build a collective history by contributing their own family stories.

We have received some foundation money for our "Ellis Island of the Southwest," and I have visited Ellis Island in New York several times for inspiration. We may pattern part of our museum after the Tenement Museum in New York on the Lower East Side. The Tenement Museum is not about cases of artifacts. It is about re-creating the apartments people lived in and about telling their stories. A simple museum, and so powerful—just as ours will be.

**PRINCIPLES BY WHICH I LIVE:** I am excited about my job as president of UTEP and about the "Ellis Island of the Southwest" project because both involve the principles around which I have shaped my life.

- *Appreciate people and cultures different from your own.* My life has been influenced immensely by the richness of the cultures in El Paso and by its people.
- *Empower others.* It bothers me to see a person denied the opportunity to do something she or he is good at simply because of that person's gender, race, or economic situation.

  By empowering others, you enrich yourself. I hired a woman several years ago as a custodian for the president's mansion where I live. It became apparent early on that she was capable of so much more than maintenance. She is now the manager of the house and responsible for organizing all of the receptions and parties we hold as part of university business. With my encouragement, she was able to end an unsatisfactory personal relationship, earn her GED, and blossom into a happy, more confident woman and mother to her children. It has been fulfilling for me to see her grow because she is so good at what she does. And now, I can be a guest at my own parties!
- *Trust yourself and who you are.* People have confidence in you if you have confidence in yourself. Although women's roles have changed in our society, I talk to young women all the time who still define themselves in terms of the men in their lives. Young women need to believe in themselves. They need the constant reminder that they can do anything young men can do, and that they shouldn't postpone or defer their dreams.
- *Express appreciation.* Too often, people hear complaints about mistakes they have made instead of appreciation for the good things they do every day. A note to someone who has made a difference in

your life—perhaps a teacher—can make his or her day.

• *Respect others.* Treat every human being as an equal. Do not assume that you are superior just because you make more money or are better educated. Many valuable talents are not the result of a formal education, and many of the most important contributions to society do not generate wealth. Teaching comes to mind.

**EDUCATING MINORITIES:** I have never lost the sense of wonder one gets from teaching and seeing humans develop. Education is about people stretching themselves to realize their full potential. Education is the only real equalizer between haves and have-nots. Some of UTEP's students achieve despite incredibly adverse circumstances. When they walk across the graduation stage, I allow myself to think, "Maybe I have played a small part in their success." That feels great!

UTEP is extremely important to El Paso. An education has given so many people from this region the opportunity to better their lives, to move from working-class situations to professional careers. And the whole family moves up with the person who accomplishes that.

As a nation, we have expected far too little from African-Americans and Hispanic-Americans. We have assumed that they could not or would not achieve in public schools and in higher education. Hispanics and African-Americans are underrepresented among engineers, physicians, and other professions. But talent is everywhere. It crosses gender, ethnic, racial, neighborhood, and geographic boundaries. As a nation, we really cheat ourselves if we don't develop that talent, wherever it is. Minority high school students are often advised to become beauticians or auto mechanics when they could become physicians, scientists, or engineers.

The challenge now is to change those attitudes and say, "Let's push the bar up. Let's offer advanced physics, chemistry, and calculus in low-income schools as well as in affluent ones." I think we cheat ourselves when we deny a growing segment of the population the opportunity to develop its full potential. UTEP is working with El Paso schools to change those attitudes.

In a lot of families, regardless of ethnicity, reading to kids just doesn't happen. Typically, if a household is filled with books and people are reading, children come out with good language skills. If a child is read to regularly during the early years, she or he gets a huge head start on language. We need to give all kids the opportunity for an enriched pre-school program and a solid K–12 education, so that by the time they take the SAT in high school, they are well prepared to succeed. High SAT scores usually correlate best with family affluence. If the preschool play-ing field isn't level, we have to work to level it by setting high standards for all children. And that should include fluency in more than one lan-guage.

**BILINGUAL EDUCATION:** Unlike our European counterparts, Ameri-cans seem addicted to monolingualism. We expect too little of American children. In Europe, people assume that everybody can and should speak more than one language. Nobody says, "Oh, it's too much for this little German child to learn French and English, as well as German."

No one should be taught that the language they speak with their par-ents is a liability, a negative. Not too long ago, when Spanish was prohib-ited in the public schools except in Spanish class, the message was "Your native language is bad. It is not a good thing to speak Spanish." By send-ing that signal, our society not only squandered the language skill itself but also suggested that something was wrong with the culture repre-sented by the native language.

Unfortunately, bilingual education is usually viewed as a compensa-tory program—something that you send people through to get to En-glish. And it has been unevenly implemented. The truth is, when chil-dren speak more than one language, another world opens to them. College graduates who are bi- or trilingual are able to move easily into the global marketplace. We send mixed signals when we tell children "English only" and then turn around, when they graduate from college, to tell them, "It's a shame you don't know another language. If you did, you could compete for more attractive jobs."

Rather than purge a second language at age five and then try to rees-tablish it at age fifteen, why not simply sustain and reinforce it? The goal of bilingual education should be to encourage children to speak their native language and to learn another language along with it, so that they can use two or more languages confidently. If all of us could achieve that with Spanish and English, everybody would be richer.

This is a dream worth working toward every day.

# VIOLETTE NEWTON

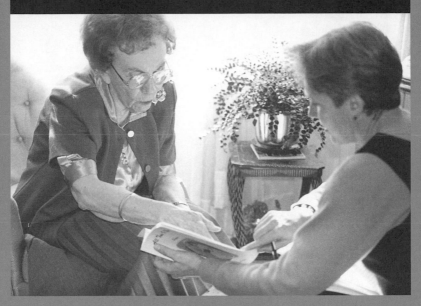

*Violette Newton, poet, with the author.*
*Photo by Summer Pierce © 1999.*

"*Sometimes a poem comes to me in a flash and needs little or no revision. Often an idea germinates for a while before I try to put it to paper.*"

*Violette Newton*

B. 1912,
ALEXANDRIA, LOUISIANA
CURRENT HOME:
BEAUMONT, TEXAS

Violette Newton is the author of seventeen books of poetry and was named poet laureate of Texas by the Texas legislature in 1973. She says her biography is in her poetry. She published her first book when she was fifty-five years old.

Although born in Louisiana, Violette has lived in Texas since she was twelve, when her family moved to Port Arthur, an oil boomtown in Southeast Texas. It was there that she discovered her life's passion: poetry. Because she missed the beauty of her childhood home and surroundings in Louisiana, she retained that other world in her mind by writing about it secretly.

But Violette stayed in Texas. She and her husband, Wilben, raised their three children in nearby Beaumont, where Violette lives today. Her husband, now deceased, was an accountant by day and a short story writer by evening. Their three children grew up to be artists, writers, musicians, and poets in addition to their day jobs in teaching and engineering. She found time to write poetry regularly during those years of family activity.

Violette's grandfather, who immigrated to America in 1850 during the potato famine, inspired her to seek her Irish roots. Her book *The Shamrock Cross* (1993) contains the resulting poems of her trip to Ireland. *A Cathedral Ringing* (1976) contains poems inspired by her experience in Guatemala.

Violette was inducted into the Southeast Texas Women's Hall of Fame in 1991 for her contribution to the arts. She travels throughout Texas as a recitalist and lecturer on poetry. Her poetry readings draw packed audiences, and her poetry and short stories appear in journals and anthologies nationwide. She speaks about poetry at universities and for many years was Visiting Poet in the public schools of Texas.

Violette has been a member of the exclusive Poetry Society of America, from which she won the coveted Medwick Award. Her work has drawn major awards from the Poetry Society of America, the National Federation of State Poetry Societies, and the Poetry Society of Texas. Her seventeenth book of poetry, *Fire in the Garden*, was released by Harp and Quill Press in 1999.

---

**AUTHOR'S NOTE** *Beaumont sits in what some people call the "swampland" of deep East Texas. The city, with its lush tropical foliage and humid air, resembles Louisiana more than it does the rest of Texas.*

*Violette fits right into the atmosphere, with her lilting Southern accent and her demure Southern-lady image. Then you notice her dry wit and the twinkle in her eye, and you understand how she came to write the following in a letter to the editor of the* Beaumont Enterprise:

*"I deplore the way those foreigners from other states look on us and the way we speak. Several years ago, I gave some lectures at a West Texas College, after which one woman said to me, 'I can tell you're from the swamps.'*

*"This didn't 'set well' with me; in fact, it was offensive. But being a Southern gentlewoman, I replied in my soft, Southern-lady voice, 'Not swamps, deah, but broad oaks and tall pines.' Then I smiled sweetly, lifted my hoopskirts and walked out of her mind."*

*Violette Newton*

**S P E A K S**

**POETRY:** I stumbled through first and second grades, not knowing what I wanted to do with my life. Then in the next year, I discovered poetry. I didn't guess that I would actually write poetry someday. All I knew was that those words on the page made me feel what they said, and the feeling gave me a strange exhilaration.

Now when I talk to students, they usually want to know how much money a poet receives for publication of his work. I tell them that few poets can make a living writing poetry, but it's a great way to live. Even if you earn your living as teacher or construction worker, if you're a practicing poet, your days will be enhanced. You will be observant and pay keen attention to everything around you—things you may later write about.

**WHAT MAKES ME FEEL ALIVE:** I feel most alive when I've written a good phrase, good line, good poem or story. Why do I spend my time at work that pays so little in money? Because it pays so much in satisfaction. I have to write.

**MENTORS:** I never had any teachers in poetry; I had to figure it out for myself. As a young teenager, I read all the poetry books in the library. I osmosed everything. I didn't know anything about writing poetry. The ability just came.

When I was in high school, everything I wrote was rhymed. When we began studying Amy Lowell, I went crazy because she was saying it without saying it. The impact was sudden and intense. I just loved it, so I began writing contemporary poetry.

**THE CREATIVE SPARK:** Sometimes a poem comes to me in a flash and needs little or no revision. Often an idea germinates for a while before I try to put it to paper.

I wrote one book of poems about my experience in Western Europe, *All the Druids Are Gone,* in two weeks, but I had thought about it for months. When I came home from a week in Guatemala, the impact of all I saw and felt was so great, I was unable to write a word about it for six months. After that, poems came in a flood.

I talked with [poet] James Dickey about it. He said an artist must sometimes distance himself enough from his subject in order to see it in perspective.

One of my best-known poems, "Texas Poetry," was waiting around in the back of my head for years, unable to form. Then one day, I was at home and it started—just out of the blue. I had to run to the bedroom and get a pen and paper. I sat down in the 1875 rocker that Mama remembered being rocked in when she was a baby. I had to hurry to get the poem down before I lost it. Then I laughed and said out loud, "But this isn't the way it was supposed to be!" I don't know what I thought I was going to write. Then I thought, "This is good."

TEXAS POETRY

Up East, they do not think much
of Texas poetry. They think Texans
have no soul for aesthetics, that all
they do is pound their own chests,
talk loud and make money.
But every time I'm nearing Austin,
I look up at a painted sign
high on the side of the highway
that says "Bert's Dirts"
and to pyramids of many-colored soils
sold by Bert, and I swell with pride
at that rhyming sign, I puff up

and point to that terse little title
and wish we could stop
so I could go in
and purchase
a spondee of sand
to make a gesture of my support
for poetry in Texas.

VIOLETTE NEWTON
PUBLISHED IN *The Scandal*, 1981
NORTEX PUBLICATION PRIZE

**WAITING FOR THE MUSE:** For the past few months I haven't written much. I kept thinking: "I guess maybe I have written myself out." Then one night, all of a sudden, a poem came to me. After all these years, I was thinking about a trip to England after my husband died, and the poem came quickly.

### THAT AUTUMN IN ENGLAND

That autumn in England, and you
not there, yet I saw your face
in those English faces
everywhere. I knew an ache
I had never known, alone
as I was in a land
I claimed my own.

I saw the ivy, reddened on brick,
and the graven saints on old
church walls, the sheep
and the heather
and always the sea
that separated me from all
we were. I walked in the air
of that English weather, slipped
as I was through the veil
of a time more rare.

But what does it matter now
that days have fled as all days do,
and I barely remember your face.
For your voice is pure in my
inner ear, speaking sometimes
in the oddest place, so those
around me may see the light
of my sudden smile
and wonder what caused
such grace.

VIOLETTE NEWTON
FIRE IN THE GARDEN
HARP AND QUILL PRESS, 1999

**WRITING POETRY:** I spend short periods of time concentrating on poetry, but I do not begin to write until the poem starts in words in my head. The way the poem starts is the form it takes. Of course, I have to follow all the way with this form.

If a poem comes fast—like "Texas Poetry"—it is "given" to me. A long poem I wrote about Great Aunt Julia took a long time. Through the years, I took it out, tried to revise, but nothing worked. It must have been fifteen years later that revision worked, and the healthy poem came out in one of my books.

**LEARNING FROM MISTAKES:** Great Aunt Julia ran a fourth-class post office in the front room of her house in Louisiana. Once when I visited her, she and I were going through family pictures. I came across a picture of a young man—very stern looking. I guess he had to keep still a long time to have that picture made. He had on a high collar, a wide cravat, and a nice coat. I said, "Who is this? He doesn't look like any of us." She said, "That was my sweetheart—the only one I ever had." That made me feel sad. I was so timid I wouldn't ask more about him.

Now I wish I had asked! I had to fictionalize some of the story for the poem I wrote.

**PERFORMING POETRY:** I insist in my talks that poetry be considered a performing art, that teachers spend less time stressing the mechanics of verse and more in having fine poetry "performed" by people who care.

**BEAUTY:** I have a need to be surrounded by beauty. Music and art have played a great part in my life. My father made canvases for me—he would make stretchers, and he would stretch white duck or sugar sack on it and paint it with a solution that he cooked on the stove. I painted in oils— even did a large self-portrait that won a prize.

I have visited the great museums of the world. I went into the National Portrait Gallery in London and saw all of my favorite people. They were looking at me.

I love to be surrounded by my history. Most of my furniture came from the Louisiana plantation where my beloved Grandmother Lunny— my mother's mother—lived. Our photos look alike. This is a poem on the generations, how we hand down our traits, our looks, our qualities.

### OUR ROOMS AND OUR LIVES

Whoever you were
I am. And for awhile
I was all there was of the generations:
the seed compounded, contained—
an instrument to extend and carry you
over our time.

When I moved here, you came too, your accents
in my voice and the days of your living
in the soft glow of old woods I brought
from your home, in the curves and turns
of their carving, the dull golds framing
plates and portraits. For as if guided
by your hands, my hands gathered and wove you
into my place, since my hands are, of course,
your hands now, and my face the face
in your fading photographs.

Who we were has been transmitted, transmuted,
transplanted, and even now blossoms
in other time zones. For wherever
my children live,
now and then among their little ones,
I see you looking at me. And I know
there is never an ending,
that we will surface somewhere
predictably/unpredictably
to build our rooms and our lives
from plans we will not know we know.

VIOLETTE NEWTON
*The Scandal,* 1981
NORTEX PUBLICATION PRIZE

**PROUDEST ACCOMPLISHMENTS:** I was pleased to be named poet laureate of Texas in 1973, but I am most proud that I've traveled the byways, highways, and skyways as a symbol of poetry in Texas. I am proud that as a woman, I write with conviction, unafraid to take a stand for my beliefs. I may have been given a flowery name, but I do not write flowery poetry.

I won the Medwick Award from the Poetry Society of America for a long poem about an elderly lady who refused to go to a nursing home. She locked herself up in her house among her treasures, survived for a while, but died alone there. It was a scandal that she hadn't been forced to go to a nursing home. My poem was in defense of her right to make her own decision.

The Medwick Award is given for a poem on a humanitarian theme. Most of the prizes in the Poetry Society of America are won by famous people. We tend to think of it as a closed circle. You can see that it isn't, for an excellent poem can win, no matter who wrote it.

**TEXAS WOMEN:** My upbringing in Texas has influenced me in my positive attitude. Though I live in the almost Deep South atmosphere of East Texas, I think the vigorous spirit of the state has affected me. I learned not to look back but to go forward and not to give up if I thought I had written something worthy of publication.

Otherwise, I don't think Texans are so different from other people. People are the same all over and from all times. People of today are no different from the people of the 1600s or the 1400s. We may know more today and live differently, but inwardly we are the same. We react in similar ways.

**HANDLING PRAISE:** When I speak at a school, I always feel good if even one girl or boy comes up to talk earnestly with me about poetry. I shall ever remember one such young woman who wrote a note to me, saying, "I love your life."

All of this brings back a bit of wisdom my father imparted to me in the last year of his life: "Anytime you think you're smart, you're not!" In other words, be humble, be humble.

**SELF-CONFIDENCE:** I've seen many a writer feel let down when his or her piece of work fails to make first place. Art cannot be measured with a yardstick, and the sooner we accept that fact, the easier it will be for us. If your piece is good, it is still good, even if one editor or judge doesn't vote for it.

Long ago I was told that it was impossible to be accepted by a university journal if you were not a member of a university faculty. I was told that no one in our part of the country could win an award from the Poetry Society of America. None of that is true. We shouldn't believe everything "they" say.

**HUMOR:** I was never humorous until I was older. My parents were grim during the Depression. There wasn't much to be funny about, so I didn't incorporate much humor in my life.

Then, in my fifties, I won a publication prize for my first book of poetry, *Moses in Texas.* A woman professor said to me, "You have a lot of humor in your poetry." I didn't know it until then.

Now, thirty years later, I have more humor than I have ever had. It's just something that comes out of the pen. I don't anticipate it.

At a gathering of Texas publishers and writers, I read one of my Cajun short stories. The audience was laughing all the way through.

**WIDOWHOOD:** I never liked the word "widow." It always painted a picture of a little gray lady alone in the world. I never considered myself like that.

My husband and I had each lived such complete lives with our writing. After he was gone, my own writing soon helped me to fill my days. There seemed never enough time to write all I had to say. I accepted invitations to go out of town to speak or read from my latest book. I read in the schools, in universities, I taught in my local poetry club.

Of course, I wish he were here with me, to talk and read to each other, as we used to do. An entire section of my newest book is about him and our family.

**GETTING OLDER:** I like the age I am now because I have already learned so much about life. I'm calm about what happens—I don't worry. I take life as it comes.

If I were a young woman starting out today, I would work against all odds to attain an extensive higher education. Somehow, life didn't work out for me to earn the Ph.D. I craved, but I have walked around Oxford and the Sorbonne, I have lingered in the Louvre and the Prado, I have read the great books. I love my life.

And now that I am eighty-six, should I at last publish my love poems? Do I dare?

# GUADALUPE C. QUINTANILLA

Guadalupe C. Quintanilla, educator and entrepreneur. Photo by Charles Cormany
© 1998. Courtesy of Charles Cormany.

"*I would never have fought that hard for myself alone. What you won't do for yourself, you will do for your children.*"

## Guadalupe C. Quintanilla

B. 1937,
OJINAGA, CHIHUAHUA, MEXICO
CURRENT HOME:
HOUSTON, TEXAS

Guadalupe C. Quintanilla has come a long way since her upbringing in San Luis, a Mexican village without streets, running water, or electricity, and with no school. Having attended grade school or high school for less than four months, today she owns bachelor's, master's, and Ed.D. degrees. She holds an impressive list of positions and honors and has accumulated wealth through savvy investments in real estate and the stock market.

Dr. Q., as her students and staff call her, is associate professor of modern and classical languages at the University of Houston. For more than twenty years she has been president of her own company, the Cross-Cultural Communications Center, through which she conducts language and cultural sensitivity training for law enforcement officers and other professionals all over the country. The training program she devised has received national recognition from the FBI Academy, the Department of Justice, and the Department of Defense as the best of its type in the country. It was also selected as part of the training of security forces during the Pan American Games.

In the 1970s, she was the first Mexican American female with a doctorate at the University of Houston. She designed both the Mexican American studies and the multicultural bilingual programs for the university and wrote grant proposals to get them funded.

Lupe has received several presidential nominations and appointments. In 1984 she became the first Hispanic U.S. representative to the United Nations, and she still serves on two United Nations committees. In 1990 she was nominated to the position of U.S. assistant attorney general, an honor she declined in order to continue with the development of her Cross-Cultural Communications Center. Recently she was honored by the Women's Chamber of Commerce in Texas as one of one hundred Texas women who have made a difference in the past century. She is also included in the Women's History Museum in Dallas. Dr. Q is a sought-after speaker.

Her success in modern American society seems an impossibility when one hears the story of her early life. Lupe was raised by her grandparents in two small villages in Mexico—first, in Nogales, where she began working in their grocery store at age five. Her grandmother taught Lupe to add and multiply so she could wait on customers. (Lupe's mother was emotionally not equipped to raise a child and disappeared from her life. Lupe's father then handed the baby over to his parents. Later he remarried.) When Lupe was seven, she, her grandparents, and her uncle, a young doctor, moved on horseback to the tiny village of San Luis, south of Acapulco. She lived there till she was thirteen. At age seven, she taught herself to read and write so she could perform her duties as nurse in her uncle's medical office. "I had to read the pamphlets for the medications, and I learned to give shots and perform X-rays," Lupe said. At age eight she organized her own "school" and taught her peers in the village how to read and write. "I have gone back to San Luis twice in the past few years and many of my 'pupils' remember me," she said.

Her grandfather lost his eyesight when Lupe was thirteen, and the family moved to Brownsville in South Texas to be close to her father. There she entered school for the first time. Everybody spoke English, a language Lupe didn't understand. She was labeled "retarded" after taking an intelligence test administered in English, and she was placed in first grade but was not allowed to take part in the regular learning because of her "retarded" status. When she spoke Spanish, she was punished. The experience was so humiliating that Lupe dropped out after a few weeks and never went back to public school. Instead, she became her blind grandfather's "eyes" and spent hours each day during the next several years reading him the classics in Spanish. When she became bored from reading aloud, she would speed-read and then paraphrase, a skill that proved helpful in her university studies later on. From her grandmother Lupe learned housekeeping, and when she was sixteen, her grandfather selected a husband for her, a man who was thirteen years older than she. "I had never dated before, but my grandparents really liked my husband because he was established as a dental technician," she said.

"They wanted somebody to take care of me." The three children came along quickly and "life was fine," she said, "until I realized that my children were having trouble at school."

They, too, were being labeled "slow learners" in the Brownsville schools because of their inability to speak English. It was 1969. Lupe took an unprecedented step for a Mexican American mother. She confronted the children's teachers and asked what she could do to help them learn. The consensus was "learn to speak English and use it at home." Determined to learn English for her children's sake, Lupe was refused at every turn because she did not have a high school diploma. Her last resort was to seek help at the local college. But she couldn't get past the administrator's secretary, who told her that without a high school diploma she couldn't enter college. She waited several hours in the parking lot next to the car of the registrar, an Anglo man. When he came out at the end of the day, Lupe, the shy Mexican American mother, confronted him, begging him to let her sit in on English classes so she could pick up the language. "I never intended to become a college student," she said. "All I wanted was someplace to learn English." But the registrar insisted that she sign up for a full load or nothing at all. She found herself taking basic English, psychology, basic math, and typing. She left with the registrar's words ringing in her ears: "Don't come back if you don't pass the first semester."

"Every day I would make breakfast for my husband, grandparents, and children, get the children off to school, go to campus on the bus, come home at noon to cook lunch for everyone, take the bus back to class, and be home in time to greet the children when they got home from school," Lupe said. "I studied and wrote papers most of the night."

With the help of her younger classmates, the thirty-one-year-old mother not only made it through the first semester, she made the Dean's List. "The dean was amazed," she remembers. "He called me into his office and told me the good news. Last year he was in the audience when I gave a speech in Dallas. Afterward, he told me he had been following my success through the years, and he is so proud." She forced herself to speak English at home with her children, and their language skills improved quickly. (Once they reached high school and were fluent in English, she switched back to speaking Spanish with them at home so they would remain fluent in both languages.)

She soon realized that the two-year degree would not satisfy her, and she enrolled in a four-year university 140 miles away, got her driver's license, and took classes simultaneously at both institutions. Within three years, she had earned both her junior-college degree and a bachelor's degree in biology. She won a fellowship at the University of Houston, 350 miles away, and she moved her children and her grandparents to Houston with her. (Her husband stayed behind in Brownsville.) Lupe's grandparents lived with her until they died years later. At the university, Lupe earned a master's degree in Spanish literature. When she graduated, the university offered her a job as interim director of the Mexican American Studies Program. She agreed to take the offer, but only on a permanent basis. The administration at the university agreed. While in that position, she earned a doctorate in education.

"My motivation for continuing my education was always for the welfare of my children," she said. "I knew that I would need to make as much money as I could so they could get the best education possible." Today Mario is a physician, and Victor and Martha are attorneys, both having earned doctor of law degrees. There are four Dr. Quintanillas in the family.

---

**AUTHOR'S NOTE** *Lupe is immediately friendly and curious about my daughter Summer, with her professional camera equipment. "Why is that lens so big?" she asks during the flow of conversation. "And don't you need a flash? No? I love learning new things."*

*Her soft voice and long, wavy hair cascading down her back paint an image unlike that of most other successful businesswomen like herself.*

*Her candor is refreshing. Lupe laughs at herself as she tells us about a predicament in which she had recently found herself. A few nights before, she had accidentally locked herself out of her hotel room with wet hair and clad only in her nylon nightgown. As there was no other solution, she had had to go to the lobby in that condition and stand in line at the front desk to get another key. Afterward, with dry hair and business attire, she was the keynote speaker at a banquet in the same hotel.*

*Guadalupe C.
Quintanilla*

**S P E A K S**

**MOTHERHOOD:** I married so young that I had to finish growing up as a wife and mother. I had been happy as a Mexican American housewife and mother, speaking only Spanish in Brownsville, until I saw that my children were being undervalued at school because they weren't fluent in English. That's when I summoned the nerve at age thirty-one to confront the registrar at the local college and beg him to admit me so I could learn English. I would never have fought that hard for myself alone. What you won't do for yourself, you will do for your children.

Motherhood is an opportunity that every woman should seriously consider. For me, being a mother has been wonderful, but it also has been very difficult, challenging, and painful at times. Being a parent is usually hit and miss because nobody tells you how. You make so many mistakes. And then you look back and you think, "Oh, I should not have done that." But you understand your mistakes only after you have already made them.

Because I was the total support for my children for so long, I have to remind myself now to step back and let them live their own lives. It took me a long time to understand that I had to respect my children as adults.

**MOTHERHOOD AND WORK:** While I was going to college as a young mother, I felt a tremendous guilt about not being with my children enough. My parents and grandparents cared for them while I was in class. But I knew in my heart that if I didn't open the doors for myself and therefore for my children, we were never going to get out of where I thought we shouldn't be.

**IF I WERE A YOUNG WOMAN STARTING OVER:** I would try to prepare myself better for life. For example, I would seek answers to questions such as "What could be the most satisfying career for me?" "What does married life really entail?" "If I become a parent, what does such a role demand?" "How can I be a better parent?" "How can I effectively manage my finances?"

Furthermore, I would write my own definition of success and take the necessary steps to achieve that success. I would not marry until I had completed at least my first college degree.

**SEIZING OPPORTUNITIES:** Although I firmly believe that I have been "the architect of my own destiny" (a quote from my favorite poem, by Amado Nervo), I have been fortunate to be in the right place at the right time. But my success lies also in the fact that I have had the right preparation, the right energy, and the willingness to do it.

**DEALING WITH AN "EMPTY NEST":** When my last child finished his medical training and was ready to support himself, I was forty-seven. My goal had always been to work to pay for my children and their education. Now that I no longer had that financial responsibility, I didn't know what to do with myself. I didn't know what I wanted for me—although I was working in several positions that I really enjoyed: as a professor at the University of Houston, as owner of my Cross-Cultural Communications Center, and on the national level as both a United States representative to the United Nations and cochairman for the National Institute of Justice. Now I wondered what I would do with the money I was making.

But again I happened to be in the right place at the right time. That was in 1984—about the same time that the oil bust hit Houston. I was fortunate to have a good mentor in the real estate business, and I decided that I would learn about how to invest my money. So I bought several properties in two upscale neighborhoods in the heart of the city. It was very scary because I had never invested in anything but my children's education. But it worked out well, and I have made a lot of money in real estate and also in the stock market.

**MONEY:** I like to make money, but it is important to be having fun and to be creative at the same time. Also, I like to be in control. Then, if I make a mistake, I am responsible for the consequences. My money-making endeavors all have those qualities. My real estate, my program at the university, and my company all require creativity, and I have lots of fun with them.

My most important mentor was a man who explained to me when I moved to Houston: "Don't use credit cards; use cash. When you see the money going out of your hands, it makes you think twice about what you spend. Don't ever owe so much money that you have to work when you don't want to work." I follow that advice even today. I use cash for everything but business expenses. I use one credit card to keep track of business records. I pay the credit card charges in full at the end of the month.

Being secure financially gives me the confidence to know that I don't have to work at a job that I don't like. And to me that is real success.

**SELF-RELIANCE:** It has been fun working with my rental houses and learning about roofing, painting, and plumbing. Now, if I can't get a repairman, I can do a lot of the work myself. I have crawled under many houses to fix broken pipes. And I have surprised a few dishonest repairmen by letting them know that they just need to clean the points instead of selling me a new furnace. These are all skills I have learned hands-on.

As I look back through the years, I realize I have become a pretty strong person. My (step)mother told me once: "You know, your eyes have become hard." It's because I have had to survive lots of challenges, and it hasn't been easy. I have always been strong, but I think I used to have a softer glove. Maybe I used to be more agreeable. But when I made the big decision to be the sole support of myself and my children, I got harder. I decided I wanted to become independently wealthy and not have to depend on anybody. And I didn't have anything to lose by trying, except maybe the softness in my eyes.

**LEARNING NEW THINGS:** Money hasn't been the sole reason I have gone into most endeavors. I am always motivated by the desire to learn something different, something new. For example, I started my cross-cultural training program for two reasons: because I saw a need and because I knew I was liable to learn a lot in the experience. I saw the need for emergency personnel in the community to learn some Spanish in order to communicate with Hispanics in trouble.

**SELF-CONFIDENCE:** My work with policemen around the country has made me realize that if I can handle the ego of a policeman, I can probably handle anybody. About twenty years ago I was teaching a class of thirty policemen. I said, "You need to make a sentence with these Spanish words." A big policeman—well over six feet tall and maybe 275 pounds—said, "I'm not going to do that." And a silence fell on the room.

I thought to myself, "What am I going to do now? If I let him get away with this, the twenty-nine others aren't going to do what I say either." So I said, "Yes, you are, Joe." And he stood up and looked down on me (I am only five feet tall) and said, "No I'm not!" I climbed on a chair, looked him straight in the eyes, and said, "Yes, you are!" Well, I was lucky. Joe started laughing and he did what I had asked. We became very good friends, and I baptized him "Chiquito." Now everybody in the department calls him Chiquito (meaning "little bitty one").

Another self-confidence builder has been my work in the United Nations. That was one of the best experiences of my life. As I sat at the discussion table with world leaders, I realized that many of the solutions they were offering were ones I had thought about as well. The confusions they experienced I had experienced myself. That experience gave to me a global view of humanity.

**WORKING TO ALLEVIATE PREJUDICE:** I like to find ways to build bridges between people from different cultures—on the international as well as local levels. In my cross-cultural training program, I get juveniles from the court system who need to do voluntary service to pay for their fine. They teach Spanish vocabulary to police officers. Both sides lose the hate and fear that they have for each other because they learn to see each other as people, not as adversaries. I employ teachers as young as five years of age. The children teach colors, parts of the body, and names of clothing, and the officers learn how to describe suspects. Both cultures are learning from one another.

**BEING MEXICAN AMERICAN:** I am a really interesting combination of culture and tradition. When I am in my parents' home, I revert to being their daughter. For example, my children and I eat with my parents after church every Sunday. If we eat at home, I am busy frying meat, and my hands are full of lard. My mother is making tortillas, and her hands are full of flour. My father comes to the kitchen from watching TV in the living room and he asks me to give him a glass of water. So I stop what I am doing and wash my hands. He is standing closer to the glasses than I am, and the water comes out of the front of the refrigerator door. But, because of tradition, he will not get his own glass or his own water. Because I care for him, I don't have the heart to tell him, "The glass is right there." My response to him comes from my being raised in the Mexican American culture.

**FAMILY:** My parents don't really understand what I do for a living. My status as a rather powerful female in today's culture is still a foreign idea to them. The less they know, the less intimidating I am to them. It is a lot more comfortable to be with somebody who is a daughter instead of a businesswoman. They know I work at the University of Houston. They know that I am respected in my community, and that I have worked very hard to deserve it. They know those things because they live here in Houston. They see me on TV occasionally, and they read about me in the paper. My mother's usual comment is "Comb your hair because it never looks combed." And my father's comment: "Buy another dress because you wear the same dress in all the pictures." Which is true. (Laughs.)

**BEING TRUE TO YOURSELF:** Worrying what other people think of you is part of the Mexican American culture. One of the most difficult things I have ever done is to conquer my fear of being disliked. I used to do things I didn't want to do in order to please people. Now I do things because I really want to do them or because something just really needs to be done. If you like yourself, it doesn't matter if other people like you. It has taken me forty years to come to that conclusion.

**NURTURING YOURSELF:** At this point in my life I am very particular about how I spend my time. I am pretty good at getting people out of my office; I have learned all the techniques over the years. I don't enjoy social functions, and so I attend very few. I don't have much free time, so I don't want to spend it frivolously.

I give myself time to think positively, to exercise and, above all, to be with people I love. I do crazy things like go to garage sales; it is like treasure hunting. For fun I read Erma Bombeck. I walk three miles every day with a friend at 5 A.M. And I go to church every Sunday.

**GETTING OLDER:** I enjoy my birthdays, but I don't feel as if I am getting older. It's not a Pollyanna attitude either. I have really just never thought about age.

Sometimes I think I am experiencing my childhood right now because I never got much of a childhood. I am enjoying this age a lot because I do what I want to do.

**YOUNG PEOPLE:** Being around young people renews my enthusiasm for life. They remind me that hope is always there. I learn not to complain about life and not to talk about problems, about my aching knees. Young people have troubles, but they don't seem to dwell on them.

Maybe because I see the cream of our youth, I find the present generation to be talented and determined. I see confident, bright, self-reliant people. However, they tend to be spoiled and not very hardworking. That worries me somewhat. I try to impart to my students the truths I have learned along the way.

**PRINCIPLES I LIVE BY:**

- Do not present a problem without offering a solution.
- Health is your most important treasure. Take care of yourself.
- If you give your word, follow through.
- Do more than expected.
- Cultivate your own garden. Appreciate what you have. Most of us have what we really need, even though we don't realize it.
- Spend less than you make. I allow myself the luxuries that I really want. I learned a long time ago not to buy on impulse.
- Tell people when they do something well.
- Find the best in those around you and tell them about it.
- Express appreciation. Learn the names of the people who park your car, who wait on you at the cafeteria, and who clean your office. Call them by their names.

- Teach by example. If you expect things of others, you must also expect them of yourself. I can't ask my assistant to stay until 6 P.M. if I am not willing to do it myself.
- Persistence is the only antidote for failure. One has not failed until one stops trying. Figure out what you want in life, plan a route to get there, and keep working until you arrive.

**HELPING THE UNDERDOG:** One of my biggest fears is not having enough years in my life to contribute as much as I want to the Mexican American community. There is still so much that needs to be done. The 48 percent drop-out rate of Hispanic students bothers me a lot. I have worked on that problem for a long time, but I still don't know exactly how to solve it.

When I die I want my epitaph to read: "She left her world better than she found it."

# LOUISE B. RAGGIO

*Louise B. Raggio, attorney. Photo by Summer Pierce © 2000.*

"*If I have done anything,
it's that I seized opportunities
to change things, especially
for women.*"

## Louise B. Raggio

B. 1919,
MANOR, TEXAS
CURRENT HOME:
DALLAS, TEXAS

Every married woman in the state of Texas owes Louise Raggio a debt of gratitude. Without her vision and hard work, women in Texas might still be victims of the laws known as the Twenty-seven Disabilities of Coverture, the worst laws in the United States concerning married women.

When Louise married in 1941 at age twenty-one, she forfeited most of the legal rights she had had as a single woman.

In 1967 Louise, the attorney, changed all that. She headed up the otherwise all-male Marital Properties Task Force in the Texas State Bar and helped push new laws through the Texas legislature. For the first time, married women in Texas could buy or sell property, secure a bank loan, start a business, and have credit in their own names.

Next, Louise headed up a twelve-year effort to streamline the jumbled Texas laws relating to marriage, divorce, and families. In the end, her committee put together the first fully codified set of family laws in the world. The Texas Family Code brought Texas out of the Dark Ages of family law, and the code has served as a model for other states and foreign countries.

Both the Marital Property Act and the Texas Family Code rank as major milestones on the path toward equality for women.

In the background, Louise was practicing family law in the firm Raggio and Raggio, which she founded with her husband, Grier, in 1956. They had two children, Grier Jr., and Tom, when her husband encouraged her to go to law school. Kenny was born while Louise was in law school and attended classes with her as a baby. Today all three sons are attorneys with Louise at Raggio and Raggio. Grier died in 1988 after forty-seven years of marriage.

Louise attributes her values and work ethics to her Swedish-German immigrant grandparents and to her parents, both of whom had to drop out of school after sixth grade. She grew up on a "plain old dirt farm without electricity or running water" near Manor, Texas, down the road from Austin.

Among her achievements: first woman ever elected as director in the hundred-year history of the State Bar of Texas; governor of the American Academy of Matrimonial Lawyers; Texas State Bar's Outstanding Lawyer Award, 1987; Dallas Bar's first Outstanding Trial Lawyer award, 1993.

Louise was diagnosed with leukemia at age seventy-four, but she hasn't let it slow her down. "It is a very slow-moving, chronic variety called lymphocytic leukemia, that the doctors watch. I don't take medication for it," she said.

**AUTHOR'S NOTE** *Dressed in a stylish business suit, Louise heartily welcomes my two twenty-something daughters and me one Saturday morning into the homelike office of Raggio and Raggio, which she shares with her three lawyer sons. The two-story building is tucked in a corner of the lovely old McKinney area near downtown Dallas.*

*Having already seen age eighty, Louise is still energetic and sharp-witted, and has laugh lines around her eyes. Her excitement about life is contagious, and she makes you laugh, even as she tells of the difficulties she has overcome in her life and career.*

*Louise stands five feet two inches tall and has a motherly quality about her that belies her reputation for being a hard-nosed matrimonial trial lawyer in the courtroom. A powerful client advocate, she is despised by many of her clients' former spouses, both male and female. Louise's compassion has always been focused on the children in divorce cases, which usually has meant that one ex-spouse or the other has had to sacrifice more than he or she had expected so the children could get what they needed. "We have always practiced 'holistic' law," she says. "We take care of the whole person, not just the legal case."*

## Louise B. Raggio

# SPEAKS

**OPPORTUNITY DISGUISED AS DISASTER:** Sometimes the events that you view as real disasters turn out to be the most significant influences in your life.

People are surprised when I tell them that as a teenager I was fat and tacky. I never had store-bought clothes until after college. Mother would get old clothes and rip them up and make them over. She was a marvelous seamstress and tailor. We were poor.

I certainly was not "date bait." (Laughs.) At sixteen, if I had had a magic wand, I would have chosen to be popular and to have boys take me to dances. But I didn't have that wand.

So I became the valedictorian of my class at Austin High School and Phi Beta Kappa at the University of Texas. If I had been cute and popular, I might not have excelled in academics. As it turned out, it was lucky for me that I was a real nerd. I had no way to go but up.

But I can remember thinking like all teenagers think: "Wouldn't it be nice . . ."

**PRINCIPLES I LIVE BY:** My principles are a combination of professionalism and the morals I was brought up with.

- In law, I practice professionalism, ethics, and confidentiality.
- You are your brother's and your sister's keeper.
- You have a duty to work on the solutions rather than just moan about the problems.

- Giving as well as receiving is important.
- We are all part of the same great spirit. We are part of the same family.

**FAITH:** I was brought up an orthodox Swedish Lutheran. I was taught that the world was created in 4004 B.C. And you were not supposed to ask questions. I accepted that discipline as a child.

Then I went to the University of Texas and took geology. When I began digging up extinct vertebrates and finding out how long those things had been there, I was disturbed. And I went to my Lutheran minister back in Manor. (Laughs.) I can understand his reaction now, but I couldn't then. He became very angry and he said, "The University of Texas is a training camp for hell. I told your folks to send you to a church school!"

Of course, when you find a crack in such a rigid belief system, the whole thing falls down. So I've had the interesting experience of rebuilding my religion. I have been Unitarian now for fifty years, and I am very dedicated to it. I attend church every week. Unitarians are flexible. They are capable of saying, "Well, that doesn't work anymore. I think I'll look at it in a different way."

If you discover DNA, you can still fit it into your religion. You find out that religion is bigger than any one book. I can read and understand about Buddhism, for example, without feeling that I am betraying my beliefs.

**VOTING:** All four of my grandparents were immigrants. They have influenced my life more than any other persons. Two came from Germany and two from Sweden. They taught me that it is a blessing to live in this country and how important it is to participate in its decision making.

My father had about a sixth-grade education, but he was precinct chair of a little community. He would get about 98 percent of the people to vote every time—the highest percentage of voters in Texas. I guess that attitude spilled over into me.

I vote if I have to crawl to the polls. Before World War II, this country was divided. But when Americans began to understand the threat of Nazism, they united to fight against it. When people feel that something is really important, they usually respond.

I wish that we could get people today to realize the importance of participating. We need to get it into the minds of our children. If people got back into informed voting, there would be no problem we couldn't clean up.

When I was a young woman, I got to know a number of the old suffragettes who lived in Austin—Jane McCallum, Minnie Fisher Cunningham, Amelia Evers, and others. They were in their seventies and eighties, and they loved to talk about the days when they were working for suffrage. These suffragettes were actually spat upon and pushed around, and some ended up in jail—all because they wanted to vote.

**SEIZING OPPORTUNITIES:** If I have done anything, it's that I seized opportunities to change things, especially for women.

Texas is a macho state. I couldn't get a job when I got out of law school because there weren't any law jobs for women. I accepted that fact. But then I got the chance to change things as chair of the Marital Properties Task Force on the State Bar of Texas. I had no idea we could change the entire law in only one session of the legislature, but we did. We struck down the Twenty-seven Disabilities of Coverture, and married women in Texas finally got rights.

Pragmatically, you do what you can. You take the talents you have and you go with them. I have taken chances as they have come to me. It has been sort of like catching on to the ring of an old carousel as it comes by. Or, sometimes, I have seen the opportunity and said, "I can do something about that."

I can't say that I've ever had plans for the future. They say that you should write down what you would like to be doing in five years. I just sort of see what there is to be done and then go do it. Opportunities just come sometimes out of the blue sky. I still look for the next ring to catch.

**MENTORS:** I really didn't have a female mentor. Sarah Hughes was not the kind of touchy-feely person we think of as a mentor. But she was there and she made it possible for me to get my first job as a lawyer. She was a gifted judge. I was probably as close to her as anybody else was, but she was not the kind of person whose shoulder you could cry on.

**ADVOCATING WOMEN IN A MALE SYSTEM:** While I was lobbying for the Bar, it was very important that I *not* be known as a feminist, although I was working to get rights for women. I was careful not to be out in front on any of the feminist activities, such as the fight for abortion rights. I would not have had the support in the Bar. I have used the Bar as an avenue to get things accomplished for women.

Let's face it: the older male lawyers tolerated me because I was not very offensive or strident. So I could do my work like a stealth bomber. They didn't even know I was coming. (Laughs.)

**EDUCATING OUR YOUNG PEOPLE:** Most young women have no idea what older women have gone through. So I give speeches. They stare at me and think, "This old lady has been out in the sun too long—telling us all these wild stories!" I hope they are listening so they don't have to repeat all those experiences.

**POLITICS:** Women need a greater voice in the U.S. government. One thing I do to help women get elected is to support EMILY's List (Early Money Is Like Yeast), an organization that raises money to cover early campaign expenses for female Democratic congressional candidates. I am a member of the majority council for EMILY's List. This morning I wrote a check for $1,000 to the organization to help start the ball rolling for the next election year.

It is important for the Republicans also to have groups to support women running for office. Their group is called WISH (Women in the Senate and House). It is proven that the women in Congress have made a difference. Although they represent different parties, Kay Bailey Hutchison, Diane Feinstein, and Barbara Boxer have all been on the same side when it comes to women.

**REPRODUCTIVE RIGHTS:** I think that most women in Congress, both Democrats and Republicans, feel that reproductive rights are important. The women who were elected from the far right wing in 1994 are an exception.

But speaking up for women's reproductive rights can get real touchy. Republican Kay Bailey Hutchison was defeated for representative in Dallas some years ago because of the reproductive rights issue. I had walked the streets campaigning for her. She was *for* reproductive rights. And her male opponent ran a dirty campaign against her.

Pro-choice doesn't mean that abortion is the only choice. Abortion is just one option. If you are against abortion, you don't have to have one.

**MOTHERHOOD:** The aspect of my life that I am most proud of is my family.

In the 1950s and early 1960s when my boys were young, I was one of few mothers working away from home. Society told me that if you were not home twenty-four hours a day, all your kids were going to turn out to be criminals or ne'er-do-wells.

I listened to all that criticism from people and it hurt. I needed to work as an attorney for economic reasons. Looking back, I realize that I was a supermom. I baked cookies for the kids' activities. I was room mother. I worked in the cafeteria at their grade school because moms were expected to take turns working shifts. I was a scout leader. If I had it to do over again, I wouldn't do those things.

**FAMILY:** Family also was important to my parents. I grew up with lots of cousins in my German-Swede community. Immigrant families all settled in clumps. Within my clump there were a lot of cousins. I was the only child in my immediate family, but I had thirty or forty first cousins who lived around me.

Today I get together with my children and grandchildren often. The nicest thing is that all three of my daughters-in-law are each others' best friends. Anytime we have a family crisis, the whole bunch of us handle it.

My husband, Grier, had several heart bypasses ten years before he died. We knew toward the end that he was terminal, and he spent his last three months at home. My sons and daughters-in-law would also come just about every day to help. It was a good experience to allow him to die in his own bed at home with his family there. But it would have been very difficult if I had not had the family support.

**WIDOWHOOD:** Widowhood has been a compelling new experience. Although Grier and I traveled the world during his last ten years of life, we were also used to traveling without each other. For most of our professional lives, one of us always stayed home with the law practice and the kids while the other attended a business meeting. So when he died, I was used to going places on my own and relying on myself.

After he died, I gained one-third more time. I had spent so much time caring for Grier over those many years. It was also the first time I had ever lived by myself, and I enjoy it. My house has become sort of a "Raggio Bed and Breakfast" with so many out-of-town friends coming in and out. I have a downstairs with a bath and den where people can spend the night, and sometimes I don't even see them.

Widowhood has opened up a new life to me. I had spent practically all my life with men—either in the Bar with law activities or with my boys and in boys' activities. And while I knew a lot of women, I really hadn't been active in women's organizations. So I have joined a few and have made hundreds of new women friends—something I had never had.

**FRIENDSHIP:** The International Women's Forum is a group of women worldwide—from Margaret Thatcher to Corazon Aquino. You have to be invited. We have a chapter here in Dallas with about seventy women— Kay Bailey Hutchison and I started the Dallas chapter.

Another group, the Summit, is about seventy-five women, half of whom are not employed outside the home. Some of these women might be champions of industry, but they all are feminine and they all have the same problems.

I am going to New York Thursday for a "Dirty Thirty" meeting— thirty self-appointed best matrimonial lawyers in the United States. We are good friends from all over the country, and we meet every year. Seven are women and the rest are men. We share things that are important to us.

**LEARNING NEW THINGS:** I am still learning all the time—things such as the value of friendship and the value of serving your community. I am finding lots of opportunities to give back to the community. I don't charge to speak. I especially like speaking to young people.

**MONEY:** I remember what life was like in Texas back in the Depression. I am still so frugal. I'll give $50,000 to my church without thinking, but I check out all the specials at the grocery store. And I watch all my pennies. But that is just a part of me, and I might as well understand it. 'Cause you don't live through what I've lived through without it making a big impression on you.

**ENVIRONMENT:** I contribute money to environmental organizations. I belong to everything from the Sierra Club to the Nature Conservancy. It makes me feel really good to write big checks to causes I believe in because it allows me to contribute to progress in many different areas.

**LOOKING TOWARD THE FUTURE:** You have to change your whole focus sometimes to make progress. You can complain about the problems, or you can say, "This is a whole set of new opportunities!"

I am really frosted at George W. Bush right now for allowing a hundred thousand zygotes to be thrown in the trash instead of being used for curing spinal injuries, leukemia, and dozens of other diseases. [President Bush has just announced his decision to allow only limited use of embryonic zygotes for medical research.] It seems like such a travesty to waste the chance for such promising medical advancement. Can you imagine what might happen on the black market now? Private groups are likely to take hold of the new technology using human zygotes and will not be held to the ethics that the government would have imposed if it had taken the responsibility.

However, I still have hope that the government will see the light on the human zygote question. Of course, I won't be around, but I am real excited about what will happen in the next fifty years. We have got to cooperate more on land mines. We can't risk a nuclear war. We must understand that people can't have everything they want and still live in this world. In a legal case, you try to leave with both clients unhappy, i.e., nobody won everything. You've got to learn to compromise.

Pollution in our country affects people all over the world. The world is one community. We've got to look at this as one well-functioning planet.

I liked the good old days, too. But the so-called good old days were sometimes dysfunctional. People who got sick were likely to die. Now we care a lot more about individuals. There is definitely hope for the future when you look at where we have been.

**TEXAS WOMEN:** Texas women have had to overcome machoism, more so than other women in this country. For instance, I was the first woman to be director of the State Bar of Texas in the first hundred years of its existence. Now, you wouldn't have had that problem to overcome in Massachusetts or New York. Women had more opportunities earlier up north than we did here. We have had to fight harder, and we have had more doors to open.

I don't know why it is that Texas women are so funny. But you take Ann Richards, Liz Carpenter, and Molly Ivins. Do you know of any other state that has such comedians among their women? I imagine it is that we have so many things to laugh at.

**NURTURING YOURSELF:** We nurture ourselves with laughter—it's good medicine. Living a long time requires paying attention to diet, exercise, and lifestyle. I've always eaten what is now considered a good diet. No fried foods, lots of vegetables and fruit and fish. I was doing that twenty years ago. I walk at least thirty minutes every day, and my weight, ever since I was a fat teenager, has taken care of itself.

I also try to go to bed at the same time and wake up at the same time. I take vitamins. I'm not on any drugs except for replacement estrogen for my bones.

I really enjoy my church. That gives me a lot of spiritual nurturing.

I also get a lot of nurturing and positive strokes by being asked to be on task forces, advisory committees, and boards.

**BRIDGING THE GENERATION GAP:** One of my granddaughters and I take a trip every year together. I was seventy-seven when we went through the interior of Alaska. We are good traveling partners.

Another granddaughter and I bought EurRail passes and spent fifteen days backpacking through Europe. We found bed and breakfasts along the way.

**IF I WERE A YOUNG WOMAN TODAY:** If I were young today, I would do what my granddaughters are doing. Spend semesters in Europe, learn to speak other languages. But I was really poor as a young woman and didn't have those choices.

**GETTING OLDER:** My favorite age is right now [age eighty-two]. (Knock on wood.) I am still relatively healthy. (My doctors tell me that I'll probably die of something else before my leukemia kills me.) I don't have the responsibilities I had with three young kids. I have enough money and enough to eat. I am comfortable.

There's a poem by Jenny Joseph that Liz Carpenter likes to read. It's about wearing purple when you are an old woman to make up for the sobriety of your youth. Well, I am doing that now. (Laughs.) I certainly speak out more because I figure that nobody is going to hit an old lady. I dare to express myself a lot more. And I travel a lot.

It's been a great trip. And you know, if I die tomorrow, it's going to be fine. I've already gotten probably more than my share of strokes and accolades.

# IRMA RANGEL

Irma Rangel (D-Kingsville), Texas House of Representatives. Photo by Summer Pierce © 1999.

"The truth is that we don't want the standards lowered for us. Once we have been admitted to institutions of higher learning, we want a first-rate education and nothing less."

*Irma*
*Rangel*

B. 1931,
**KINGSVILLE, TEXAS**
CURRENT HOME:
**KINGSVILLE, TEXAS**

Irma Rangel, the first Mexican American woman ever elected to the Texas House of Representatives, has held office since January 1977. She has chaired the House Committee on Higher Education since her appointment in 1995, the year after she retired from her successful private legal practice in Kingsville to devote all of her time to the legislature. She is "pro-choice" and a Catholic. "I love being Catholic, and I became 'pro-choice' when I was assistant district attorney in Nueces County, Texas, and I saw the toll illegal abortions were taking on young women. No health services were available to women who became pregnant from rape and incest. The only thing available in 1971 was a prison term for those who sought an abortion. They had no 'choice.'"

Irma, who makes sure that Anglos pronounce her name correctly (Earmah Ron-hel), was one of three daughters born to parents who both had been orphaned at early ages. Although neither parent had completed grade school and neither spoke fluent English, each was an entrepreneur. Her father, Presciliano, owned a barbershop and became known as one of the most successful business and political leaders in the community. Her mother, Herminia, owned a dress shop. Even though Anglos had circulated a petition to keep the "Mexicans" out of their side of town, Irma's parents were the first Mexican Americans to live on the "other side of the tracks," where they built a five-bedroom house.

Irma and her sisters, Olga and Minnie, learned English in first grade, and all three girls graduated high school at age sixteen. Their parents stressed education, and Irma and Olga earned B.B.A. degrees in business administration from Texas A&I College (now Texas A&M at Kingsville). Irma added to her résumé both an elementary and a secondary teaching certificate. Minnie earned a B.S. degree in pharmacy at the University of Texas. All three daughters entered the public service arena. Olga became a schoolteacher and earned a master's degree in education, and Minnie became a pharmacist.

After fourteen years of teaching public school in South Texas, California, and Venezuela, Irma entered St. Mary's University School of Law in San Antonio, Texas. While teaching the children of Stanford University professors in Palo Alto, California (1964–1966), Irma observed Mexican American activist Cesar Chavez and became inspired. "I felt I could help my people better as an attorney than as a teacher," she said.

The desire to better the lives of her people in South Texas was also the impetus that made her run for state representative when she was forty-five years old. During her years in the legislature, Irma's major emphasis has been to improve both public and higher education systems. In 1993 she was instrumental in passing legislation that netted border colleges and universities well over $400 million. In 1997 she opened the doors of opportunity to a higher education for all students in Texas by passing landmark legislation, House Bill 588, which mandates that the state's colleges and universities automatically admit all high school seniors who graduate in the top 10 percent of their senior class. She passed another bill that allows certain *colonia* residents to connect to utilities so that they may live in healthier and safer conditions.

Some of the many awards and achievements she is proud of include the following:

- 1977 and 1979—Judicial Nominating Panel for the Fifth Circuit U.S. Court of Appeals—appointed by President Jimmy Carter
- 1993—Matt Garcia Public Service Award from the Mexican-American Legal Defense and Education Fund (MALDEF) for her efforts to promote equal opportunity and treatment in education for minorities
- 1994—Texas Women's Hall of Fame—inducted by Governor Ann Richards
- 1997—G. J. Sutton Award from the Seventy-fifth Legislative Black Caucus for her efforts to promote equal opportunity and treatment in education for minorities

- 1998—Margaret Brent Women Lawyers of Achievement Award from the American Bar Association's Commission on Women in the Professions, for contributions to women's rights
- 2000—Women in Government Award from *Good Housekeeping* magazine

Irma refers to herself as Mexican American because "that is what I am," she explains. The word "Hispanic" comes from the Latin word for "Spanish" and is a generalization to indicate Cuban, Puerto Rican, and Mexican American.

"My parents always told us that the word 'Chicano' was a crude term, and I find it difficult to accept, even today. I don't know why the younger generation resorted to the use of the word 'Chicano,'" she says. ("Chicano" comes from the word *(Me)chicano,* a phonetic misspelling of *Mejicano,* a Mexican.)

The memory of her parents is with her daily, not only in her thoughts, but also in her home. Irma still lives in the five-bedroom house in Kingsville that her parents built on the other side of the tracks. She also maintains an apartment in Austin, where she stays when she is working at the Capitol.

**AUTHOR'S NOTE**   *One thing you don't forget about Irma Rangel is her deep, contagious laugh that comes often and easily. Another is her distinctive style of dress: bright-colored scarves, big earrings, and big eyeglasses. All of that draws you in.*

*But her most amazing trait is her sharp mind. I am awestruck when, without notes, she is able to reel off her schedule of meetings for the coming week—several a day. "How do you remember all that?" I ask. "I don't know," she says, smiling. "I've always been able to remember things."*

*She is known for keeping constant eye contact with her audience when she speaks. For any speech under twenty-five minutes, she doesn't use notes. Her steel-trap mind is one reason she has been able to work her way into the "good-old-boy" system of Texas politics and to get much of her legislation passed over the years.*

*I find Irma to be an interesting combination of forcefulness and humility. Before I leave, she thanks me: "I appreciate what you are doing. You are sharing with others what I can't do. I am not a writer, I am just a talker. We women appreciate what you are doing to share our existence." That is a humbling thought.*

*Irma Rangel*

## SPEAKS

**TEXAS WOMEN:** I certainly see myself as Texan, but my identity as a Texas woman is quite different from that of my Anglo friends. Growing up Mexican American in South Texas shaped who I have become. I feel a pride in my people and my culture. My people have a special bond to this land; we were living here centuries before the Anglos came to Texas.

My outlook is influenced also by the poverty I am exposed to near the border. South Texas has more poor people than most other parts of Texas, and certainly more than in most other parts of the United States.

And I have been shaped by the discrimination that we Mexican American women face when we forge our way in the Anglo world. Enduring that prejudice has played a part in making me a stronger, more compassionate person than I might have become otherwise.

**BEING MEXICAN AMERICAN:** When we were little children, my two older sisters and I didn't experience prejudice. We lived in a predominantly Mexican American community, and we were surrounded by our own culture, so we didn't know about discrimination until we started public school. We loved growing up Mexican American in Texas.

Our family was very close-knit, and our parents did not allow us to go on dates or to dances until we graduated from high school. They wanted us to concentrate on our schoolwork. On the other hand, our house was full of guys all the time because we had a Ping-Pong table, and my parents were very welcoming of our male friends. They felt that by being around all of us as a family, the boys would learn respect for us as girls.

Other fathers were very strict with their daughters and wouldn't let them bring guys to their houses, so the guys never got to see those girls interact with their families. Many of our girlfriends would meet the guys at our house and go out with them from there.

**MENTORS:** We were raised with a great sense of responsibility, a lot of obligations, and a very big conscience. We grew up with the expectation of having to work hard for our money.

Our father was unusual for a Mexican American man of that era. He didn't hold us back from pursuing our dreams. Instead, he encouraged us to undertake challenges, whether or not they were seen as traditional for girls.

My mother was also much ahead of her time. She was very ambitious, and with my father's encouragement she started her own dress shop. Even though our father had never been to school and my mother went only through fifth grade, they made sure that we got all the educational opportunities. We felt as if we could go out and achieve—reach for anything we wanted.

My uncle told my mother that she was wrong to give us so much freedom. But her intuition told her differently.

I became an attorney because I had had a role model in that field. Gus Garcia was an attorney who used to visit in our home when I was a young girl. He advocated for Mexican American workers at the King Ranch near Kingsville, and I never forgot all the good he was able to do for our people. Since my parents had instilled confidence in me, I eventually found the nerve to go to law school.

**PREJUDICE:** The sting of racism continued into college. At Texas A&I, all the sororities, cheerleaders, and most football players were Anglo. But we learned to combat the discrimination by trying to excel in sports and academics.

We began to learn that if you place yourself in a position of recognition, such as being an attorney or a state legislator, people might see you on their own level. You might have to do twice the work and learn twice as much as someone with white skin or a different gender, but you must not resent having to put forth that effort. You will be the recipient of that much more knowledge. However, if you aren't being paid the same as the other person, you had better complain.

Our parents told us, "If you are faced with discrimination, the best thing you can do is to ignore the person's ignorance. Laugh it off. The thing is to prove that you can do better than they can."

**HUMOR:** I have found that it is easier to survive in this world if you have thick skin and are not easily offended. A good sense of humor has come in handy in most situations, not the least of which has been surviving the rigors of the Texas legislature.

**PROVING YOURSELF AS A MEXICAN AMERICAN:** When I got to the legislature, I knew that I was being regarded with some suspicion, as I was the first Mexican American woman to be in that leadership position. I had to prove that not all Mexican American women were in the kitchen making tortillas or in the bedroom making babies. I had to combat the myth that Mexican Americans are all asleep under a cactus in our *sombreros*. And I had to show nonbelievers that Mexican Americans are smart and very hard workers, as well as very loyal and dependable.

**WORK ETHIC:** It's a good thing that I enjoy working hard because for the first seventeen years that I was in the legislature, I had to continue running my law practice in order to make a living. (Legislators in Texas earn only $600 a month.) During the legislative sessions, I worked seven days a week—three days in Austin in the legislature and four days, including the weekends, in Kingsville as a lawyer. That work ethic came naturally to me because as a child I watched my parents work hard and enjoy what they were doing. I learned that when you work hard to earn something, you value it more than if it had been given to you.

**POLITICS:** Aside from their daily jobs, our parents also put a lot of their efforts into local politics. They knew that if Mexican Americans could be represented in government, they would have a chance at better lives. Improving education for the children was key. So our parents worked on the grassroots level, informing our people about the candidates and getting them to vote.

That same desire to help my people is why I am in politics today, with education as my main focus in the legislature. When I became chair of the nine-member Higher Education Committee in 1995, five were Republicans and four were Democrats. I said to myself, "My God, how am I going to get any legislation out of this group?"

(South Texas is mostly Democratic, and most Republicans tend to isolate themselves from the problems of the Mexican Americans of South Texas.) But it turned out to be the most beautiful year that I have had. Most of the time we arrived at all of our decisions by a unanimous vote. I found out that it is possible for Republicans and Democrats to agree and to work together for good results. I was able to enhance their knowledge about Mexican Americans and to convince them that, as legislators, they had a choice: to spend more money on educating our people or to spend more money on penitentiaries. It costs approximately $5,000 a year to educate a student in our public schools, as opposed to the $25,000 a year it takes to house a prison inmate.

That year we passed legislation allowing children on welfare free tuition for their first year at the university. As an added incentive, we allowed them $1,000 toward their first year of college if they finished high school in three years. To fund their second year of college, they can apply for grants and scholarships.

**PROUDEST ACCOMPLISHMENTS:** Over the years, I have introduced and carried through many pieces of legislation I am really proud of. Some of them are:

- A program to educate and train women on welfare so they could become self-supporting, productive citizens. During my first session, the legislature had just voted down Sarah Weddington's bill to legalize abortion. I came to the podium next and said, "OK, members. You say you want us to have babies. Now you must provide us education and training to support these babies that you want us to bring into the world." My bill passed right away.
- A bill providing free tuition to teacher aides who wish to become certified teachers. This bill was designed to ease the teaching shortage in Texas.

- A bill making it easier for migrant workers to be able to vote absentee. The migrant workers would have to leave in April—before the May primaries—to pick crops up north. Governor Briscoe assisted me in the passage of that bill.
- A bill to protect big grocery chains from liability if they gave their outdated products to food banks (unless the stores were grossly negligent or malicious). That law allowed food banks to get food that otherwise would have been thrown away.
- A bill allowing the top 10 percent of each high school graduating class to be accepted automatically to state universities. That bill took over two hours to debate on the House floor. If those accepted to college don't make the grade the first semester, they are out. We passed this "top 10 percent" bill after affirmative action had been struck down in Texas in 1996.

**AFFIRMATIVE ACTION:** Many people don't understand the concept of affirmative action. They believe that preference has been given to minorities—that we are asking for lower academic standards. The truth is that we don't want the standards lowered for us. Once we have been admitted to institutions of higher learning, we want a first-rate education and nothing less. The admission standards need to be lowered, and once we are admitted we can prove our academic abilities and prove that we can earn a degree. I said to the board of regents of the University of Texas, "I took the same bar exam as those attorneys who work for Jaworski, and all the other fancy law firms."

If minorities don't become educated, it will be not only a horrible economic disaster for Texas but also a very inhumane cruelty that must not continue. It makes sense for the State of Texas to start investing in the education of minority students so that they can become productive and ultimately put money back into the economy with their taxes.

The population of Texas is soon to become 40 percent Mexican American (up from 27 percent in the mid-1990s), and the African American population will become at least 20 percent (from 11 percent in the mid-1990s). The growth among these two "minority" populations will knock the Anglo-American population to below 40 percent.

The leadership is going to be elected by the majority of voters. So it is reasonable to believe that the future leadership in Texas will come more

and more from the Mexican American and African American populations. And I hope they are educated.

**PRINCIPLES I LIVE BY:** This great sense of responsibility I feel toward others is heightened because I realize that we all have only a short
time on Earth to make a positive impact. Some of the principles that
guide my efforts are

- Honesty.
- Compassion for others.
- Integrity.
- Humility. I remember my father saying, "Look back and see who
  has not been able to achieve as you have. Then try to make sure that
  it won't be as tough for them as it was for you. Give them a helping
  hand and share your wealth of education."
- Equal treatment for everyone. The person who pays $100 a year in
  taxes and the person who pays $100,000 should get the same
  opportunities and the same respect.

**NURTURING YOURSELF:** In order to help other people, you have got
to take care of yourself. So I try to eat well and keep myself in shape
physically. I have a treadmill at my apartment in Austin and a stationary
bicycle at home. I play some golf, I shoot baskets once in a while, and I
walk at the mall.

**PUBLIC SPEAKING:** Part of nurturing myself is allowing myself to say
"no" when I absolutely can't be there for people. But then my conscience
bothers me. It would be wrong of me not to take the time to explain
legislation that I have passed, so when groups ask me to speak, I try to
juggle my schedule around so I can do it. In my job, it is important to be
accessible.

**INDEPENDENCE:** I think that being single helps when it comes to being accessible to others. If I were married, I wouldn't have been able to
devote so much time to my work, and I probably wouldn't have been able
to accomplish so much for so many people. So I look on being single as a
luxury.

I was engaged three times when I was a young woman, but I stayed single through what I suppose were acts of God. One fiancé was killed in an airplane crash two months before we were to marry, another was killed in a car accident, and the third convinced me that marriage would be a mistake.

The older I got, the more particular I became. I became involved in the law profession and in traveling, and I began to value my independence more than I valued the prospect of a husband. I couldn't find anyone who would allow me the freedom that I had gotten used to. My two sisters did get married and have children, so I have nieces and nephews that I enjoy.

Being single allows me to be impulsive. I have no specific plans for the future, but who knows? Tomorrow I might discover a new path for my life, and I wouldn't have to compromise with a partner. I like it that way.

# ANN RICHARDS

Ann Richards, former Texas governor. Photo property of Ann Richards 2001.

"*There seems to be a general feeling that if you are funny, you're not serious. But people don't know how many brain cells it takes to be funny.*"

*Ann
Richards*

B. 1933,
LAKEVIEW, TEXAS
CURRENT HOMES:
AUSTIN, TEXAS,
AND NEW YORK CITY

As the only child of Cecil and Iona Willis, Dorothy Ann Willis took expression lessons, in which children memorized poems and presented them at a recital. "I was nothing but a little-bitty first grader, but I was taught early to stand up and say my piece," said Ann.

Her dad, a truck driver for a pharmaceutical supply house, was known for telling good stories. "I learned that people liked you if you told stories, if you made them laugh."

Her humor, storytelling, oratory skills, and logical mind helped Ann to become one of the most effective and respected politicians in America.

As a teenager, she built a reputation as a brilliant debater at Waco High School and at Baylor College (now Baylor University).

Ann was nineteen when she married her high school sweetheart, David Richards, in 1953 after their junior year in college. She earned a bachelor of arts degree at Baylor in 1954 and a teaching certificate at the University of Texas in Austin after that. While David finished his law degree at UT, Ann taught social studies and history for a year at Fulmore Junior High School, in 1955–1956. She still maintains that teaching is the hardest job she has ever had.

While raising four children in Dallas, Ann involved herself in grassroots Democratic politics, "making phone calls and stuffing envelopes." She remembers, "I was running a household, catering the local Democratic Party, being everything to everybody."

The Richardses moved to Austin in 1969, and Ann was determined to stay away from politics. But two years later, a young Sarah Weddington persuaded her to help run her campaign for the Texas legislature. When Sarah won, Ann became her administrative assistant.

In 1975 Ann's friends urged her to run against the three-term incumbent for a seat on the Travis County Commissioners Court. She won that election and, at age forty-one, became the first female commissioner of Travis County.

Her success as commissioner did not translate into success at home. Her political life interfered with her marriage, and she began drinking heavily. Friends and family members confronted her, and she agreed to go into a hospital for treatment. Two months after she left the hospital, Ann and David separated. They divorced in 1984 after thirty years of marriage. "Getting divorced was the hardest thing I have ever done. Harder than alcoholism, harder than treatment, harder than politics."

Ann was the first woman to win a statewide office in fifty years when she became treasurer of Texas in 1981. She made more money for the state than all the previous treasurers combined—more than $2 billion. In 1988, she delivered the keynote address to the Democratic National Convention.

Ann was elected governor of Texas in 1990 at age fifty-seven. As governor, she stressed education, public safety, economic development, and efficiency. She authorized audits that saved the state $6 billion, held the line against new taxes, and brought home a record $17 billion in federal funds for Texas—up almost 75 percent from the previous administration. She appointed more minorities and women to state posts than the previous two governors combined. Although she was a popular governor, Ann was defeated by George W. Bush in 1994. "I mourned for maybe five or six seconds," she said.

From 1995 to 2001, Ann was a senior advisor with Verner, Liipfert, Bernhard, McPherson, and Hand, a Washington-based law firm with offices in Austin and Houston. Now a senior advisor for Public Strategies, Inc. (PSI), a public relations firm based in Austin, Ann divides her time between Austin and New York City. She is opening an office for PSI in New York with the aim of expanding the company's influence into the international market.

A sought-after speaker, Ann spends about one-fourth of her time on the lecture circuit. Her favorite topics center around women's health issues, including taking care of yourself physically, emotionally, and financially.

She is a founding board member of the Foundation for Women's Resources and sits on the boards of J.C. Penney, T.I.G. Holdings, and the Aspen Institute.

The story of Ann's life before her gubernatorial years can be found in her 1989 book, *Straight from the Heart.*

Today Ann has seven "nearly perfect" grandchildren.

**AUTHOR'S NOTE** *"I hate talking about myself. That subject bores me," Ann informs me as she settles down at her mahogany desk. We are in her modern office suite overlooking Town Lake and downtown Austin.*

*But when Ann finds out that I am more interested in her wisdom than in her life's story, her enthusiasm takes over. And the wisdom begins flowing.*

*She has promised only an hour of her time, but when the hour is over, Ann still has more to say about what really is important in life. "Let's just get these questions answered!" she says.*

*So we continue the interview. When I finish asking questions, Ann fixes her attention on my daughter Heather, age twenty-four, who has taken a day away from her advertising career to be my technical assistant.*

*"So, what are you doing with your life?" Ann asks her. The two fall into a fifteen-minute discussion about careers. Ann's words to Heather speak to all women and are included below, in the "Changing careers" section.*

*Ann
Richards*

## SPEAKS

**SETTING PRIORITIES:** When I was defeated in the gubernatorial race in 1994, it was a dramatic change in my life. I was no longer in public service. My mother was getting old and more demanding of my time, and I wanted to spend quality time with my children and grandchildren.

So, for the first time, I realized that I probably needed to measure the number of years I had left to live—something that people rarely do—and that I'd better decide how I wanted to live those years. I had the opportunity to shape my last years to my liking. I could finally do what I wanted to do. Until then, I had always done what was expected of me or what I felt obligated to do.

I think I have approximately twenty years left. My mother died last year at the age of eighty-six, and I figure I have twenty years to live with all my faculties in place. It was a new experience to be able to see a finite end to my life, rather than living from goal to goal.

So I made a list of the ways I would parcel out my time, because, after all, that's what life is. It's how you spend your time. I decided to make a checklist against which I could weigh how I said yes or no. I put five things on the list (more than five makes it a cluttered exercise) and each of the phrases begins with "I want." They have to be affirmative desires. I didn't include my children on my list because they are always number one.

The list is:

1. *I want to work.* I want to make a living. The goal is that I don't end up in a trailer in my daughter's driveway. I have no desire to be rich,

but I want to work and produce enough income so that I don't have to worry. The older I get, the more I value work. It is something I really like to do.

2. *I want to add to the world that my grandchildren will inherit. I want to be socially responsible.* I don't want to feel like I need to save all the starving children of the world, but I am going to involve myself in social causes that are important and interest me.

3. *I want to work with people I like.* I spent most of my professional life working with people I didn't like. I worked with people I had to work with. So now that I have a choice, I want to be discriminating.

4. *I want to travel for fun, not just for work.*

5. *I want to learn new things.* I have no desire to keep repeating what I already know how to do.

The list has been a real help to me. If I am asked to do something that doesn't meet four out of five of the items on my checklist, I don't do it.

Now there are still obligations, such as doing favors for friends because I owe them something. There are enough of those to take up an awful lot of time. But, by and large, that list is sacrosanct.

**Seizing opportunities:** I've never set goals. People say that if you don't set goals, you can't succeed. But I think a lot of life is serendipitous. It's about seizing opportunity when it occurs.

I want to be open to anything that comes along that might interest me. Right now that is difficult to do because my job takes a lot of time. Time is so precious to me.

**Being true to yourself:** My best advice is be true to yourself. Start doing what makes you feel good.

I am trying to do that for myself. But it has taken awhile. Now that I'm over sixty, I don't feel like I have to "win friends and influence people" anymore. I don't have to mind all the clichés. I don't have to remember the "seven habits of highly successful people" every day. I am finally old enough to realize that all those grandiosities are for somebody else.

I am trying to give myself permission to do what I want to do. It takes a conscious effort to stop and think, "I don't have to do that just because somebody else wants me to. I don't have to think the way other people think."

**TRUTHFULNESS:** One of my strongest suits has always been telling it like it is—being truthful. But it is also my weak suit because sometimes people wish I wouldn't tell it like it is. Sometimes the truth is too harsh.

I have always had integrity and a good grasp of right and wrong and morality—all of those things. But that doesn't mean that I was satisfied with myself as a person. That didn't come until much later. It took me a long time to develop self-respect.

**SELF-RESPECT:** Alcoholism treatment was a great school. It provided me a great opportunity for self-examination and for self-acceptance. It helped me identify the three most important things in my life: the love my children have for me, my own integrity, and my self-respect.

**FAILURE:** If you respect yourself, you learn to see your own failure as a form of success. I've learned a lot of lessons from failure. I can always tell you the things that I didn't do right. For a good part of my life, I always figured that when I succeeded, I had just gotten lucky. That was because I was carrying around the "Willis guilt" that my mother instilled in me.

**GUILT:** To some degree, I still carry that guilt around. I grew up under the pervasive influence of penance. If I was having fun, I felt that I must not be working hard enough. Mama always told me that if you sewed on Sunday you would have to take the stitches out with your teeth in heaven.

Even though I tried not to inflict the "Willis guilt" on my kids, I think I did. You can't overturn a lifetime of influence you got when you were a child, during your most formative years. But during the last fifteen to twenty years, I have tried to butt out of my kids' lives, not in the positive things I do for them, but in interfering ways. And when I do interfere, they are nice about it. (Laughs.)

**GRANDMOTHERHOOD:** I like watching my children and their families develop. I like my seven grandchildren, and they like me. But I am not a baby-sitting grandmother. I have absolutely no interest in that role. I am the grandmother who writes a check.

The things I do with my grandchildren have a purpose. I'm not good at just chatting. I like to spend short periods of time with them. We go to the movies. I like to travel with some of them.

**SIMPLIFYING LIFE:** One thing I hope to instill in my grandchildren is to keep their lives uncluttered—one of the many things I learned from my mother's death.

I learned that your *things* don't matter. The only things that matter are people. My mother was a collector of all kinds of stuff—anything that was worth a penny. When she died I found gold fillings from her teeth. She was so afraid that someone would steal her things that she hid them, and then she would have to make a list of where she hid them, and then of course she would lose the list. I found lots of lists.

She was so afraid that none of us would "appreciate" the stuff she had laboriously collected. She was exactly right. I mean, I couldn't care less about all that cut glass.

It doesn't matter what kind of car you drive. If you are going to run over the neighbor's gas meter, you might as well do it in a Ford rather than in a Mercedes. Toward the end of Mama's life, those things didn't matter to her either. Her cabinets were full of them. All she really cared about was when we were coming to see her.

So my kids and I are going to have the world's biggest garage sale. I'm getting rid of all my stuff—the silver services and the junk that you keep up there in those cabinets that you never use. I'm going to sell a lot of stuff that has been in storage for years. And I'm trying to clear out some of the intellectual and psychological baggage that I have carried around all my life.

It's really kind of sad when I think back about the way Mama did it. She could never go much of anywhere cause she either had to water the yard or feed the dog. I own nothing that I have to feed or water. I don't own a plant. When I come in from out of town, I go to the grocery store and get a flower or something.

**NURTURING YOURSELF:** The best thing I have done for myself and my body is to get a personal trainer. Lifting weights has had a dramatic effect on my health. I didn't have anything specifically wrong with me, but I had the little signs of aging. Now those signs are gone. I had a little heart arrhythmia and that has disappeared. My bone density has improved, and I no longer have signs of arthritis in my hands. My cholesterol is normal for the first time in about fifteen years.

**HUMOR:** Another way I have nurtured myself is with humor. It is a powerful tool. I have always been able to make people laugh, but I honed my humor further in the political arena. Humor clears the air. Once you laugh, your mind opens up and then you are able to hear the other things that are being said.

There seems to be a general feeling that if you are funny, you're not serious. But people don't know how many brain cells it takes to be funny. I've watched [Texas politician] Jim Hightower cut opponents to shreds with humor.

**TEXAS MEN:** Jim is just one example of a Texas politician who has learned the power of humor. Because Texas men (as well as women) tend to have a funny streak, they can make fun of their own stereotypical image of being bubba, backwards, and macho. In spite of that stereotype, Texas men are far more accommodating toward the needs of women than anyone on Wall Street.

**TEXAS WOMEN:** Texas, in general, has been a very accommodating place for women. Back in the 1970s, when I was on the County Commissioners Court, I remember a cover photo on *Parade* magazine. In the picture were several Texas women who were influential in state and national politics at the time: Austin mayor Carole Keeton Rylander, Liz Carpenter, Lady Bird Johnson, Texas legislators Sarah Weddington and Wilhelmina Delco. The number of women in high offices in Texas over thirty years ago was newsworthy enough to be on the cover of that national publication.

My upbringing in Texas has influenced the way I have lived my life. No doubt about it. When you grow up on the frontier, or close to it like I did, you believe there is nothing you can't do. Texans don't seem to abide by the rules. We have a tradition that says rules are made to be broken. That attitude has certainly permeated my life.

**MENTORS:** Texas women have been my most important mentors. Most are part of a group of women ten years younger than I am. No matter what happens to me, it is to that group of women that I turn when I need help. They have been the most influential to me politically, the greatest support to me personally. Cathy Bonner, Janie Hickie, Mary Beth Rogers,

Judith Guthrie, Martha Smiley, Sarah Weddington. This unique group created the Foundation for Women's Resources, a national nonprofit organization started in Austin to further the advancement and achievement of women.

**POWER OF THE FEMALE:** Females with power are willing to pull other women up behind them and help them achieve. Powerful men tend to hoard their power. But women have found that your power grows when you are willing to give it away. I think compassion is innate. Most males can't learn the compassion I'm talking about. Most anybody can grow the intellectual ability.

The female ability to build consensus is a tremendously powerful tool. Women who combine their compassionate nature and their intellectual ability in equal measure have an advantage over most males.

**MOTHERHOOD:** Motherhood has been a powerful way to build both compassion and a consensus-building ability. An added bonus of being a mother is that now that my children are grown, they are my mentors. They are the most supportive, encouraging, and loving support system that anybody could have. They don't smother me and they don't patronize me. They give me my freedom. That is a huge thing.

And I think I have been a pretty good mentor for them, perhaps especially for my daughters. The greatest favor a mother can do for her daughter is to set an example. Next to that, she should make sure that her daughter gets the best education possible, no matter what the cost.

**CHANGING CAREERS:** If you have a good, well-rounded education, your career possibilities are endless. And in today's world, you need to be flexible because you may change careers many times.

Let me tell you something that no one tells you when you are growing up. It's hard to conjure up a career that you don't know about. And so you tend to limit yourself to what you already know.

There is a great world out there. There's a lot of stuff that you don't know about at all. My experience has been that if you are open to change with no restrictions, you have fought half the battle.

We usually make a list of things that make it impossible for us to change. The list might include:

- I have to make as much money as I am making now.
- I have to include my health care benefits.
- It has to be in a neighborhood that is easily accessible.
- I have to be off by three.

If you restrict your choices to what you are used to, the only job that can feel right is the one you are in. A fairy godmother is not going to come down and touch a wand to your head. Good jobs don't come easily, but if you are persistent, you will find the right job. And when you find it, don't talk yourself out of it because it means you might have to make major changes in your life.

If that job turns out to be rotten, well, then, do something else. 'Cause you're going to change careers—not jobs—probably five times in your life. It's really staggering. We don't even know what the careers of the future will be. If we had to list likely careers for young women getting out of business school in five years, we wouldn't know half the jobs. They haven't been invented yet. We don't know enough about the nature of the global economy to envision what the business world is going to be like.

**FINANCIAL SECURITY:** I once heard Gloria Steinem say, "Every woman's greatest fear is that she will be old and poor." And I thought, "Man, if Gloria Steinem is worried about it, then that must mean all of us should be!"

I encourage all young women to think seriously about the importance of financial security. If I were a young woman again, I would train in a field that pays a good salary. In my generation, you trained to be a teacher not because you really intended to teach, but for insurance in case your husband left you and you had to make a living.

Our society encourages women to think that we are supposed to save all the children and take care of all the old people. That message serves the male half of our society well because if women believe it, women will be the only ones providing abundant cheap or free help. And the world of business, economics, and money will always be reserved for the men. While being a full-time caretaker may offer satisfaction, you gain a much greater sense of security and self-sufficiency if you are financially prepared.

**INVESTING MONEY:** Young women need to learn how to manage money and invest it wisely. Mothers should give their daughters money and open a bank account for them. Mothers should introduce children to stockbrokers when they are very young. Girls eight, nine, and ten years old need to start investing money and begin learning how it works. They need to think that money is important.

I am just now learning to deal with stockbrokers. You don't need to have a lot of money to start investing. Stockbrokers will teach you a lot if you are willing to spend the time with them to try to learn it.

**THE POWER OF MONEY:** Now that I am out of office, I have the time to make good money. And I can't tell you what a thrill it is to be able to write a big check as a gift to one of my kids!

If I can write a check to a charitable organization, it means a whole lot more in the long run than if I went down there and gave two hours a day of my volunteer time. In the end, they name the building after the person who wrote the big check, not the one who gave two hours of volunteer time a day.

**LEARNING NEW THINGS:** The stock market is just one area that I am learning more about lately. I learn new things all the time. It's in the nature of my work. For instance, I am on some corporate boards now. Before, I knew nothing about business, other than from a governmental perspective. And now I am really learning from the inside how business works. It has been a fascinating experience. It enables me to push my limits.

**GETTING OLDER:** I keep thinking that I am supposed to be planning for retirement because that's what I read everywhere, but the thought of retiring really bores me.

I'm excited about where my energy and new ideas will have taken me five years from now!

# MARY LOU ROBINSON

Mary Lou Robinson, federal judge. Photo by Summer Pierce © 2000.

"*I learned that you have to deal with the world just the way it is. That doesn't mean that you have to* accept *it the way it is. When you get the opportunity, you can change things.*"

## Mary Lou Robinson

B. 1926,
**DODGE CITY, KANSAS**
CURRENT HOME:
**AMARILLO, TEXAS**

∿

A well-known and respected figure in Amarillo, Texas, since 1950, federal judge Mary Lou Robinson was thrust into the national spotlight in 1998 when her most famous defendant, Oprah Winfrey, spent six weeks in Amarillo during the *Cattlemen v. Oprah Winfrey* trial. A group of Texas cattlemen was suing Oprah for suggesting in a 1996 show that "mad cow disease" might affect beef in the United States.

Despite the media and hype surrounding the celebrated trial, Mary Lou bent no rules and kept her typical stern demeanor in the courtroom. She chastised Oprah once when the TV star caused the courtroom audience to burst into laughter. Oprah commented on having to wear the same few skirts over and over because "Judge Mary Lou wouldn't allow women to wear pants in the courtroom." But later Mary Lou contended that, in fact, she has no such rule in her courtroom. "I have absolutely no idea where Ms. Winfrey got that idea. I wear tailored pantsuits as frequently as I wear skirted suits myself."

To keep the trial from becoming a circus, Judge Mary Lou put a gag order on the participants in the trial. They weren't allowed to talk to anybody outside the courtroom about the case. And the judge's ironclad rule disallowing cameras in the courtroom stood its ground for the trial. Oprah won the six-week case, citing the First Amendment right of free speech.

Oprah said later, "I was totally scared of the judge, totally scared."

But to her grandchildren who live next door and down the block, Mary Lou is just "Grandmother." To her many friends in Amarillo, Mary Lou and her keen sense of humor are fun to be around, though many haven't forgotten that she was the first woman to achieve most of the positions she has held—from judge to Rotary Club member.

Mary Lou has been called a "champion of women's rights" and was a frequent speaker about laws that discriminated against women before the Marital Properties Act was passed in 1969.

She earned her B.A. and law degrees each in less than three years at the University of Texas at Austin and did clerical work to pay her way through school. Mary Lou and her husband, also an attorney, moved to Amarillo in 1950 to set up the law practice of Robinson and Robinson.

At age twenty-eight she was appointed to serve as judge in the County Court at Law—the first woman in Amarillo history to serve in that capacity. During the next twenty-one years she was the first woman to be elected justice of the Court of Civil Appeals and the second woman in Texas, after Sarah Hughes, to become state court district judge.

From 1979 until today, she has been judge of the U.S. District Court for the Northern District of Texas. She was appointed to that position by President Jimmy Carter.

Her oldest child, Rebecca, was born when Mary Lou was in private practice in 1954. She took two weeks away from the bench in 1957 when her second child, Diana, was born. Three years later she delivered Matt, a few days after she had won a district court election. "A judge's robe makes a mighty good maternity garment," she remembered.

Her children—all children—are important to her. Mary Lou was co-founder in 1972 of Opportunity House, a facility in Amarillo for teenagers needing a home. The program eventually housed thirty teenagers in three complexes and, if necessary, allowed them to stay until they graduated high school.

She has had to curtail some of her volunteer work. "Well, now I get tired," she said. "I get to the office about 8:30 A.M. and leave about 6:30 P.M. most days."

She realizes that retirement is somewhere in her future. "I'll step down from the bench sometime," she said. "I think I'll know when that time comes."

**AUTHOR'S NOTE**    *In almost twenty years as a federal judge, Mary Lou Robinson has not given a personal interview until today when I sit down with her. And it is one of the few times in all those years she has allowed a camera on the second floor of the federal courthouse in Amarillo.*

*My photographer daughter Summer and I have no trouble finding a parking spot in front of the courthouse on this cold morning in January. As we find out later, this is the last day an unoccupied parking space will be available within several blocks of the courthouse for the next two months. At the end of our interview, Mary Lou mentions the pretrial hearing to take place tomorrow. "We are getting ready to have a case that involves Oprah Winfrey, and apparently everybody in the world is interested in it. . . . Ms. Winfrey is apparently a highly publicized person. I'm probably the only person in the United States who has never seen one of her shows. They apparently come on in the afternoon when I am working."*

*After the interview as we walk out the front door of the courthouse with our tape recorder and camera equipment, two photographers from New York are trying to talk their way past the guards. They know the rest of the national media are getting ready to descend on this courthouse, and they want a sneak preview. The New York photographers aren't successful at getting past the guards. We just smile at them.*

*Mary Lou says she learns something new every day. As we drive away, I am thinking about the lesson this studious, down-to-earth judge is getting ready to learn about modern pop culture.*

*Several months after the trial's conclusion, I interview Mary Lou again, this time by phone. Her comments about the trial are included in this chapter.*

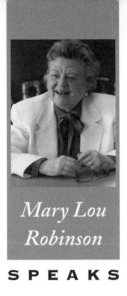

## *Mary Lou Robinson*

## SPEAKS

**SETTING GOALS:** When I was quite young, I decided to become a lawyer. In most people's eyes, that was a strange goal for a woman. But I had encouragement at home.

**MENTORS:** My mother was my best mentor. She expected a high degree of performance from me, particularly academically. She was extremely supportive of the things I wanted to do, and she encouraged me to go to college and then to law school. Before my mother died, I had become a federal judge. She was very pleased.

I think my dad was somewhat amazed that his daughter wanted to do such things. He didn't actively discourage me. He just stood back and watched.

**SEIZING OPPORTUNITIES:** Although women lawyers couldn't get positions in major firms back then, I found out that becoming a lawyer was indeed possible. After law school, my husband and I practiced law together in our own firm, and when I got the chance to become a judge, I took it. I really hadn't planned on being a judge all my life, but when judgeships just seemed to open up along the way, I would think, "Well, I can do that!"

**JUST DEALING WITH IT:** There were many chances to feel thwarted in my early career, but I didn't spend much time being frustrated with the way things were. I learned that you have to deal with the world just the way it is. That doesn't mean that you have to accept it the way it is. When you get the opportunity, you can change things.

**THE CHANGING STATUS OF WOMEN:** When I became a judge, women in Texas could not serve on juries. A married woman could not enter a contract or sue for her own wages. Her husband had to sue for her, and if he declined to sue, she couldn't collect.

Things are dramatically different today for women. It's just a whole new ball game. And that's the way it ought to be.

I think that juries are quite comfortable now with women lawyers in the courtroom. When I first came to the federal bench in 1979, it took the jury a little while to get used to a woman lawyer in the courtroom, not to mention a woman judge! One assistant U.S. attorney said she knew that the first thing the jury did was check out her clothes. But I don't think you see that now. The professional problems women face now are more the glass ceiling type, in which they are thwarted in their attempts to achieve the upper levels in management.

**LOOKING TOWARD THE FUTURE:** I think women are going to do well in the future. However, in the meantime, I am seeing our society being thrown into a crisis because of all these changes in sexual and racial politics, and in technology. In the long run, however, I think change will be good for us. The challenge is to get along with each other amid all the transition. Our laws are lagging a little behind all these changes in society and technology, but I think we'll get there.

My own children are sharp. They are a part of what I am talking about because they are going to meet those challenges. When my grandchildren have to show me how to program a VCR, I realize that what seems really remarkable to someone my age is not so remarkable to the younger generations.

**WHAT MAKES ME FEEL ALIVE:** Computers and VCRs may perplex me at times, but what I really like is to plunge myself into a difficult legal question. I am exhilarated when I get to work really hard and to see the question start to resolve itself. I enjoy interesting courtroom trials; I like managing the docket and moving things along.

**CAREER CHALLENGES:** I am lucky that I get to do work I like. When I come to work in the morning, I never know exactly what is in store. My cases are different every day, and I learn new things every day. I never get bored.

Recently we tried a case involving contracts for an unmanned plane that would replace U2 spy planes. I see on the horizon lawsuits dealing with "designer genes." Those things are pretty interesting and exciting. In law we are on the cutting edge of what's happening.

Of course, we also try a lot of less exciting cases, but those cases are very important to the litigants.

**OPRAH WINFREY TRIAL:** One recent case was exciting to the whole country, it seemed: *Cattlemen v. Oprah Winfrey*. Although the daily scene outside the courthouse was full of national media and others wanting to get a peek at the television star, inside the courtroom was business as usual.

Since the trial was so highly publicized, we imposed the gag order well before the trial started and carried the gag rule through to the end of the case. No one involved in the case was allowed to speak about it outside the courtroom because we felt that irreparable harm would occur if the jury were tainted by continuing comment by participants.

There was simply no problem in the courtroom. We had good lawyers. Recesses did take a few more minutes because usually there was a large crowd, and we had to get people in and out.

The trial itself was interesting because of the questions involved. You had the First Amendment question of freedom of the press; you had Ms. Winfrey, who is a national public figure; and you had the cattle industry, in which there is a high level of interest in the community. But there was nothing in the courtroom that would reflect that it was a sensational trial. And it was certainly not the most demanding trial we have ever tried.

I can't emphasize enough that it takes incredibly good staff to make things run smoothly under such circumstances. The clerk's office handled the media, the courtroom deputy handled the jurors, and the marshal's office guarded the perimeter and the spectators coming into the courtroom. That team of staffers knew what I wanted and they made it happen.

The back parking lot was a "no trespassing" area, and we had permitted Ms. Winfrey to come in the back if she chose so she could avoid the crowds. There was always a group of cameramen outside the fence. Because I was not personally accessible to the press, they seemed to really want to get a picture of me, so they would take my picture through the fence. I didn't object to it. They had a job to do. And it was a significant case.

**GRANDMOTHERHOOD:** During the Oprah trial and all the others, I have always been able to make the transition from the courthouse to home quite easily.

Away from work, the biggest part of my life is my family. I spend a lot of time with my grandchildren. Three grandchildren live next door, two down the street, and two in Dallas. The Amarillo children are always coming and going in my house. If for some reason they are spending the evening with me, it's not as if I am baby-sitting. They are just there a little longer than usual. They like to play in my backyard—I still have the swings and playhouse.

All my children and grandchildren were here for Christmas. It was pretty wild. In fact, the first grader left a chemistry experiment on my kitchen table and it exploded and sent olive oil and broken glass flying all over my kitchen in the middle of the night, just last night. (Laughs.) I was late to this interview because I was cleaning it up, and my hands are still slick with the oil.

Of course, I get a lot of pleasure from my children, too. When you talk about your grandchildren, sometimes you forget to mention your children. But the fact is, I was a mother before I was a grandmother, and I still feel very motherly.

**MOTHERHOOD AND WORK:** The traditional thing for working mothers to say is, "Oh, I wish I had spent more time with my children," or "I wish I hadn't worked so late," or something like that.

But I really can't say that. I have never wished that I hadn't worked late that night. But then, nothing terrible has happened. I spent a lot of time with my children while they were growing up. But I was working full time also.

Work—either at home or away from home—is important. Doing what you do and doing it well. I know of no substitute for long, hard hours.

My daughter-in-law spends a lot of time chauffeuring. I didn't have to do that. For one thing, we very deliberately moved close to the school so our kids could walk to school. And my children weren't involved in as many lessons and sports as today's kids seem to be.

I think every parent has to organize family life differently depending on what resources they have at their disposal. It's helpful to have other family members near enough to pinch-hit. It also helps to bring in the salary of a professional, because then you can hire someone to come in to help.

**COOKING:** I was able to hire someone to clean and do everything but cook. I have always cooked. I like to cook, but I'm not crazy about fixing meals. There is a big difference.

**CHILDREN:** I don't think it hurts children to know that Mother or Daddy has important things to do, and that they can't be present at a certain time because they have to work. Children certainly shouldn't feel that they are not important.

It's kind of nice to be the boss at work. If you need to leave during the day, you can. The work was always there, so I could reschedule my hours when I needed to.

**SETTING PRIORITIES:** When we were raising our family, our two major activities were working and tending to our children. Everything else fit in around those two things. You have to know what comes first.

My kids have chosen lifestyles very similar to mine. They are doing work that they enjoy. They are very involved with their children.

**YOUNG ADULTS:** I'm excited about young people today. I am working with some young lawyers just out of law school, and they give me faith in what young people are doing. Not only are they bright and capable, but they want to do what is right. Their motivation is in the right place.

**SELF-CONFIDENCE:** My advice to young people is this: don't build cages for yourself and don't let other people build cages for you. Decide what you want to do and give it a try. Maybe you can and maybe you can't, but find out if you can.

**TEENAGERS:** I like teenagers; I think they are funny. Through the Rotary Club, I have mentored high school students for many years. The students follow me around and find out what it is like to be a lawyer and what really happens. They get to be a bug on the wall. They have lunch with us here in the office and listen to our conversations.

**SENTENCING:** On the other hand, I deal with young people who are on the other side of the law. Young men make up the majority of defendants, both first-time and repeat offenders. The extremely long prison sentences for some crimes, such as crack cocaine, seem inappropriate to me and to many other judges. We think that most young men probably can be rehabilitated.

Some of the laws and sentencing guidelines that come down from Congress are too severe for the crime. Not every defendant deserves that severe a penalty. However, our role as judges is to follow those rules. Quite often we feel we don't have enough flexibility.

We have to render decisions based on the law, sometimes in spite of our gut feelings. It leaves us uncomfortable. The judges, together with the sentencing commission, have gone to Congress and asked them to modify those guidelines, but so far it hasn't happened.

**FAITH:** I view every person—a criminal defendant or anybody else—as a child of God. I am responsible for what I do to God's child. Now I am sure that a lot of criminal defendants don't think I feel that way, but I really think that each of them is important.

**HELPING THE UNDERDOG:** Young people are important. Helping young people has always seemed an appropriate thing for me to do. So when I see a chance to do that, such as helping to found Opportunity House or mentoring teenagers, I do it. And I enjoy it.

I don't have pretentious feelings about why I do these things. I don't think that we need to solve all the problems in the world and solve them permanently. We just need to do what we can do while we are going along.

I have learned that things are not going to stay fixed. We, as a community, have to keep working on societal problems all the time. The price of most any worthwhile endeavor is eternal vigilance—continuing work, continuing interest. You find that there are a lot of people out there who have the same desire to see things work out well. When my husband was ill, I had to step back from much of my community work to care for him, and others took over and continued where I left off.

**WIDOWHOOD:** It was really hard to lose my husband. I would find myself thinking that there was something I needed to tell him, or something that he would enjoy—even long after he passed away. It is hard to adjust to the fact that someone who has always been there and who's been a part of your life for nearly forty-five years just isn't there anymore. But of course you have no choice but to move on.

You reach a new stage of life where you must find compensations to make up for the losses. You can find certain advantages. Let's face it, typically, women are always taking care of someone, be it children, husbands, or parents. There is something to be said for living alone. There is a certain freedom. You do not always have to plan what you do to accommodate other people.

**ENJOYING LIFE:** I have enjoyed each part of my life as I have gone through it. And I'm still having a good time! Some of my best advice is this: Don't lose today in trying to get to tomorrow!

Sarah
Weddington

B. 1945,
ABILENE, TEXAS
CURRENT HOME:
AUSTIN, TEXAS

Sarah Weddington is a nationally known attorney and spokesperson on leadership and public issues. In 2000 *Texas Lawyer* named her one of "102 of the 20th century's most influential lawyers" and the *Houston Chronicle* called her "one of the most important Texans of the century."

Sarah is best known for successfully arguing the landmark *Roe v. Wade* case before the U.S. Supreme Court in 1971 and in 1972 when she was twenty-six and twenty-seven years old. She is thought to be the youngest woman ever to win a case in the Supreme Court. (No records are kept on the age of lawyers who go before the Supreme Court.)

By a seven-to-two vote on January 22, 1973, the court announced its decision: a constitutional right to privacy gives women the right to choose whether to continue or terminate a pregnancy. The court then added dictum (suggestions) about how states might implement the new decision. Dictum suggested the "trimester" system of regulation, which allows the right to an abortion in the first three months of pregnancy if the abortion is performed by a physician. During the second and third trimesters, each state can make more restrictions, even prohibiting abortion in the last trimester. Since 1973, these standards have been changed by subsequent decisions of the Supreme Court. In general, however, the government still cannot make abortion in the first trimester illegal.

With the help of attorney Linda Coffee of Dallas, Sarah had filed the case in 1970 to overturn a Texas law prohibiting all abortion, except if necessary to save the woman's life. They hadn't expected their lawsuit to reach the Supreme Court. But when a state law is overturned in the Supreme Court (as the Texas abortion law was in 1973), the decision automatically applies to all states.

A few days before the decision was announced, Sarah had begun her first term in the Texas legislature. At age twenty-seven, she had just become the first woman from Austin to be elected to the Texas House of Representatives, a position she had sought in order to fight for women's issues on the state level. Ann Richards, who later became governor of Texas, served as a campaign manager and then as Sarah's administrative assistant. Sarah served three terms in the legislature before going to Washington as U.S. Department of Agriculture general counsel in 1977. From 1978 to 1981 she served as an assistant to President Jimmy Carter, "the most exciting job I ever had," she said. From her office in the West Wing of the White House, she directed the administration's work on women's issues and appointments of women to government posts. She was also in charge of outreach to public leaders across the country.

In an autobiography published in 1992, *A Question of Choice,* she tells of her upbringing in West Texas, of an abortion in a Mexican border town in 1967 when she was a frightened law school student, and of the events leading up to arguing her first contested court case, *Roe v. Wade,* before the Supreme Court. Sarah was a founding board member of the Foundation for Women's Resources, which created Leadership Texas in 1983. Leadership Texas provides women leaders with essential information, an awareness of ongoing changes, sharpened skills, and the initiative, where necessary, to rewrite the rules. Over the years, the programs have attracted over two thousand women of diverse experience.

She grew up Sarah Catherine Ragle in the conservative environment of the small West Texas towns of Abilene, Munday, Canyon, and Vernon. She was the oldest of three children of a Methodist minister father and a mother who had been a high school basketball coach and a college teacher before becoming a minister's wife. Sarah earned a B.A. in English and speech at McMurry College in Abilene when she was nineteen and was one of forty women among the sixteen hundred students in the University of Texas School of Law in 1965 when she was twenty. At age twenty-two, she married fellow law student Ron Weddington. Although no longer married, the two remain friends.

Today Sarah heads the Weddington Center, which she founded. The center focuses on expanding the world for women and teaching women and men leadership skills and attitudes. She travels extensively, speaking on the development of leadership skills and about women's issues. Sarah is an adjunct associate professor at the University of Texas at Austin, where she teaches courses that include "Leadership in America" and "Gender-Based Discrimination." She is presently working on a book about leadership and self-renewal.

Sarah is one of thirty-nine Unforgettable Women honored with special display cases in the Women's Museum, which opened in September 2000 in Dallas. Memorabilia from her work on *Roe v. Wade* share a display case with memorabilia of two other honored American women, Babe Didrikson Zaharias and Amelia Earhart.

Sarah's biggest challenge, however, has been her fight against breast cancer. She was diagnosed in April 2001 and has experienced six weeks of chemotherapy, followed by six weeks of daily radiation. Her radiation treatments are being administered as this book goes to press.

**AUTHOR'S NOTE** *Fresh off her twenty-fifth anniversary of* Roe v. Wade *speaking tour, Sarah is in the process of switching career gears this hot Austin afternoon. The walls of her office, in an old Victorian house not far from the State Capitol, are being painted, and the books and papers are stacked from floor to ceiling. The heat is stifling, and, because the paint is drying, all the doors and windows stand open. But Sarah, dressed in her typical business suit with long sleeves, isn't bothered. Her makeup is fresh, and her graying hair is pulled back in her trademark French roll.*

*Nonplussed by the chaos the painters have made of every room in the house, Sarah pushes aside stacks of files on the table to make room for our interview and begins chatting as if we are old friends. I recognize the West Texas friendliness. She graduated high school in Canyon, a town just down the road from my hometown.*

*She talks about trying to get her new book off the ground, about trying to learn more about the computer, about starting a workout program. She has the summer to reorganize her life before classes start again in the fall.*

## Sarah Weddington

# SPEAKS

**ROE V. WADE:** *Roe v. Wade* is my proudest accomplishment. It is probably the best-known case in the United States today, and I am proud that it has given women more choices about their bodies and their lives.

When I toured the country in 1998, speaking in celebration of the twenty-fifth anniversary of *Roe v. Wade,* I started my speeches with the words, "If anybody had said to me in 1973, 'In twenty-five years, you will still be fighting for reproductive rights,' I would never have believed it." I thought (naively) that since the case had been decided by the U.S. Supreme Court, we could move on to other fronts. But since 1973, a major part of my day-to-day work has revolved around preserving pro-choice and working for progress on other women's issues. Even today, there are a lot of forces trying to push back the advances that we made with *Roe v. Wade* and other groundbreaking women's rights achievements. It is a lot more fun to be making forward progress than being bogged down defending past gains, as we are today.

Some women of my generation remember our fight for rights as being like isometric exercises. We got stronger because we were pushing against resistance. A fifty-five-year-old woman said to me recently, "I feel that to work on women's issues, you need to wear a steel hat and have spiked boots." Well, maybe not, but vigilance and persistence are definitely required.

**REPRODUCTIVE RIGHTS:** Many young women today are pro-choice but lack the passion of the older generation because they have never experienced a time when reproductive choice wasn't their own. They perceive no obvious threat to that right. In fact, the opposition is still there, but it is often more subtle, more difficult to pinpoint. The truth is that women in their age group would be most affected by a defeat of pro-choice principles.

A woman on a college campus recently said to me, "What is the big deal? Why are you still talking about this? If I need an abortion, I know where I can get one." She wasn't thinking (or may not know) of the decreasing number of doctors who perform abortions. The shortage is due, in part, to the violence and harassment aimed at those who work at clinics that include abortion among the services offered. That young woman doesn't realize that rural and poor women are gradually losing access to abortions because of fewer funds and limited access. Women with money and sophistication can still easily receive a safe, legal abortion today. But those who are young or poor or in military service or in rural areas often run into roadblocks.

**FLEXIBILITY:** I have finally let go of the idea that if I work hard enough and am organized enough, I will get everything straightened out. The minute I thought everything was straight, something always messed it up. Learning to be flexible makes life a lot easier in the long run.

One thing I have learned is that the abortion issue simply is not over. I wish we could declare a final, lasting victory, but there are constant skirmishes. I won't give up my goal, but I will be more flexible about the time frame of that goal. When Gerald Ford spoke at the LBJ Library in Austin a few years ago, he told this story: President Johnson invited Everett Dirksen, (former) senator from Illinois, down to the White House in hopes of passing a certain measure that Dirksen didn't really like. LBJ finally said, "Senator, you should give me what I want if you want to have any hope of getting what *you* want." Dirksen drew himself up to his full height and said, "Mr. President, I *never* vary from my principles. I am always true to my principles. But one of my principles is flexibility."

**OPTING OUT:** After you have given a demanding project or job your all, it is reasonable to opt out for a while. An Olympic runner would never be expected to run the same race the next day. It would not be possible. Many boards have built "opting out" into their bylaws. An organization's past president continues to be a member of the board but is not expected to be in charge of anything. She is called on for her wisdom.

Although I will always be involved in the ongoing battle for pro-choice, it is time for me to step back and let members of the younger generations step into that leadership position.

**LEADERSHIP:** My biggest focus right now is teaching, writing, and speaking about leadership, a skill I have honed during the first half century of my life.

Leadership takes years of practice. You don't become a leader overnight or by reading a book. You can learn leadership skills in lots of different contexts. I talk about leadership not being a matter of title, but being an element within a person. Leadership occurs when a person sees a need and determines to find a better way.

**TAKING CHARGE:** I like to tell about Wilhelmina Delco of Austin, who began her public career in the early 1960s because she wanted her kids to have more streetlights on their way to school. She decided that the PTA would be the best place to start. After successfully chairing the PTA, she was elected to the school board, and then to the state legislature—becoming influential because she wanted to find a better way to educate kids. Most of the women who go into politics do so because they see problems that need fixing. That's why I went into the state legislature—to fight for women's issues and other issues that I cared about.

In speaking about leadership, I encourage people to step up and offer to take charge when they see need. But they shouldn't expect to carry all the weight themselves. Being in charge requires putting together a team and delegating responsibilities. Otherwise, the leader gets bogged down and burns out quickly. Each person should create her own best style of leadership as she progresses. All leaders are different, but the most effective ones know how to delegate.

**HANDLING CRITICISM:** When you are in a leadership position, you are going to spark attacks and jealousy. An old saying goes, "The pioneers take the arrows." Other people have talked about the "crab theory" of leadership. It says that one never has to put a lid on a bucket of crabs because as soon as one crab looks like it might be climbing over the top, the others pull it back. The farther one gets out in front, human nature makes others say, "She is not so smart after all."

A lot of women, including myself, care what other people think. We were taught to please others and to make them feel comfortable. I had to unlearn that "skill" when the need to accomplish issue goals required it.

**TEXAS WOMEN:** Texas is known for the unusual number of its women leaders who emerge on the national scene. People I meet from outside of Texas often see Texas women as being outspoken and self-confident. In my travels I'm often asked, "What do they *do* to you Texas women?" They are usually thinking of women like Ann Richards, Molly Ivins, Liz Carpenter, Lady Bird Johnson, Linda Ellerbee, and Barbara Jordan, and perhaps me. I usually reply, "Maybe it is that Texas is still a pioneer state. No one ever says to anybody here in Texas, 'Who were your parents?' Your ability to accomplish things is not based on what your family heritage is, as it so often is in the East. It's just based on what *you* can do."

Now that Texas is becoming more homogeneous because so many people are moving in and out of the state, many of us don't have as pronounced a Texas accent as we used to. And we probably don't have as pronounced a Texas character either.

**LEARNING FROM MEN:** A survey by Leadership Texas a few years ago found that the majority of women CEOs in their thirties and forties had been raised by very supportive fathers. That's not to say that mothers were not important, but rather that when these CEOs were young, their fathers were the role models that set the pattern for work outside the home. Most women of that generation grew up and were hired into companies where men were the dominant participants. Perhaps while those female CEOs were young, their fathers gave them the confidence to deal effectively with men in the other contexts.

I found that survey very interesting. I was close to my father, and my mentors were men. I am wondering if, in years to come, women will be using their mothers as role models for their leadership skills because their mothers will have been in such positions themselves.

**FEAR OF FAILURE:** I find that women, more than men, are reluctant to try things they can't do perfectly. So a lot of women hold themselves back from things that they actually could do very well. When I left the White House, I decided to go skiing. I had never skied, so I took lessons. They taught me to keep my skis parallel, to bring my shoulders around, and the other basics that make one a good skier. I went up on the baby slope and tried to come down perfectly. Finally, after reaching the bottom of the hill, I said to the instructor, "I have come all the way down and I did not fall once!" And he said to me, "Then you will never be any good. The only people who become skilled are the ones who will go a little faster than they know how to control, but who, if they fall down, have learned how to get back up."

I don't want my students to be like the inexperienced skiers who come off the top of the hill, going ninety-to-nothing and yelling, "Help, I can't ski!" But I do want them to practice and to take some risks. I tell them that you don't have to be perfect. And no matter how old you are, you should always be in a learning mode.

**TOOTING YOUR OWN HORN:** Women, especially, need to be willing to take risks and to get back up when they fall down. Women are usually more self-critical than are men. When something goes wrong, a woman in a leadership position will typically say, "What did I do to cause that?" Whereas a man in the same position typically says, "Who did that?"

We women can usually outline our faults better than our strengths. That's why, when I facilitate a group of midlevel women leaders, instead of always having them introduce themselves, I sometimes ask, "Will you please introduce the person next to you?" Traditionally, women have made other people feel good. It is a good skill we have acquired. We are very good at pushing someone else into the spotlight. But we also have to learn how to spotlight ourselves. A Hispanic congressman once said, "He who tooteth not his own horn, his horn goeth untooted."

**MENTORS:** Among many other valuable lessons, my male mentors taught me to "toot my own horn." I was on the front edge in the 1970s and 1980s when women were finally emerging as leaders in traditionally men's fields such as law and politics. There weren't many women who held the positions to show me how to do things, and I was lucky to have a series of men who were helpful in letting me just watch them do their jobs.

John Sutton, my former UT law professor, was the first lawyer who hired me to work for him. He knew that, because I was a woman, no law firm would hire me. He also knew that I was both a good writer and researcher and a hard worker. The relationship was "employer-employee," but I used that opportunity to ask him questions and to observe him and the other men on the committee we worked with. He also had been an FBI agent and a trial lawyer, so he could tell me a lot about developing the skills of a lawyer.

My most important mentor was Bob Johnson, the parliamentarian when I was in the Texas House of Representatives. He taught me the importance of human relations skills. For example, one day I saw him heading over to see Lieutenant Governor Bob Bullock. I said, "What are you going to talk about?" He said, "I don't know. It depends on what kind of mood he is in." Now that thought would never have occurred to me. I would have prepared my list of discussion topics, and I would have gone through it, regardless of what kind of mood Bob Bullock was in—and he was famous for mercurial moods. Of course, that would have been a mistake.

My speaking style comes in large part from watching my father preach while I was growing up. He was an excellent speaker. I use a lot of that storytelling heritage to illustrate principles in my speeches today. People tell me that those stories help them remember the points I make.

I also use lots of humor in my speeches, a trait I learned from Ann Richards, one of the funniest women around. I used to be too serious about everything, and she taught me the value of humor. I learned one-liner techniques watching Ronald Reagan.

**NURTURING YOURSELF**: You must build in more laughter, more enjoyment, more time with friends. It's easy to say, "I don't have time to relax with friends because I have too much work to do." But as I get older, I realize that you have to recharge your energy in order to remain effective.

**STARTING OVER**: Although most of my mentors have been men, most of my support networks are made up of women. They have been there for me at critical crossroads, both professional and personal. I have discovered over the years that life is a series of course corrections. Each of us sets off in a carefully planned direction, but a lot of things happen along the path that we never foresee.

I have had to start over a few times. For many years, my life was on an upward trajectory. My legislative years gave me the springboard to go to Washington as general counsel of the Department of Agriculture, which gave me the springboard to go to the White House as an assistant to the president. When President Carter was defeated, I thought, "Now what do I do?" No upward trajectory was readily apparent. Later I came back to Austin, helped my sister through the last days of her cancer, and began reinventing myself through teaching at the university and writing.

When you reach a crossroads and need to make a transition, the first thing to do is to sit down with people you really trust and say, "This is the situation I am in. What would you do if you were in my shoes?" You can get some really helpful ideas.

**GETTING OLDER:** As I get older, I listen to younger people differently because I realize that they are inheriting the world. People who are now in their thirties and forties are going to have more impact in the next ten years than I will. They are in their years of greatest energy and opportunities. The thirties and forties seem to be the "do it" years, when you are so busy that you don't have as much time to read and reflect and think.

In the past I thought of myself as a principal actor. Now that I am in my fifties, I am becoming more reflective, a little more internal. I am beginning to think about conserving energy and financial resources. I am thinking about what wisdom I have acquired and how to share it with somebody else.

Whether you are writing, speaking, or teaching, I think you are in a "guide role." You are saying, "I have been down this path. Here are the things I saw." It's almost like being a travel-book writer. You are trying to figure out how to save people some heartaches or some wrong paths— how to share with them what you have been through so they can get further down the road faster. You can tell them where the detours are and how to avoid roadblocks.

**CANCER:** That's what I'm doing now, since I have been experiencing the biggest challenge of my life: breast cancer. I am writing a series of first-person op-ed pieces for the *Austin American-Statesman,* sharing my thoughts, emotions, and the lessons I am learning along the way.

Everything I've learned underlines the importance of early detection. Women whose cancers are found early have the best treatment options and survival rates. If my tumor had been small, surgery would have been less invasive and chemotherapy probably not necessary. Women must understand how important it is to do self-exams regularly and correctly.

I have shed many tears through these past few months, but my "let's-do-something-about-this" self has reemerged. I volunteered to participate in a study comparing various chemo treatments to see which one was best. Let's hope the results from the current fifteen hundred volunteers will help those diagnosed in the future.

**LOOKING TOWARD THE FUTURE:** For many months I've been thinking about how to design the memorial for my Texas State Cemetery plot close to Big Foot Wallace, a bachelor and early Texas raconteur. When I recently asked friends for suggestions, I didn't connect those queries—as they did—with my newly found cancer. They worried that I was much more upset than I was letting on. However, we all shared a good laugh when they learned I recently bought five pairs of earrings from a woman designer. They decided I had faith in my future if I was willing to buy so many earrings.

I certainly am not in any hurry to spend my days next door to Big Foot. I'm eager to get back to dancing country-western at the Broken Spoke.

# JUDITH ZAFFIRINI

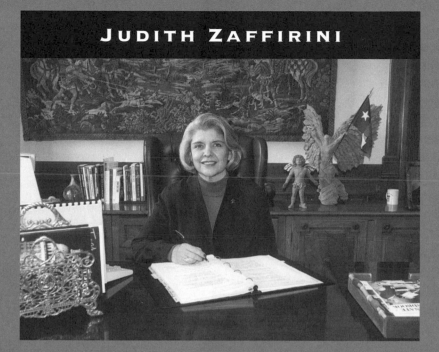

*Judith Zaffirini (D–Laredo), Texas Senate.*
*Photo by Senate Media Service.*
*Courtesy of Judith Zaffirini.*

"*Do not ask anyone to do anything that you would not do yourself. My staff works hard, but not harder than I.*"

B. 1946,
LAREDO, TEXAS
CURRENT HOME:
LAREDO, TEXAS

~

Judith Zaffirini (D-Laredo) began serving in the Texas Senate in 1987 when she was forty years old. She was the first Hispanic woman to be elected to the state senate and has won in landslide elections each time she has run. In recent elections, Senator Zaffirini has carried all counties in her large, diverse district of South Texas, a feat no one else has ever accomplished.

She serves as chair of the Senate Human Services Committee and is a member of the Senate Committee on Education and the Special Committee on Border Affairs. The only senator with career-long 100 percent attendance and 100 percent voting records, Senator Zaffirini has cast well over 22,000 consecutive votes in her Senate career. She has sponsored and passed more than 360 bills, and cosponsored and passed nearly 200 more.

Among them are bills to immunize all Texas children, to restrict minors' access to tobacco, and to reform Medicaid, indigent health care, welfare, nursing homes, adoption, and child support. Calling herself a "pro-life feminist," Judith crossed party lines and played a key role in passing a 1999 bill mandating parental notification before minors have abortions.

Fellow senator Jeff Wentworth (R-San Antonio) once said, "She does her homework and lines her votes up ahead of time. I don't think she ever is unprepared or surprised."

Judith has received more than 350 awards and honors for her legislative, public service, and professional work. In 1997 she became the first Hispanic female and only the fifth woman to serve as Governor-for-a-Day, an event that attracted more than three thousand Texans. An elementary school in Laredo is named in her honor. *Texas Monthly* named her one of the Ten

Best Legislators for 1997. The Women's Chamber of Commerce of Texas named her one of the 100 Texas Women of the Century. She is also known around the Capitol as the senator who bakes desserts to share with everyone.

Judith owns her own business, Zaffirini Communications, through which she provides professional communications services, including consulting, workshops and seminars, one-on-one coaching, and keynote addresses. She holds bachelor of science, master of arts, and Ph.D. degrees in communications from the University of Texas at Austin—all of which she earned with a 3.9 grade point average.

Judith was the third sibling of four sisters and was raised in a close-knit family in Laredo. She went to mass on Sundays with her family and every day at St. Peter's Elementary School. Two of the four sisters went to college and earned advanced degrees. She credits her discipline, work habits, and values largely to the influence she received from her high school teachers, the nuns at Ursuline Academy in Laredo. Today Judith is a lector at Blessed Sacrament Catholic Church in Laredo. She and her husband, attorney Carlos Zaffirini, have been married since 1965. Their son, Carlos Jr., was four years old when Judith began her first term as senator in 1987.

Carlos Jr. has inherited the Greek and Mexican heritage of his mother, as well as the Italian and Mexican heritage of his father. "Zaffirini is an Italian name," Judith explains. "My paternal grandfather came from Greece to Laredo and married a Mexican American woman at approximately the same time that my husband's grandfather came from Italy to Laredo and married a Mexican American woman. They all made Laredo their home, as have Carlos and I throughout our lives."

**AUTHOR'S NOTE**   *It is unusual for Judith Zaffirini to leave in the middle of a Senate committee meeting, but she makes an exception today to meet me for our scheduled interview at the Capitol. It is between legislative sessions, and she is in Austin for a day of meetings at which agendas are being planned for next year's session. (The Texas legislature meets in regular session every other year for five months.)*

*In typical Zaffirini fashion, she wears a business suit, silk blouse buttoned at the neck even on this warm spring day. "My idea of informal wear is an open collar," she says. "As a senator, you are always on, and you have to dress appropriately." She wears flats instead of heels, a practice she has kept since 1980. "You also have to be comfortable," she adds.*

*Judith doesn't spend a lot of time outdoors and explains that most of her exercise occurs on the treadmill each evening in her hotel room in Austin or at home in Laredo. "Ursuline girls never sweat. We perspire," she says with a smile.*

*Judith Zaffirini*

## SPEAKS

**BEING MEXICAN AMERICAN:** Growing up in a bilingual, bicultural, binational border town broadened my perspective, increased my understanding of diversity, and enriched my outlook. The dominant population of Laredo is Mexican American, so we have never been the minority in our community. I had never felt discrimination and oppression, as did some of my Senate colleagues who consider themselves "minority" senators.

So I was shocked when I ran for office for the first time and realized that some of the people from the northern counties of my district had negative attitudes toward Mexican Americans, especially those from Laredo. Then I began trying to consider the problem from their perspective. Frankly, I decided that they just didn't know any better; they had had limited experiences. Of course, now many of them are friends and supporters who help me carry all of the counties in our district at election time.

**PROUDEST ACCOMPLISHMENTS:** My proudest accomplishment as a state senator is having passed legislation that literally will save lives and diminish tragedies in Texas. Legislation I am most proud of includes establishing a statewide emergency medical services program, suspending the driver's licenses of drunk drivers, setting up a program to eventually immunize 100 percent of Texas children, and helping defeat the multimillion-dollar tobacco lobby by restricting minors' access to tobacco. My anti-tobacco bill finally passed, and it has been called one of the

toughest anti-smoking laws in the nation. The law penalizes both tobacco companies and retailers for advertising and selling tobacco to minors and penalizes teenagers, themselves, for using tobacco.

**LEARNING FROM YOUR CHILDREN:** It is interesting that midstream
in my fight against tobacco companies, I changed my perspective. For
four years, I had argued that the entire blame should be placed on the
tobacco companies themselves. After all, it was the tobacco companies
who were luring our children to their product and then deliberately ad-
dicting them. I felt that children who smoked were victims who should
not be punished. Governor Bush agreed with me, just as Governor
Richards had agreed with me earlier.

Then one day I asked a fourteen-year-old boy (who didn't smoke)
why so many of his friends did, even though they knew that smoking was
against the law. He answered, "Because everyone knows that if you get
caught, nobody does anything to you. That's why nobody respects the
law."

Hearing those words from that child hit me like a ton of bricks. In
that instant, I changed my attitude and my position on the issue. I used
that example to convince the governor, lieutenant governor, and my colleagues that the law must hold minors accountable if they use tobacco. In
future debate on the issue, I used the words of that fourteen-year-old
boy. What I failed to mention was that he was my son.

**MOTHERHOOD:** I have gained enormous insights from my son on other
issues as well. One thing he helped me realize was the importance of
constructive discipline and of love. I have never spanked him in my life,
and some of his friends think that is so unusual. I can look at the world
through his eyes, and I become more understanding of children and more
tolerant. As he has grown up, I have tried to instill in him the principles
I live by.

**PRINCIPLES BY WHICH I LIVE:**

- Keep your priorities straight. My top four (in order) are faith, family,
  public service, and business. If your home life is happy, you have set
  the foundation for happiness elsewhere.

- Treat others the way that you want to be treated. Emerson said, "The best way to make a friend is to be a friend." This philosophy has worked well in the Texas Senate, as well as elsewhere in my life.
- Set higher standards for yourself than for anyone else. Do not ask anyone to do anything that you would not do yourself. My staff works hard, but not harder than I.
- Handle both victory and defeat with equal grace and dignity. Because they are both short-lived, you should consider them both learning experiences.

**FEMINISM:** Two other strong beliefs I hold are that

- life is sacred, and
- men and women should have equal opportunities.

I am a pro-life feminist. Some people believe that a feminist, by definition, is pro-choice. However, I do not believe that abortion is the dividing issue. I believe that abortion is an "issue," and I do not believe that there is any issue on which all feminists agree. A "feminist" is simply a male or female who believes that men and women should have equal opportunities, including equal pay and equal access to equal jobs.

**SEX DISCRIMINATION:** Sex discrimination does not fit into my belief system. The most difficult time in my life was when, as a young junior-college administrator, I experienced sex discrimination when I was denied the professional and financial privileges offered to men in comparable positions. When the situation finally became intolerable, four of us sued Laredo Junior College (now Laredo Community College) for sex discrimination and civil rights violations. The biggest disappointment was when the judge forced us to settle out of court for $250,000 instead of being allowed to win the case outright. We didn't want a financial victory; we wanted a favorable verdict. We were convinced that we would have won the case.

**ADVERSITY:** Several people who were my adversaries in that lawsuit are my friends again today. Now, more than twenty-five years later, I have a very positive relationship with the community college in Laredo. I have learned through adversity that today's friend may be tomorrow's enemy and vice versa. It's not a matter of turning on the charm that has brought us back together. We have built a new relationship by working on issues on which we agree.

**VOTING:** Other struggles in my career include having to separate my personal perspective on certain issues as I meet my responsibility of voting to represent the needs and interests of my constituents. The most difficult time was when I felt I had to vote *for* the concealed weapons bill, an extremely difficult thing for me to do because I would have preferred voting *against* it. Voting that day made my hands perspire. It really bothered me.

Sometimes I have to vote one way in the Senate and the opposite way at the ballot box. In the Senate, I voted against raising salaries of state legislators because the idea was unpopular in my district. But on election day, I exercised my individual right and voted for raising salaries.

**MENTORS:** As a child, I never imagined that one day I would be casting votes in the state legislature. My childhood was a time when few women, especially those in the Mexican American community, aspired to political and professional careers.

My mother looked forward to our marrying successfully and having a good marriage. She encouraged us to learn to type in case we needed to work as secretaries, as she did. She also encouraged us to learn good manners, to speak English with an American accent and Spanish with a Mexican accent. Those were her standards. She personified the word "lady" in every way.

**IF I WERE A YOUNG WOMAN TODAY:** I would enroll in a greater variety of courses, including computers, business, and law; participate in lifelong sports and exercise programs; concentrate on writing and publishing; and develop good nutritional habits. I wish I had completed my Ph.D. studies earlier and had secured a law degree.

**BEING FEMALE IN A MAN'S WORLD:** As a woman studying and working in areas dominated by men, I often have had to work harder to prove myself and to succeed. In fact, since the 1970s, I have had a book in my Laredo office opened to a page that includes Charlotte Whitton's statement "Whatever women do they must do twice as well as men to be thought half as good." Then she added: "Luckily, this is not difficult."

**BEING FEMALE IN THE TEXAS SENATE:** When I was Governor-for-a-Day in 1997, not only did I have to do the job of the senator and pass seventy-nine bills that year, I also had to help plan my own Governor-for-a-Day celebration. When I walked into the first planning meeting, the committee members looked at me in surprise, and said: "The senator never comes to these meetings; usually his wife does." And I said, "Well, I *am* the wife." (Laughs.)

Working my way into the power structure of the traditionally male Texas Senate was a slow process. Often it takes a woman a lot longer than it takes a man to become a committee chair. I have worked my way up through hard work and discipline and by addressing the issues. It really is very easy: all you have to do is outwork men and outsmart them. (Smiles.)

To be perfectly frank, a lot of times the greatest advantage is in being underestimated, not only as a woman but especially as a Mexican American woman from Laredo.

**MARRIAGE:** My husband is the person whose opinion I value most. Carlos has been my major influence since high school. I first had a crush on him in fifth grade, but he wouldn't even look at me. I started going with him when I was thirteen and he was sixteen, and I married him five years later. I don't remember *not* knowing him.

From him I learned the importance of peace and harmony at home and at work, of love and loyalty, of ethics and honesty. I think that our friendship and understanding of each other makes our marriage strong. We grew up together. We developed our habits, attitudes, and our standards together. There are a lot of couples like us where we come from.

We are both busy and fulfilled in our separate professional lives; he enjoys the practice of law. When I'm not in legislative session in Austin, Carlos and I get to spend most of our time together in Laredo. We office in the same building, and we eat lunch at home every day, a time we have come to consider our time.

**FAMILY:** Before we had our son, we were the ultimate professional couple. Carlos would pick me up at my office every day, and we would eat lunch out. Often we would fly in our own plane to Acapulco for the weekend or to San Antonio or New Orleans for dinner. Having a child changed our lifestyle. After Carlitos was born, we started eating lunch at home, vacationing as a family at the beach, and reserving Sunday as "family day." Now, almost twenty years later, Sunday is still "family day."

When I was a child, we would gather at my grandfather's house every Sunday morning to share lunch together. My family continues that tradition, except now we gather at my sister's house. We all contribute to the meal. Last Sunday I brought "Zaffirini spaghetti," a special recipe developed by my husband's grandfather, and flan for dessert.

**COOKING:** Baking is my hobby, and I usually enjoy it on Sunday mornings. My husband loves cake, so I try to bake one every week, cut it into pieces, and flash-freeze them so he will have fresh cake every day. He can usually select from a variety of six cakes in the freezer.

I don't cook on a daily basis; our housekeeper does. I cook "fun" foods like desserts and party foods. My pimento cheese and chicken salads are popular (from my own recipes), and I am organized about making them. If I tell my housekeeper that I plan to make pimento cheese, for example, she will have everything ready when I get home—the proper bowls and measuring utensils on the counter, the ingredients organized, and even the cheese grated and onion chopped. It takes me three minutes flat to put it all together.

**DELEGATING:** No one can do everything herself. Telling the housekeeper to have the proper ingredients ready for me is one example of how I have learned to delegate. Our housekeepers organize themselves to cover household duties seven days a week, including buying groceries, cleaning, and running errands.

I expect staff members to be initiators and to have things ready so I can step in and do my job efficiently. I don't direct every step for my administrative assistant in my Senate office, for example. She gives me recommendations of possible meeting times, and I choose which time I would rather meet.

**ORGANIZATION:** Learning to prioritize tasks is important. Unless you realize that there are *x* number of hours in the day and *x* number of purposes to accomplish, you can lose control of your life. If there are too many things to do that day, instead of trying to do absolutely everything, you have to stand back and say, "What *must* I do and what can I reschedule?"

**TIME MANAGEMENT:** When I am in session, I wake up at 2:45 A.M. and arrive at my office in the Capitol at 4 A.M. I sometimes work till 7 P.M., but I usually don't take paperwork from the office back to the hotel. I spend my free time calling home, reading for pleasure, and walking on the treadmill. Typically people say, "How do you do so much and not look tired?" My answer: "Because of discipline, because of schedule, and because of priorities. That is the key."

I try to focus on my Senate work while I am in Austin and in transit, so that when I get home to Laredo, I can concentrate on my communications business and family activities. I have learned to use my travel time productively, and I typically have an agenda for the four-hour car trip between Laredo and Austin. A staff member always drives so that I am free to work. When my assistants take phone messages, they ask callers for after-hours numbers so I can call the person back from the car in the evening on my way home. When I'm not on the phone, I read work-related documents, sign letters, confer with the staff member, or sleep.

**SLEEP:** I'm lucky that I don't need much sleep. If I'm involved in a big project, three hours of sleep is sufficient. I usually sleep five hours, but I can sleep all day on the beach when I'm on vacation and not feel bad about it. I work hard, always with specific projects, goals, and deadlines in mind, but I do not consider myself a workaholic. I can turn my work off just as easily as I can turn it on.

**READING:** Allowing myself a schedule is part of how I assure myself relaxation time—time after work to think about something else. Reading offers me that pleasure. Away from work, I always have a book nearby. I mark in all my books, making comments here and there. You should see my books; there is no doubt that I have read them!

I like a variety of genres, including classics and books by popular authors such as John Grisham and Tom Clancy. During last session, I read fifty books for pleasure, mostly at night. I try to keep a journal about the books I read, quoting favorite passages, which I sometimes use in my speeches or perhaps in my writing. I reread my journal from time to time. As the years progress, I have found appropriate times to quote much of the wisdom I have jotted down in my journals.

**GETTING OLDER:** I am enjoying getting older because I have a happy life. I don't think that happiness is automatic. You have to focus on being happy.

Many people have urged me to run for governor or lieutenant governor, two jobs I would love. But I haven't figured out how I could meet my responsibilities on that high a level and still prioritize the two things that make me happiest: faith and family.

# EPILOGUE

FROM AN AGING PHOTOGRAPHER'S
FIELD NOTES ON LATE LIGHT

Sun     leaving the landscape
lingers warm on curves of hills
caressing voluptuous contours
alive under velvet.
Like sentinel torches
backlit autumn poplars glow.

Silent sheep watch     unmoving
silhouetted in shimmering haloes.

And I     bathed in slanted gold
must capture this pulsing moment
of clear echoes     woodsmoke scent
long shadows
stirring in me another time
almost remembered     an early
morning vista     elusive now in evening.

But unbidden     a midday scene
emerges     floating on fluid.
Under a harsh high sun these very hills
teeming with traffic     come

into focus      stark and lack-luster
the lighting flat and washed-out.

Now in this day-end hush
with sun leaving the landscape
I marvel at mellow transformations
of the terrain      and I must
capture these sensuous subtleties
revealed by late light.

—PAULINE DURRETT ROBERTSON,
*Field Notes: Poems on Late Light*
(PARAMOUNT PUBLISHING COMPANY, 1987)

This poem, a favorite of mine, turns out to be an appropriate conclusion to *"Let me tell you what I've learned"*—insights gained from living a long, productive life.

My mother wrote the poem several years ago. She used her perspective as a photographer who appreciates the advantage of the low, glowing light emanating from the western horizon—a special enhancing light that makes the landscape appear richer and more beautiful than it did at midday. Now, in her later years, she uses the concept as a metaphor—for the wisdom of appreciation that can mellow in the last years of life.

Her wisdom has influenced my life and those of countless other people, many of whom have admonished me for not including this woman of accomplishment as one of the wisewomen in this book. I have taken their advice to heart, and I am proud to include a bit about my mother here.

# PAULINE DURRETT ROBERTSON

"*Early child-hood nurture might be the most important work that anybody does in the world. In our country, nurturers of children are some of the lowest-paid workers. Our society has its priorities upside down.*"

*Pauline Durrett Robertson, historian and poet.*
*Photo by Summer Pierce © 2000.*

To Leta —
best wishes

— Pauline Durrett Robertson
11-17-02

## Pauline Durrett Robertson

B. 1922,
AMARILLO, TEXAS
CURRENT HOME:
AMARILLO, TEXAS

Pauline Durrett Robertson is well known in the Texas Panhandle as author, photographer, historian, poet, entrepreneur, and community activist. At age seventy, this mother of ten children decided that, after editing several of her children's master's theses and doctoral dissertations, she really should finish her own college degree. So she graduated from St. Edward's University at age seventy-two with a bachelor's degree in English writing.

Before that, she had written four books of poetry and four books about the history of the Texas Panhandle. The big book, *Panhandle Pilgrimage*, has been called by critics "the definitive history of the Texas Panhandle" and is still in print, after selling out in four previous printings.

Pauline is one who has never stopped being productive. She has taught poetry writing for twenty-one years at Amarillo College, a job she recently relinquished to concentrate on completing several writing projects. At age eighty, she continues to write books and to win regional and national awards for her poetry and photography.

Recently she was named Woman of the Year in Amarillo, and also the Mayor's Friend of the Young Child. In 1977 West Texas State University conferred on her the Texas Panhandle Award for Distinguished Service.

For as long as I can remember, my mother has reached out to others, particularly in the areas of women's issues, child advocacy, and the environment. She has embraced pioneering, sometimes controversial, causes. For instance, with a rather small group of citizens, she succeeded in keeping the Department of Energy from building a high-level nuclear waste dump in a fertile farming area of the Texas Panhandle, although Chambers of Commerce were pushing for the DOE to succeed. She was cofounder of the Children's Cottage for homeless black children (before integration), a summer camp for poor children of all races, a treatment center for cerebral palsied children, and a transition home for troubled teenagers. I can't count the times that my mother and father have opened their doors to young people temporarily needing a home.

Like most of the mothers and grandmothers in this book, she delights in her family, including now nineteen grandchildren and six great-grands. She has been married to my father more than sixty years.

By following my mother's example, I've learned valuable life lessons. Be passionate. Think big. Generosity is expected. However, it's not the size of the gift; it's the act of giving. Tell the truth. Be nice. Play fair. You won't always win, but you'll be able to live with yourself. Make good choices and then make the most of the path you choose. And finally, no matter what you accomplish, your greatest achievement will be raising happy, productive children.

Although she discouraged me from including her in these pages because "it would be embarrassing to have your mother in your book," she did allow me a lengthy interview, which I have recorded for her descendants. I share a few of her insights with you here.

*Pauline*
*Durrett*
*Robertson*

**S P E A K S**

**TEXAS:** I have been affected by growing up in the Texas Panhandle where the land is flat or gently rolling, and there is nothing to obscure the horizon. There is something liberating about being able to see into the distance; we people on the High Plains can become claustrophobic when too many trees or mountains block the view.

**POETRY:** I am drawn to poetry—both the reading and writing of it. I tend to think in poetic terms, to see metaphors in life and in nature. I see how nature reflects the human condition and the whole plan of the universe. Poetry expands your mind into realms of creativity. A poem is a sort of celebration—truth distilled into a few words. The best poems have that aspect of truth.

**MARRIAGE:** John Ciardi wrote a poem entitled "Most Like an Arch This Marriage." The premise is that the arch is the strongest form in architecture. The two sides come up singly and are weak by themselves, but when they bend and meet to form an arch, they lean against one another, completing the strongest architectural form. I think it is a good analogy for a marriage. I believe in a marriage that blends your life, your goals, your love, and your daily work with somebody else who is supportive of you. If children are involved, a strong marriage is important to their nurture.

**EARLY CHILDHOOD NURTURE:** Early childhood nurture might be *the* most important work that anybody does in the world. In our country, nurturers of children are some of the lowest-paid workers. Our society has its priorities upside down.

It is essential to nurture young children so they will have the ability to realize their potential in life. It is amazing how much learning takes place between birth and age four! Nurtured children usually escape the penchant for violence that abused and neglected children often display when faced with conflict. Violence can be seen as killing another person with a gun or killing another person's spirit or self-image with words. Children need to learn to nurture others in their words and actions and to maintain a positive, inclusive attitude.

**CONFLICT RESOLUTION:** Beginning in kindergarten, children should be taught conflict resolution as a required, graded subject, so that it will be taken seriously. That instruction should continue throughout their school years in incrementally comprehensive courses, so that when they graduate from high school, they will have internalized how to resolve conflicts peaceably with others. Universities should enhance conflict resolution studies to a real art.

If we took conflict-resolution education seriously, we would have a more gentle, civil society. Road rage and domestic violence would be rare incidents, and war would not be the inevitable solution for unresolved conflict.

**WAR:** I remember working in the war effort in World War II, right there where they repaired bombers that went overseas and killed people. But it didn't weigh on my mind then as it does now.

War is uncivilized, barbaric, unnecessary, and the ultimate tragedy. I can't stand to look at Arlington Cemetery or to think about my classmates in high school who didn't come back from World War II—my dear friends. It seems like such a travesty of human nature to kill each other deliberately.

Peace. It is our most urgent need. I didn't appreciate peace enough until I began getting older.

**RESPECTING OTHERS:** Every year I continue to learn more about the sacredness of the human personality. And I learn not to trivialize anybody's aspirations, abilities, accomplishments, or hardships, even though I may not agree with them personally. I find almost everyone has a part of the truth that I need to learn.

**SENSE OF COMMUNITY:** I do believe it is important to seek out people who share your same goals, who are committed to your truths, and who are willing to give of themselves to bring those principles to fruition.

I find a sense of community when I am with people who are centered on something larger than themselves—people who have a common purpose they think is worthwhile, and who are willing to put their shoulder to the wheel of a goal that has drawn them together. For example, one of the many groups I associate with is the League of Women Voters. We work together to promote better citizenship. Church-related groups are important to me, too.

**NURTURING YOURSELF:** One perk about being my age is that you are free to choose your obligations, your priorities, and how you spend your time and energy. But there's one slight drawback: At this age, you don't have quite as much energy as you used to have.

One sage bit of advice I got from a friend a few years ago is this: Get horizontal at least twenty minutes every day so that the blood can get to your brain. (Laughs.) When I lie down for just twenty minutes to rest, I feel refreshed whether I have slept or not.

**CHOOSE/LOSE:** As I look back on my life, I see things that I wanted to do that are still undone. Because I chose another route, I wasn't able to accomplish those things. The road not taken, you know. For example, instead of raising ten children and squeezing my writing in when I could, I could have been a full-time writer my whole life. And although that career would have been fulfilling, I would have lost a great joy by not having my family.

Presently I am writing a book called *Choose/Lose*. The premise is that when you choose one thing, you lose another. It is just part of the package, a given. When you choose to pass up an opportunity, you need to truly *lose* it. Bid that thing good-bye and put it out of your life or you will be miserable harking back to what might have been. It helps to realize that you can't accomplish everything you would like to do in this life. If you missed becoming a singer or a scientist or a minister, enjoy and celebrate those who have done it, while appreciating what you've been able to accomplish. I'm happy with the choices I've made.

# Appendix A

**ARTISTS**

Carmen Lomas Garza—San Francisco, California (b. 1948, Kingsville)
Glenna Goodacre—Santa Fe, New Mexico (b. 1939, Lubbock)
Violette Newton—Beaumont (b. 1912, Alexandria, Louisiana)

**ATHLETIC COACHES**

Jody Conradt—Austin (b. 1941, Goldthwaite)
Barbara Jacket—Prairie View (b. 1934, Port Arthur)

**ATTORNEYS/JUDGES**

Louise B. Raggio—Dallas (b. 1919, Manor)
Mary Lou Robinson—Amarillo (b. 1926, Dodge City, Kansas)
Sarah Weddington—Austin (b. 1945, Abilene)

**DENOMINATIONAL REPRESENTATIVE**

Marj Carpenter—Big Spring (b. 1926, Mercedes)

**EDUCATORS**

Juliet Villarreal García—Brownsville (b. 1949, Brownsville)
Amy Freeman Lee—San Antonio (b. 1914, San Antonio)
Diana Natalicio—El Paso (b. 1939, St. Louis, Missouri)
Guadalupe C. Quintanilla—Houston (b. 1937, Ojinaga, Chihuahua, Mexico)

ENTREPRENEUR

Ninfa Laurenzo—Houston (b. 1924, Harlingen; d. 2001, Houston)

HISTORIAN

Pauline Durrett Robertson—Amarillo (b. 1922, Amarillo)

JOURNALISTS

Liz Carpenter—Austin (b. 1920, Salado)
Linda Ellerbee—New York City (b. 1944, Bryan)
Sarah McClendon—Washington, D.C. (b. 1910, Tyler)

LAWMAKERS AND POLITICAL OFFICEHOLDERS

Wilhelmina Delco—Austin (b. 1929, Chicago, Illinois)
Kay Bailey Hutchison—Dallas (b. 1943, Galveston)
Barbara Jordan—Austin (b. 1936; d. 1996, Austin)
Irma Rangel—Kingsville (b. 1931, Kingsville)
Ann Richards—Austin (b. 1933, Lakeview)
Judith Zaffirini—Laredo (b. 1946, Laredo)

PHYSICIAN

Edith Irby Jones—Houston (b. 1927, Conway, Arkansas)

# APPENDIX B

1. What makes you feel most alive?
2. What are some principles by which you live?
3. What have you found that really matters about life? And, conversely, what did you once think important that you since have found to be unimportant?
4. What are some of the most difficult things you have ever done?
5. In one sentence, offer your most sage bit of advice to generations coming behind you, and then elaborate.
6. Reflect on your proudest accomplishments and, if you wish, your most bitter disappointments.
7. Has your upbringing in Texas influenced the way you have lived your life? Do Texas women tend to be different from other American women?
8. If you were a young woman starting out to build your life today, what would you do or not do again? Or, what might you do differently?
9. What have you learned from your successes and mistakes?
10. What are you still learning?
11. Did you (do you) have a mentor? Female? Male? What have you learned from her/him?
12. Cite instances when you have felt especially successful and satisfied.
13. Has there been a moment in your life when perceived failures disheartened you and you thought you couldn't go on? If so, how did you get through it? What did you learn? From failure? From persistence in the face of discouragement?
14. Do you have specific advice about nurturing yourself physically, emotionally, and spiritually, setting boundaries, balancing your life?
15. What new insights have you learned since you have gotten older?
16. Which age have you enjoyed the most? Why?
17. Where do you find a real sense of community?

18. Where do you find spiritual comfort?
19. What excites you about the future?
20. What else is there for you personally to conquer in this lifetime?
21. What do you do to recharge your energy?
22. Is there anything else you would like to impart to readers?

# BIBLIOGRAPHY

The information I used to compile this book came in large part from personal interviews with every woman except Barbara Jordan. The quotes of Barbara Jordan came from various sources, all documented in her chapter. Sources for the biographical sketches included information supplied by the subjects, newspaper and magazine articles, résumés, personal biographical sketches, and books written by or about the subjects.

These books include the following:

Brew, Lydia E. *Edith: The Story of Edith Irby Jones, M.D.* Houston: NTR Publishing Company, 1986.

Carpenter, Liz. *Getting Better All the Time.* New York: Simon and Schuster, 1987.

———. *Unplanned Parenthood: The Confessions of a SeventySomething Surrogate Mother.* New York: Ballantine Books, 1994.

Chrisman, Kent, ed. *To the Ends of the Earth: Mission Stories from Around the World: As Told by Marj Carpenter.* Louisville: Presbyterian Publishing Corporation, 1995.

Edson, Gary, ed. *Glenna Goodacre: The First 25 Years.* Lubbock: Museum of Texas Tech University, 1995.

Ellerbee, Linda. *Move On: Adventures in the Real World.* New York: G. P. Putnam's Sons, 1991.

Garza, Carmen Lomas. *A Piece of My Heart/Pedacito de mi Corazón: The Art of Carmen Lomas Garza.* New York: New Press, 1991.

McClendon, Sarah, and Jules Minton. *Mr. President, Mr. President!: My Fifty Years of Covering the White House.* Los Angeles: General Publishing Group, 1996.

Newton, Violette. *Fire in the Garden.* Harp and Quill Press, 1999.

Richards, Ann, and Peter Knobler. *Straight from the Heart: My Life in Politics and Other Places.* New York: Simon and Schuster, 1989.

Robertson, Pauline Durrett. *Field Notes: Poems on Late Light.* Amarillo: Paramount Publishing Company, 1987.

Rogers, Mary Beth. *Barbara Jordan, American Hero.* New York: Bantam Books, 1998.

Weddington, Sarah. *A Question of Choice.* New York: G. P. Putnam's Sons, 1992.

# INDEX

academics, 52, 131
adversity, 50, 75, 121, 140, 279
advocating for
    African Americans, 63
    children, 74
    the underdog, 129, 173, 212, 258
    women, 123
    women in a male system, 219
affirmative action, 233
American Dream, the, 16
anger, 26
animals, 161
art
    the business of, 100
    Chicano, 95
    realism vs. abstract, 108
    sculpting vs. "art," 111
assertiveness, 86

baseball, 181
beauty, 196
being
    African American, 141
    different, 64, 72, 164, 171
    Mexican American, 154, 209, 229, 277
    a stay-at-home mother, 88
    true to yourself, 210, 242

being female in
    male art world, 107
    male business world, 87
    man's world, 280
    Texas Senate, 281
bilingual education, 188
biliteracy, 85
business, growing a, 149

cancer, 75, 271
career challenges, 37, 144, 255
careers, 27, 142
    changing, 27, 38, 246
    preparing for, in art, 108
Catholicism, 99
challenging yourself, 16
change, 75
Chicano heritage, 97
children, 40, 257
choose/lose, 292
church, 39
coaching, 49, 131
    in the Olympics, 133
communicating, 63
competition, 48, 128
conflict resolution, 291
confrontation, 50

Constitution, the, 17
cooking, 28, 150, 257, 282
corporate world, 27
creative spark, 193
creativity, 111, 159
criticism, handling, 52, 267

dance, 99
Day of the Dead, 99
delegating, 282
diversity, 18, 51
divorce, 110

early childhood nurture, 290–291
educating
    children, 161
    males, 174
    minorities, 64, 187
    young people, 174, 219
education, 96
El Paso, 185
empty nest, 207
enjoying life, 134, 151, 259
environment, 222
equality, 17
ethical behavior, 17

failure, 52, 243
    fear of, 268
faith, 19, 29, 39, 75, 143, 158, 170, 217, 258
fajitas, 150
family, 40, 84, 119, 152, 210, 220, 282
fear of flying, 163
federal government, 175
federal secrets, 175
feminism, 73, 279
financial security, 247
flexibility, 266
friendship, 30, 41, 77, 89, 160, 173, 221
future
    investing in, 86
    looking toward, 39, 101, 114, 124, 144,
        164, 222, 254, 272

generation gap, bridging, 31, 223
getting a job, 28
getting involved, 16
getting older, 32, 42, 53, 77, 113, 124, 152,
    173, 199, 211, 224, 248, 271, 284
goals, setting, 37, 49, 182, 253
grandmotherhood, 84, 243, 256
growing up
    Chicana in Texas, 96
    with boys, 129
guilt, 72, 243

harmony, 18
hate, 26
help, asking for, 83
humor, 26, 42, 76, 107, 183, 198, 231, 245

if I were a young woman starting over,
    89, 109, 207, 223, 280
independence, 163, 234
Irish Famine Monument, 112

journalism, 170
just dealing with it, 253

leadership, 174, 267
learning
    from men, 87, 268
    from mistakes, 195
    from setbacks, 120
    from your children, 278
    new things, 100, 109, 208, 221, 248
lifelong skills, 47
light, 164
living one day at a time, 19
love, 160
loving a younger man, 76

marriage, 18, 31, 65, 84, 100, 123, 142, 281,
    290
    the second time around, 110
medicine, women in, 141
men, 142

menopause, 101
mentoring, 60, 140, 151
mentors, 25, 36, 49, 59, 110, 120, 140, 151,
    160, 192, 218, 230, 245, 253, 269, 280
Mexican American, proving yourself as,
    231
Mexico, 185
money, 59, 111, 208, 221
    investing, 248
    power of, 248
motherhood, 30, 72, 153, 171, 206, 220, 246,
    278
    and work, 73, 88, 141, 206, 256
muse, waiting for, 194

networking, 62
    with females, 88
nurturing yourself, 41, 65, 76, 88, 102, 123,
    165, 210, 223, 234, 244, 270, 292

opportunities disguised as disaster, 216
    seizing of opportunities, 66, 151, 207,
    218, 242, 253
Oprah Winfrey trial, 255
opting out, 266
organization, 283

parents, dealing with aging parents, 119
patience, 19
persevering, 83, 121, 148
poetry, 192, 290
    performing of, 196
    writing of, 195
politics, 17, 25, 60, 74, 219, 231
poverty, 128
power, 46
    of the female, 16, 246
praise, handling, 53, 198
prayer, 143, 159
prejudice, 97, 129, 230
    working to alleviate, 209
principles by which I live, 26, 36, 59, 134,
    139, 158, 172, 186, 211, 216, 234, 278

priorities, setting, 65, 165, 241, 257
privacy, 53
proudest accomplishments, 41, 85, 122, 132,
    153, 197, 232, 277
public speaking, 163, 234

reading, 283
reproductive rights, 219, 265
respect, 171
respecting others, 17, 150, 291
retiring, 32
risks, taking, 183
*Roe v. Wade,* 265
roots, remembering, 130
rubbing elbows with
    the famous, 150
    First Families, 175

Sacagawea dollar coin, 112
San Antonio, 164
satisfaction, 28
self-confidence, 18, 72, 172, 198, 209, 257
self-reliance, 208
self-respect, 243
sense of community, 292
sense of place, 98, 111
sentencing, 258
sex discrimination, 279
silence, 19
simplifying life, 244
sleep, 283
solitude, 184
speaking out, 74
sports
    girls in, 182
    growing up in, 48, 130
    women's basketball, then/now, 51
    women's sports and society, 47
    women's sports, then/now, 131
standing up for what you believe, 37, 61,
    72, 162
starting over, 270
success from failure, 107

taking charge, 267
teaching, 18, 49, 132
teamwork, 50, 123
teenagers, 174, 258
Tejanas, 98
Texas, 98, 154, 163, 184, 290
    men, 245
    women, 24, 42, 46, 64, 71, 120, 172, 184,
        197, 223, 229, 245, 268
time management, 111, 283
Title IX, 51, 126, 127
tooting your own horn, 269
travel, 38, 152
truthfulness, 243

Vietnam Women's Memorial, 112
voting, 61, 217, 280

war, 175, 291
wealth, sharing your, 151
what makes me feel alive, 49, 95, 162, 170,
    192, 254
what really matters in life, 165
White House, reflections from half-cen-
    tury, 174
widowhood, 31, 40, 143, 153, 199, 220, 259
women, the changing status of, 254
work ethic, 182, 231
    teaching of, 153
writing your own job description, 27, 38,
    148

young
    adults, 257
    people, 18, 211